GREAT
FRM THE
START

HOW CONSCIOUS CORPORATIONS
ATTRACT SUCCESS

JOHN B. MONTGOMERY

NEW YORK

GREAT FR◗M THE START
HOW CONSCIOUS CORPORATIONS ATTRACT SUCCESS

JOHN B. MONTGOMERY

ISBN 978-1-61448-148-5 Paperback
ISBN 978-1-61448-149-2 eBook

Published by:
MORGAN JAMES PUBLISHING
The Entrepreneurial Publisher
5 Penn Plaza, 23rd Floor
New York City, New York 10001
(212) 655-5470 Office
(516) 908-4496 Fax
www.MorganJamesPublishing.com

Cover Design by:
Rachel Lopez
rachel@r2cdesign.com

Interior Design by:
Bonnie Bushman
bonnie@caboodlegraphics.com

In an effort to support local communities, raise awareness and funds, Morgan James Publishing and the author donate a percent of all book sales for the life of each book to Habitat for Humanity Peninsula and Greater Williamsburg. Get involved today, visit
www.HelpHabitatForHumanity.org.

DEDICATION

To entrepreneurs

I discovered that the best innovation is sometimes the company,
the way you organize a company
—Steve Jobs, Co-founder of Apple, Inc.

Author's Note

Great from the Start uses the male third-person pronoun *he* as shorthand for *he and she* when referring to an entrepreneur. This usage is solely for convenience to streamline the writing by avoiding the use of *he or she* and *him or her,* and to avoid confusion by alternating the use of these pronouns. This book celebrates entrepreneurs of both genders. The English language, unfortunately, lacks a third-person singular pronoun that includes both genders, and publishing convention requires this usage.

CONTENTS

FOREWORD

As I sit down to write this, I have just returned from an offsite planning session with our management team in Shanghai. Ten of us spent three days in Lijiang, in Yunnan Province, at the Banyan Tree, only miles from the eastern edge of the Lower Himalayas. It's a beautiful spot with majestic views that formed the perfect backdrop for a strategic offsite. We spent a day focused on the respective personalities of the individual team members and how, like instruments in an orchestra, they all work together to produce something greater than the mere sum of the parts. The second day we talked about the culture (or values) of our organization, the extent to which it is real, and the gap between what it is and what we aspire it to be. On the third day, we talked about our purpose and how that translates into a strategy, or long-term plan, and how our business, or short-term plan, helps us advance the strategy, bringing us closer to realizing our purpose. It was a great trip, and when we summarized at the end, we all felt that a number of important things had come out of it.

We felt that most of the people in our organization are there for a reason. They have chosen our company as much as it has chosen them. Their reasons for having chosen it are in some regards typical: They believe that we will be successful, and they want to be associated with a successful company. Accordingly, they believe that we will be able (and willing) to pay them fairly, meaning a market rate. They also like the nature of the work, and they like the person they report to. Their most important reason, however, is not typical: They feel that they fit the corporation and that, culturally, it fits them. In other words, their values and the values of the company are similar, making it possible for them to identify with it. And, most importantly, they feel that the organization has a sense of purpose, that its purpose is a good one, and that that purpose gives them a purpose, as well.

In our case, purpose goes beyond the obvious, meaning beyond making money. When I was in business school 30 years ago, it seemed that if the professor called on you and you hadn't read the case, you could almost always get by with an answer that included the phrase "shareholder value." Making money *was* the sole purpose of the corporation in that era, or so it seemed. Implicit to the subjects we covered and the way in which we covered them was a highly mechanistic view of the corporation. Our discussions revolved around which levers to pull to achieve a given result, and that result invariably involved increasing "shareholder value." In 30 years of business, I have learned that corporations are far more like living, breathing, evolving organisms than they are like machines; that understanding people is far more important to success than understanding numbers (or even "algorithms"); and that purpose needs to go way beyond increasing shareholder value—and all the more so if increasing shareholder value is part of your purpose.

For if our shareholders are to have any chance of increasing the value of their holdings, that will have to be accomplished for them by and through people. And people are far too complex and sophisticated, both as individuals and even more so as members of groups, to be motivated solely by a desire to make money, either for themselves or for their shareholders. First and foremost people today—in America, in Europe, and in Asia—want to affiliate with companies that have a purpose that goes beyond increasing shareholder value to include helping their employees self-actualize and making the world a better place. They want to work with and for managers who care about them, their development, and their opinions. They want leadership that leads by generating trust rather than fear. In short, they expect the companies they work for to treat them as the complex and sophisticated human beings that they are; and then, and only then, are they likely to do their best to increase shareholder value. Having said that, they expect to be treated as ends unto themselves, not as means to other ends.

In this book John Montgomery has recognized and captured all of this and more. Having spent his entire professional career working with startups, and having observed hundreds if not thousands achieve some level of success, John has, with the assistance of a number of his colleagues and collaborators, put down on paper the patterns that he and they have seen. I believe that he has produced a book of immense value, perhaps the best of its type that I have ever seen.

The patterns that he has disclosed—and the wisdom he has gleaned from doing so—are more important today than ever before. Centers of innovation have sprung up around the world; and thanks to the increasing breadth and depth of our global knowledge base, there are more fundable ideas, capital is in abundance, and the level of need for innovation in the world at large, particularly in the areas of clean tech and life sciences, is higher than ever before. All that is missing is management talent, particularly in developing countries and newer markets. This book addresses that shortfall. Everyone and anyone who organizes training sessions and boot camps for entrepreneurs should embrace this book. With management talent, as elucidated herein, we can optimize our knowledge base, our capital, and our impact on the world.

Ken Wilcox,
Chairman of Silicon Valley Bank

PREFACE

I wrote this book because I want you to experience the joy of building a successful company. I want every business to succeed. As a lawyer who supports startups, I know that great companies are not only more profitable to represent but also are more exciting and meaningful to work with. Having experienced the joy of successful companies and the pain of those that have failed, I want to work with successes. This book was written so that you can have one of the successes and so that we can work with more great companies.

The book walks you through the thought process of building a successful company. Unlike most business books which provide examples of successful companies and leave you to figure out how those are relevant to you, *Great from the Start* shows how to start with a solid foundation and build from there. All of this requires that you be conscious so that you understand what is needed, what your choices are and how to reach your goals.

I want you to design your company as a conscious corporation for several reasons. First, a corporation needs to be awake so that it can make conscious decisions with people who are engaged and united by a common goal. Second, a corporation needs to be aware of the interdependencies and complexities of today's world. Without this awareness, the limited concept of the corporation existing solely to enrich stockholders will limit your success. Finally, because the law endows the corporation as an entity with many of the rights of personhood, a corporation must be conscious so that it can act appropriately as a responsible citizen of the world in which we live.

Great from the Start is both a primer about how to start a great company and a reference resulting from the collaboration between a wide range of industry experts and a Silicon Valley veteran. The book models an adaptive approach to company building by providing a variety of expert voices on aspects of building successful companies. Because building a company is a team sport, I used a team approach to demonstrate the methods outlined in the book with stories from the experts' successful businesses.

A conscious corporation engages similar experts and applies their expertise in a sequence that suits its unique needs and personality. To build a great company, you must skillfully apply a variety of disciplines and employ a team of talented people. There is, however, no prescribed formula or proper sequence in which to deploy these disciplines and talent. No company starts perfectly formed, but every company is constantly evolving. As a conscious leader you need to be flexible and cultivate your ability to remain in the present moment to apply the exact skill or engage the right person to handle your current priority.

In addition to being a guide to help you build a successful company, the book contains three additional levels of meaning. At the second level, *Great from the Start* helps you build a socially responsible business based on the tenets of conscious capitalism or meeting a third party standard of social responsibility such as B Lab's certified B Corporation standard. The legal architecture suggested in Chapter 20, which incorporates purpose and core values in a company's articles and bylaws, is especially helpful if you are a social entrepreneur who desires to build a business that will have a positive impact on society and the environment.

At the third level, *Great from the Start* shows you how to strategically build a business that not only optimizes profit but also does good. There has never been a more urgent need for a better way of building businesses because a truly sustainable economy requires an entirely new way of thinking about corporations. *Great from the Start* shows you how to make three simultaneous paradigm shifts necessary to build and lead a smarter corporation that can help create a sustainable future:

1. **Corporations exist to optimize profits *and* provide a material positive impact on society and the environment instead of existing solely to maximize profits for shareholders.** A conscious corporation makes money, and does good. This advances Google's "do

no evil" to the next level by enabling corporations that not only make money for shareholders but also have a positive effect on society and the environment. The traditional concept externalizes many costs of doing business, such as pollution, on society and the environment. In the new paradigm, corporations will responsibly minimize and manage these costs.

2. **A model of the corporation as a complex ecosystem of multiple interdependent stakeholders supplements the traditional model of the corporation as a duality of management and stockholders.** A conscious corporation adopts a multiple stakeholder model, and empowers its directors to consider the interests of all stakeholders, not just stockholders, in the exercise of their fiduciary duties and business judgment. Public corporations such as Whole Foods Market and Southwest Airlines have established the efficacy of this new approach to doing business.

3. **Leaders will not only develop traditional business aptitudes and skills but also cultivate successively more complex states and stages of cognitive development and consciousness.** A conscious corporation requires leaders who are passionately committed to personal and professional growth. Numerous models of human development have emerged ranging from Abraham Maslow's hierarchy of needs, to Robert Kegan's six stages of equilibrium, to Don Beck's spiral dynamics model, to Ken Wilber's integral theory. Each of these models uses a different framework to describe the same phenomena of development. Leaders will increasingly use such models to complement the development of traditional business acumen.

Finally, at the deepest level of meaning, *Great from the Start* shows you how to build a successful and trustworthy corporation designed for humanity that runs on love and trust instead of alternating between hope and fear. For the first time in human history, we have sufficient knowledge about biology, neuroscience, psychology and organizational development to design our commercial organizations for how humans work best. This book provides a tentative blueprint for designing and building a corporation that is optimized for how our brains work best.

Social neuroscience has spawned the field of neuroleadership, which uses an understanding of the brain to develop better leaders. This book complements neuroleadership by providing you with a framework to build an organization based on some of the fundamental principles of neuroscience. At its essence the book shows you how to create a supportive working environment based on love and trust. In a business context, love is simply the intention to help others succeed. A workplace that runs on an operating system of love and trust is more productive and stable than one that alternates between hope and fear. Because the human brain is hardwired for survival, however, many of us spend much of our work day in a flight-or-fight response rather than engaging enthusiastically in the job at hand.

Neuroeconomist Paul Zak has demonstrated that humans perform best in environments where they are loved and trusted. His research shows that when we work in supportive workplaces, our brains produce oxytocin, a neuro-chemical that makes us feel happy and helps us enjoy our work and co-workers. On the other hand, when we work in unsupportive or hostile work environments, our brains produce cortisol and adrenaline, stress producing chemicals that make us feel miserable. *Great from the Start* is a preliminary blueprint to design humane corporations that will enable the ultimate paradigm shift:

A sustainable global economic system designed for humanity that runs on trust succeeds the prevailing economic system that alternates between hope and fear. This shift will be difficult because it requires business leaders to develop enough mental and emotional stability to respond confidently to business challenges instead of being victimized by fear into reactivity or tempted by greed into unethical behavior. Such conscious leaders can then lead corporations which are inspiring environments for creativity and collaboration that run on love and trust, which neuroscience confirms is conducive to optimal human performance. Such corporations will activate their collective consciences to act as responsible global citizens. Ultimately, such conscious corporations will transform the global economic system so that it too runs on love and trust.

To help you imagine how to create a positive working environment in your business, I profile my mentor, venture capitalist Gordon Campbell, and several of the companies he produced in his Techfarm Ventures technology incubator from 1994 to 1997. During this period Campbell produced one successful company after another with relative ease. He intuitively applied a consistent method to build a portfolio of successful startups, including Cobalt Networks, 3Dfx Interactive, and NetMind Technologies.

Gordon Campbell is a genius of organizational development because he understands how to organize groups of people to optimize their individual and collective intelligence. In the language of the emerging field of social neuroscience, which studies what happens in the brain when people interact, Campbell is a master of social intelligence. Daniel Goleman and Richard Boyatzis define *social intelligence* as "a set of interpersonal competencies built on specific neural circuits (and related endocrine systems) that inspire others to be effective."[1] Campbell applies an intuitive system to design organizational structures that create extraordinary value by supporting effective business behaviors such as cooperation, collaboration, and creativity.

Campbell has achieved enough business success to satisfy his ego and enough financial security to permanently transcend his Maslovian survival needs. As a result, he operated confidently from a place of abundance in his roles as chairman of the board and mentor to Techfarm's portfolio companies. Campbell's cup runneth over, and his positive, optimistic mood energized every company with which he worked.

Neurobiology has identified a phenomenon called *mood contagion*, whereby a leader's positive behaviors literally trigger corresponding chemical changes in followers' brains that cause similar positive moods. On a neurological level, Campbell infected his companies with confidence. His mentees replicated their mentorships' basis of trust throughout their companies to create environments that promoted optimal brain function.

By intuitively selecting founding teams with a visionary, a technologist, and a salesman with established relationships, Techfarm's companies spent less time in fight-or-flight reactivity and more time enjoying the challenge of realizing their visions. Having whole-brain cultures that celebrated the diversity of perspectives provided by logic, emotion, and intuition intelligence encouraged people to remain in the frontal cortex to solve problems together rather than trigger the defensive regions of the brain like the amygdala and limbic system to engage in conflict.

---

1   Goleman, Daniel and Richard Boyatzis, "Social Intelligence and the Biology of Leadership," *Harvard Business Review*, September 2008.

As an experienced executive, Campbell was able to help the chief executive officers (CEOs) of his portfolio companies maintain the balance to optimize collaboration and creativity. Simply put, his social intelligence enabled him to organize the people in each company so that they operated collectively and effectively as a single system.

Social neuroscientists are beginning to understand how the neurons in our individual brains function to form a single system out of a group of people. Scientists have recently discovered several kinds of neurons that play a significant role in organizational behavior. *Mirror neurons* are the brain's "monkey-see-monkey-do" cells that cause us to recognize others' behaviors and intuitively reproduce them in our own actions. Ken Wilcox's story in chapter 6 about the first president of Silicon Valley Bank, Roger Smith, demonstrates the power of mirror neurons. When Roger Smith swore, everyone swore. When clean-talking John Dean replaced Roger as CEO, the swearing disappeared because mirror neurons automatically caused everyone to mimic the new leader's speech.

From a neurological standpoint, most leaders unwittingly rely on mirror neurons to create their corporate cultures when they expect the company's core values to be deduced from their own behavior. Because mirror neurons operate on a subcognitive level, the result is a culture that is experienced only subconsciously.

On a fundamental level, defining core values is critical because it allows the culture to become visible at a cognitive level. When leaders define the core values and hold themselves accountable to them, they create powerful alignment because the mirror and cognitive brain neurons fire complementarily. When properly structured and enforced, core values literally create positive neural pathways in followers' brains that are reinforced by mirror neurons.

Scientists have also found another class of neurons called *oscillator neurons,* which regulate how people move together. These neurons enable synchronized movement like dance that requires coordinated teamwork. When Steve DeWitt rang Cobalt's bell to celebrate the sale of a server, as discussed in Chapter 8, it likely fired oscillator neurons in people's brains that made them feel and act as one.

A third class of neurons called *spindle neurons* seems to be the agent of intuition. Spindle neurons are large cells with thousands of connections to other neurons that enable quick judgments and optimal decisions. Effective leaders such as Campbell and Wilcox likely rely on their spindle neurons when they intuitively organize people as a team.

Each chapter of this book describes a developmental pattern that can be optimized to support optimal brain function. A well-designed brand, for example, literally causes neurons to fire positively in a customer's brain to predispose him to buy the associated product. When optimized and combined, these subdevelopmental patterns create a corporate structure that supports the genius of the human collective. Understanding the underlying social neuroscience is essential to tapping the full power of a human collective, but ultimately it's about love and trust. When we are loved and trusted in a startup, we spend less time in the survival-oriented parts of our brains and more time engaged in building a successful company.

Finally, this book is a memoir of one man's 28-year career as a corporate lawyer in Silicon Valley. The book does not directly cover the stories of the seminal technology companies of this era—Intel, Apple, Cisco, Netscape, Google, and Facebook—but features those that my colleagues and I helped build. It is my gift to the ecosystem that has sustained me.

Introduction

THINKUP BEFORE STARTUP TO AVOID BEING A F#@KUP

You probably have a good idea for a great company. If you already know how to turn your idea into a successful business, you don't need this book. This book is for people who are interested in building a successful company. You need this book only if you are looking to be one of the *best* companies. The purpose of this book is to show you how to create the most value for the least effort by intelligently designing your concept into a company that has a higher probability of success.

The Inspiration

In February 2002 I realized that my client, venture capitalist Gordon Campbell, had intuitively applied a common methodology to all the portfolio companies of his Techfarm Ventures incubator. These companies shared a common developmental pattern, which caused many of them—including Cobalt Networks (acquired by Sun Microsystems for $2 billion in four years), 3Dfx Interactive (initial public offering with $500 million in market capitalization in three years), and NetMind Technologies (acquired by Puma Technologies for more than $750 million in four years)—to succeed quickly and to attract the best resources. This repeated pattern of success inspired me to uncover the underlying system. My belief was that understanding how the pattern worked would yield a blueprint for building great companies.

This book is the result of reverse-engineering the success of Techfarm and its portfolio companies. Using what I understood about the pattern, I built a corporate law firm, which became a laboratory for testing the principal ideas in this book. I shared elements of the pattern with such clients as Solaicx and 3Tera, which used them in their businesses. The process eventually revealed Campbell's blueprint and suggested a number of improvements to make it even more effective.

Campbell applied the approach he had used to start and build two public semiconductor companies—Seeq Technology and Chips and Technologies—to his Techfarm portfolio. He succeeded in scaling his approach from one company at a time to doing so simultaneously with a portfolio of companies. His method was difficult for his partners and portfolio companies to follow, however, because it was entirely in his head. This book makes Campbell's method visible so that you can follow it.

If you are an entrepreneur starting a business who wants to improve your chances of success, this book is primarily for you. Any business organization—including partnerships, limited-liability companies, benefit corporations, and even not-for-profit entities—can use it to intelligently design its business. This book is also for venture capitalists in search of a consistent one-to-many approach to building their portfolio companies. It can serve as a textbook for a college or business school course in entrepreneurship and as a guide for entrepreneurs building businesses based on the tenets of conscious capitalism or that have a social purpose.

What Is This Book?

No idea gets turned into reality until it's ready.

—David Wolfe, *Firms of Endearment*

This book is a blueprint for turning your idea into a successful company. Each of the 23 chapters covers an essential aspect of creating a company. Although the main ideas are arranged in a linear sequence, they provide a flexible framework for company building. You can use the ideas that are most helpful and ignore the rest. The material shows you how to fully develop your business idea before you rush off to launch your company.

This is also a workbook with exercises to help you turn your concept into a company with as much clarity and precision as possible. Each chapter ends with a summary of key points and a collaborative exercise that demonstrates the "how." The exercises give your founding team an opportunity to practice working together. The bibliography lists additional resources for exploring a particular topic in depth.

This book is not a complete guide for navigating your startup company through *all* of its developmental stages, as it focuses on the time between idea and incorporation and largely ignores later stages of growth.

You should, however, understand what's next. I like to think of startup companies as having five distinct stages:

- The *concept stage* is the time between idea and incorporation.
- The *startup stage* is when a company builds its product.
- The *build stage* is when a company starts selling its product.
- The *growth stage* occurs when a company has developed a reliable and repeatable sales process that allows it to achieve an exponential rate of growth in sales. Every startup aspires to achieve exponential sales growth because that is what creates extraordinary value.
- The *maintenance stage* occurs once the company has evolved into a profitable business with a positive cash flow, robust revenues, and consistent quarter-to-quarter results.

This book is a prequel to David G. Thomson's *Blueprint to a Billion* and complements two of my favorite books about how to build a startup company: Guy Kawasaki's *The Art of the Start* and Rob Adams's *A Good Hard Kick in the Ass.* This book is a companion to two books that every entrepreneur should read: Jim Collins and Jerry I. Porras's *Built to Last* and Jim Collins's *Good to Great.*

The Blueprint

The common developmental pattern displayed by progeny of Techfarm's incubator and recorded here forms the basis of the blueprint. Companies like Cobalt, 3Dfx, and NetMind shared three common traits that gave them an advantage:

- They achieved their objectives rapidly and went public or got acquired in less than five years.

- They were capital-efficient.

- They effortlessly attracted the resources necessary to grow.

Successful execution infused these companies with an infectious positive spirit that attracted the best talent, customers, partners, and investors. These traits were a powerful lodestone that drew the right resources to the companies like a magnet.

This book uses the stories of Cobalt, 3Dfx, and NetMind to identify the key patterns of behavior that combined to create strong attractor patterns that pulled in the best resources. Several of the contributing experts were co-founders or executives of these companies. The intention is to enable entrepreneurs and venture capitalists to replicate similar attractor patterns in their companies.

Attractor Patterns

The blueprint forms an organizational development pattern comprising many component subpatterns. Each chapter generally describes a particular subpattern; and each subpattern exerts a subtle power that attracts resources helpful to building the company.

British doctor and philosopher David Hawkins articulated the phenomenon of attractor patterns in *Power vs. Force*. Hawkins observed that developmental patterns either support life or destroy it. The magnetizing power of a particular attractor pattern increases with its ability to support life.

The attracting power of a particular subpattern can be strong or weak. A company with a culture whose values have been expressly defined, for example, will tend to attract more employees that are aligned with them than one whose values are deduced from management behavior. Strong attractor patterns pull companies together and support alignment.

On the other hand, weak patterns pull companies apart and support entropy. A founder who is unwilling to have a mentor and listen to expert advice, for example, creates a weak attractor pattern.

This book encourages you to create strong attractor patterns. The basic premise is that strong attractor subpatterns combine to create a strong collective attractor pattern for a company as a whole. My observation is that the power of the collective attractor pattern to draw in high-quality resources increases as the number of strong individual attractor subpatterns increases. Cobalt, 3Dfx, and NetMind, for example, enjoyed strong collective attractor patterns. As the preface suggests, there is likely a neurological basis for these patterns.

David Rock, one of the pioneers of the field of neuroleadership, has developed an eloquent and simple framework, which is useful to explain the efficacy of the individual attractor subpatterns described in each chapter. Rock has identified five factors that influence whether or not a person will remain conscious and proactive in the frontal cortex of the brain where higher human cognitive functions generally occur. Humans need status, certainty, autonomy, relatedness and fairness in order to function at their best. In general, the stronger a particular attractor pattern, the more it supports one of these needs.

Building a Conscious Capitalism–Based Company

This book is also a guide for building a company based on *conscious capitalism*. A company that embraces conscious capitalism embodies three principles that set it apart from other companies:

- A deeper metapurpose in addition to maximizing profits
- A recognition not only that it is a complex ecosystem comprising numerous interdependent stakeholders in addition to stockholders but also that it needs to deliver value to all stakeholders
- A chief executive officer who is the steward of his company and its ecosystem, working for the benefit of all the stakeholders, not just for his own enrichment

Companies built using these three principles are better companies. *Firms of Endearment: How World-Class Companies Profit from Passion and Purpose* by Rajendra Sisodia, David Wolfe, and Jagdish Sheth shows that public companies using the principles of conscious capitalism significantly beat the performance of the S&P 500 over a 10-year period. Executives like John Mackey, co-founder and co-CEO of Whole Foods Market, and Kip Tindell, cofounder and CEO of The Container Store, lead their companies using the principles of conscious capitalism.

Venture capitalists such as Gordon Campbell understood intuitively that building a great business required following the principles that have become conscious capitalism. As an executive chairman, Campbell served as the steward of his portfolio companies, guiding them as an experienced mentor. He encouraged founders to imagine and build out their companies as fully developed ecosystems. And he made sure that each company had a compelling purpose in addition to making money.

I suggest three additional principles for the model for conscious corporations:

- A clear and precisely defined culture
- A sophisticated internal conscience
- A deliberate cultivation of consciousness

The blueprint explains how to define a company's culture with precision, suggests how to raise consciousness for competitive advantage, and explores how to create an internal conscience that balances short-term survival with long-term sustainability.

In general, the emerging class of for profit corporations with a social purpose such as a California benefit corporation are conscious capitalism–based companies. Benefit corporations focus particularly on the organization as an ecosystem of interdependent stakeholders and are designed to increase the ability of business to have a positive social and environmental impact.

B Lab, a nonprofit organization and the proponent of this new kind of company, has designed a certification program—the Certified B Corporation—to combine an ingredient brand for good business with transparent and comprehensive performance standards to enable corporate stakeholders to identify and support businesses that are aligned with their values. The B Lab certification creates transparent standards that make it easy to tell the difference between a company that is walking the talk and one that has only a green marketing veneer. Just as the organic food industry promulgated standards that make it easier for consumers to identify healthy organic food, B Lab established similar standards to identify truly sustainable businesses.

Benefit corporations and Certified B Corporations contain elements of the principles of conscious capitalism in their charter documents. Certified B Corporations, for example, amend their articles of incorporation to require them to consider the impact of their decisions on their employees, the community, and the environment. These provisions also provide directors with legal protection when they consider the interests of multiple stakeholders when making corporate decisions. The blueprint allows conscious capitalism-based companies, benefit corporations, and Certified B Corporations to incorporate their fundamental principles into their articles of incorporation and bylaws to create more-robust legal frameworks that support their companies.

Regardless of whether you are building a company that will require venture capital, a conscious capitalism–based company, or a corporation for a social purpose, you will need to apply traditional business disciplines to succeed. At the end of the day, your business must be profitable to survive. A mastery of traditional business disciplines is still the foundation upon which a successful business is built. My intention is to offer you a method for building a sustainable company that also uses the best of traditional business disciplines.

Chapter 1

A COMPELLING PURPOSE

Great companies have great purposes.

—John Mackey, co-founder and co CEO, Whole Foods Market

The power is in your purpose. Purpose answers the question: *Why build your company?*

A powerful purpose is imbued with enthusiasm, meaning, and relevance. A successful entrepreneur is enthusiastic about what his company proposes to do. What the company intends to do gives meaning to both the founder and the employees and is relevant to customers and the marketplace. Enthusiasm, meaning, and relevance combine to create a compelling purpose.

Although purpose is best discovered *before* the company is incorporated, entrepreneurs are often in love with their ideas but blind to a company's highest purpose, which can be a disadvantage in the search for backers. Venture capitalists are eager to invest in businesses with stellar products, customers, and teams, but what they are really searching for are game-changing companies capable of generating billion-dollar valuations. Which companies are game changers? Those with a powerful purpose.

A business is worth pursuing only if it has a big, compelling purpose. Developing an inexpensive, rechargeable, long-running, nonpolluting power source for use in electric cars is a compelling purpose, but forming another company to make and sell gasoline-powered automobiles is not.

Articulating your business's purpose allows it to realize its full potential. If you fail to identify the big purpose and communicate it clearly to your team, you may build a $100 million business but miss the billion-dollar opportunity. You will attract a team capable of building a $100 million business but not one capable of changing the world. Generally, the best people are inspired only by meaningful, game-changing work—the kind that arises from a compelling purpose.

Enthusiasm

To be successful as the founder, you have to relish the job of building the company that answers your "why" question. You must love your company's purpose and your role as its leader because a genuinely enthusiastic founder who loves his job can promote his company and its benefits to almost anyone. Your competitive advantage increases and your sales expand in proportion to the heart-to-heart connections you make with your customers.

Enthusiasm is a closer. When faced with a choice between buying a product from a salesman who loves what he's selling and one who merely likes it, the customer will almost always buy from the most enthusiastic person, even if the other product is better. Genuine enthusiasm drives sales.

Leading a startup company is a difficult job. Being passionate about your work helps you bear with grace the enormity of the responsibilities and the constant challenges. The founder who loves his job generates the enthusiasm needed to stay the course.

Passion with a Purpose: Cobalt Networks

The founders of Cobalt Networks provide an example. They were not completely enamored of their initial idea to provide in-flight entertainment. They made no lasting impression when they first presented it to investors because they lacked enthusiasm. Why? Because in-flight entertainment held a small purpose.

Nevertheless venture capitalist Gordon Campbell recognized the Cobalt team's great potential and challenged it to come up with another, more compelling idea. Cobalt's founders then identified a game-changing business opportunity in the computer server market, in which very expensive gear impeded the growth of the Internet. To add capacity an Internet service provider (ISP) was forced to buy $75,000 servers from vendors such as Sun Microsystems. Buying the equipment ate up scarce operating capital, and the ISPs got more capacity than they needed.

Cobalt solved this problem by developing an easy-to-use server appliance that cost just $1,000. Suddenly, the world of Internet access exploded. Cobalt seized an opportunity to create a paradigm shift by delivering products that were orders of magnitude less expensive than what were then available in the server market. The big purpose behind Cobalt's new idea, called the Qube, was to help democratize the Internet by making access available to everyone.

After Cobalt's founders came up with the Qube, their enthusiasm was boundless. The team was animated by their shared belief in the new purpose, and they devoted themselves to expanding Internet access worldwide. Their second product, a server formatted for server racks and also priced at $1,000, allowed ISPs to economically scale capacity as needed.

Sun Microsystems took note of Cobalt's newly ignited big purpose and the game-changing competition it represented. Sun bought Cobalt for $2 billion only four years after it was incorporated. A big purpose gives impetus to the possibility of building a billion-dollar business.

Meaning

Happiness comes from doing work that matters.

—Rajendra Sisodia, co-founder and chair, Conscious Capitalism Institute

People crave meaningful work. In Abraham Maslow's hierarchy of needs, as described in his book *Motivation and Personality,* the need for meaningful work is seen as an expression of people's need for self-actualization, or realizing one's full potential. Successful startups meet their employees' basic financial needs by paying them for their work but forge an even deeper bond by providing them with work that is truly meaningful. People work harder, are more productive, and feel happier when they do work that makes a difference. The simplest way to provide meaning is to articulate a company's highest purpose.

Three Components of Meaning: Ken Wilcox

Ken Wilcox, Chairman of Silicon Valley Bank, based in Santa Clara, California, explains what employees want out of work. "Essentially, people have three basic drives regarding the workplace and its culture," he says.

The need to belong. "People want to be part of a tribelike group," says Wilcox. Studies have shown that the ideal factory size is between 50 and 75 people. When a group surpasses 200, its members are less engaged and happy. When people are put together in small enough groups and allowed to freely express themselves, they'll naturally create a tribal family spirit on their own.

"Successful tribes have rituals," Wilcox continues. "Every year Silicon Valley Bank takes about 100 people on a team-building retreat with lectures and small-group discussions. Invariably, we end up on a scavenger hunt in groups of five or six. At the beginning the people are strangers because Silicon Valley Bank has 1,400 employees, but after a few hours together this group transforms into a small tribe that has developed its own rituals and slogan, like 'We're the Wolverines. We always win.' People love saying these slogans to each other because they give them a feeling of belonging."

The need to win. People want to win. Winning helps them feel accomplished and important. "Competitive people want to win," says Wilcox, "but if they are the collaborative type, it's not about beating the competition but about team success. They want to be part of a group that accomplishes something great. If they are in business, they want to do something meaningful for the shareholders, their families, and the world."

The need to celebrate. People want to celebrate their accomplishments. "When they succeed, they have a deep-seated need to put down their weapons," says Wilcox. "They want to eat and drink, celebrate, whoop and holler, pat each other on the back, and jump up and down for joy."

Relevance

Your company's purpose has to be compelling to both its customers and its marketplace. To be meaningful to customers, the purpose must be related to solving a customer need because that's why customers buy products in the first place.

Mark Zawacki, the founder and managing partner of Milestone Group, shares five rules of relevancy that he believes will refine a company's purpose in ways that will make customers love the product enough to buy it.

"The five things that make early-stage companies relevant," says Zawacki, "are an addressable market, finding a voice, partnerships and alliances, picking the right ecosystem, and focus." His criteria are very different from the standard venture capitalist's refrain, which Zawacki describes as "'Show me a great management team and your unfair competitive advantage.' Those things are necessary, but a company needs to be relevant to succeed."

Five Rules of Relevancy: Mark Zawacki

1. **A startup needs to be relevant and stay relevant.** An early-stage company must first discover and understand its addressable market, which is not the same as the target market that venture capitalists will ask about. The typical early-stage business isn't aware of its addressable market or its customers' needs. Too many startups aren't in tune with, and therefore can't address, real customer pain. They build features, not companies, thus creating a stage full of bit players because they never solve real problems.

   The tech industry is the easiest industry to enter. It would be easy to start a Web 2.0 video search company. You could be in business tomorrow; but unless you have done your homework, you would be inviting a train wreck. Not understanding the size of your addressable market and the customer's pain point is a recipe for disaster. The world doesn't need its seventy-ninth video search company. YouTube has already cornered the market.

2. **A startup needs to find a voice relevant to its ecosystem.** The fledgling startup must first identify and foster a community that will support its business. Most startups are too quick to begin selling when they should be educating targeted supporters. It's better to take the opposite approach.

   Selling too early is counterproductive because it triggers people's defenses and drives them away. Everyone hates being sold to; we all prefer to buy. A company that focuses on educating sets itself up to be a powerful presence in its community.

An educated group of journalists, partners, and venture capitalists can provide a startup with a much-needed voice in its chosen milieu. With a bit of legwork, you identify journalists with an interest in your company and its purpose and acquaint them with your product or service. If a company does a good job educating journalists about its market, it can become a source for quotes and comments that will appear in published articles.

Although educating requires more time and effort than selling, developing solid relationships can help sustain a company in the long run. Building a community today sets the stage for a customer order tomorrow. If your company gives Rebecca Buckman at the *Wall Street Journal* insights into what's happening in venture capital, she may well turn to you in the future as a knowledgeable and trustworthy source. That door has opened because your company has shown Buckman its unique point of view about its ecosystem. She may mention your company by name in her articles—and publicity like that is invaluable. A company that develops its authentic voice and creates its community will gain greater relevance than it ever could by flogging yet another video search engine in a crowded field of look-alikes.

3. **A startup must gain traction.** Zawacki's not talking about sales traction but rather developing the proper balance among resources, product, and customers.

An early-stage company has to balance on a three-legged stool. The first leg represents resources—financial and human—that it must assemble. The company needs money and great people who are willing to deliver every day. The second leg is product. The company must produce a winning product, take it to market, and, ultimately, sell it. The third leg represents customers, who must be recruited and educated. No company can succeed unless all three legs are even. If one leg is shorter or longer than the others, the stool will tip over. A company's resources, products, and customers must be in balance.

If a company builds its products without getting customer input, it will soon regret its mistake when customers choose a competitor's offering that contains all the features they want, based on customer feedback. If a company builds products without adequate financial resources, it risks bankruptcy sooner rather than later. Even if a company raises up-front capital, it still needs to build products and find customers. Companies often spend too much time recruiting customers when they don't have a product to deliver. All three dimensions must remain in balance.

4. **A startup must form partnerships and alliances within its ecosystem.** Companies often pay lip service to strategic partnerships, but if they don't follow through by building them, they put themselves at risk. Today's ultracompetitive global environment demands that you make alliances. In the technology industry, partnerships within ecosystems have created a zero sum game. Three platforms—SAP's NetWeaver, Microsoft.net, and Oracle's Fusion middleware—have overtaken the market. If a company is writing software, it must place a bet on one of these three platforms. It can't choose to work with two, let alone all three.

    A business needs to identify which ecosystem and partner strategy will work best for it. The company should develop the strategy that fits its long-term vision and execute it flawlessly.

    A client of ours recently received two acquisition offers, and he asked us for an introduction to SAP as another potential buyer. The introduction would have been a waste of time because our client hadn't created a strategic partnership with SAP and shared no common customers. Without a common customer, there was no integration with SAP's platform and no commitment to NetWeaver and SAP's ecosystem.

    The right partnership strategy can make a company relevant. If it starts getting traction with a strategic partner, it will get a lot of support from a Microsoft or a Google or a Salesforce.com. If a partner sees a company gaining traction within its ecosystem, it will take care of that company. Properly structured alliances are a great way to help grow a business.

5. **A startup must maintain focus.** Too many early-stage companies are so desperate for customers and customer traction that they operate in a frantic sales mode. They get 10 customers but without any discernable pattern. There's nothing unique about their business, they're selling into too many different verticals, and their customer case studies are so different as to be nonsensical. Apparently, the vice president of sales

had a good contact list and sold through his friends and family, but what's next? Where will he find customers 11 and beyond?

Most startups are not focused tightly enough on a primary market and are pursuing too many vertical markets. A company can't develop a repeatable, scalable sales process if its efforts are scattershot.

If there are three potential vertical markets, smart companies will focus on just one. Perhaps for now the focus will be on financial services. It's a logical place to start because financial services spend the most on information technology (IT). The best companies will focus even more narrowly—midsized commercial banks, for example—a segment that is well defined.

About 100,000 software companies exist in the world, each of which has five or more employees trying to sell into financial services. All want to call on Wells Fargo Bank, Credit Suisse First Boston, J.P. Morgan Chase, Bank of America, and so on. It's easy to imagine that those on the receiving end would like to hide under their desks when they see another salesperson coming.

The glut of salespeople makes focus particularly important to early-stage companies—and not just those trying to sell to the big banks—because they can rarely sell to more than one vertical market. If a startup tries to sell into too many markets, its sales team won't have enough relevant examples to credibly show how its solution fits into the customer's context. The new kid on the block will likely have a hard time understanding every potential customer's business process if too many unrelated vertical markets are included.

The sales story will not hold together if, for example, a company tries to sell simultaneously into manufacturing, pharmaceuticals, and financial services. Customers want to know what a company has done in their niche. Even though a company might have a horizontal application, the customer wants a relevant case study in its own vertical.

Summary

A corporation's ultimate purpose creates a powerful unifier by providing people with meaningful work.

A compelling purpose has three components:

- Enthusiasm for the purpose and the job of fulfilling it
- Meaning, which is critical to providing work that gives people a sense of belonging, allows them to win, and gives them a reason to celebrate
- Relevancy, which gives a startup an addressable market, a voice that educates the customer, strategic alliances, a chosen ecosystem, and a laser focus on its target customers

Call to Action

Answer the following questions to clarify your company's compelling purpose.

Enthusiasm

- Why is your company worth building?
- What is its purpose?
- Does the purpose generate enough enthusiasm to sustain you for years?

Meaning

- Will the purpose provide your employees with meaningful work?
- How will you design your culture to give people a sense of belonging and a reason to celebrate when you succeed together?

Relevancy

- What market will your company address?
- What voice will your company have to educate its market?
- Who are the right strategic partners for your company?
- What is your company's ecosystem?
- On which customers will your company focus?

Chapter 2

A WINNING BUSINESS MODEL

Create as much value to all stakeholders as possible without resorting to tradeoffs.

—R. Edward Freeman, Professor,
Darden School of the University of Virginia

How are you going to sell your company's product and make money? Your business model answers the "how" question. It connects your company's purpose with your customers by delivering products that meet their needs. To be successful your company needs a solid business model to complement its purpose.

Creating a Successful Business Model: Nilofer Merchant

"A winning business model is critical to a business's success because it drives the economic engine," says Nilofer Merchant, founder and CEO of Rubicon Consulting and author of *The New How*. Merchant offers six simple questions whose answers provide a logical process for creating a dynamic business model.

Question 1: What Are You Offering?

What problem is the business actually proposing to solve? This is the difference between aspirin and brain surgery. Does your customer have a headache or a brain tumor? Does he need aspirin or surgery?

Entrepreneurs should look for the highest level of pain, says Merchant. When Juniper and Cobalt created the market for networking equipment in the late 1990s, their enterprise customers had storage pain. They had severe pain because they were spending millions of dollars on new equipment that lacked adequate storage.

What is the actual pain? Sometimes the pain is not obvious. Apple's iPod and its surrounding ecosystem are tremendously successful, but it wasn't obvious that the world needed the iPod. At that time an MP3 player was a cheap commodity product that was perceived as a low-value, discretionary purchase.

Apple created the iPod by capitalizing on several trends in the music business. First, copying prevented the monetization of a large volume of music transactions. Second, Apple recognized that customers pay full value for a well-designed product that delivers a memorable experience. Apple knew that it could create real value by combining product innovation, a memorable experience, and its brand. Apple combined those elements to create a business model that turned a commodity market for disposable $49 products into a huge premium retail market for $400 products.

Says Merchant:

> *Entrepreneurs often confuse domain expertise in technology with customer knowledge and create products without identifying the customers' fundamental pain, which may not be obvious. Talented entrepreneurs often create products that are great technologies but that don't solve real customer problems. Sometimes that approach works because there is often a market if the underlying technology is good enough. Do the customers really have a problem? The key point is whether customers will spend money to solve it.*
>
> *Companies usually ask prospective customers if they really want the product but often fail to ask them how much they are willing to pay. The pain has to be acute enough for customers to pay for it. The offer must solve a real problem.*

Logitech's Harmony product solved a hidden problem. No one likes remote control devices, but consumers especially dislike having several remote controllers for multiple devices. Logitech unified multiple remote controls into one handy consumer device to eliminate this pain.

The market doesn't have to be huge; it just has to be big enough. Logitech studied customer sets but didn't expect everyone to buy its controller. It built the product for a small but profitable market segment. Logitech targeted highly educated, gadget-oriented consumers with discretionary income.

Question 2: What's the Competition?

What is so unique about the product that no competitor can buy itself into it? Each company does something unique that sets it apart from the competition. A company's talent or perspective may make it unique. The difference might be the ability to see an opportunity that nobody else sees.

"Entrepreneurs often articulate too small a purpose and define too small a market," says Merchant. "A company can win against the small players but not against the giants. Entrepreneurs need to include in their competitive market analyses everyone who could potentially enter their markets; and they must anticipate how the competitive landscape will look in three years if they all entered the market."

It is a good thing to lead with the vision, but unfortunately markets change. If an entrepreneur fails to adjust the vision when the market shifts, he will commit the company to the wrong path. Entrepreneurs must anticipate how their markets could change so that when it happens they can quickly make adjustments. For example, a company may need to adopt a strategy to be acquired because suddenly expansion capital is no longer available.

Question 3: Who Are Your Customers?

What is the market, and who are your customers? Startup companies often try to be too many things to too many people. A startup can be only one thing to start. This feels contrary to a compelling purpose, but this limitation actually dovetails with the vision.

The vision can be huge—solve world hunger—or it can be big: feed everyone in Malaysia this year, which is still a stretch but is more reasonable and doable.

Says Merchant:

> *Entrepreneurs need to think about their customers in the same way. A company can have a really big vision, but it must start selling to a small, focused subset of customers. For example, the vision might be solving climate change by putting a product that manages utilities—lights, heat, and water—in 80 percent of the buildings on the planet. Solving global warming is a compelling purpose but not one that can be accomplished quickly. To go to market, the company might target buildings in North America because that's the most accessible market with the highest rate of growth.*
>
> *A great way to gauge whether a business is pursuing the right initial market is to answer the question: Who is not the customer? Most entrepreneurs cannot answer that question the first time, but they must know who the customer is not. It's tricky because someone may not be your customer today but might be in the future.*

Merchant recommends that entrepreneurs use the "murder boarding" technique to identify their ideal customers and the correct initial market. *Murder boarding* means putting every possible idea about a product, the market, and the customer on a whiteboard. Entrepreneurs always have plenty of ideas but often can't decide among them. The goal of murder boarding is to eliminate ideas and identify one or two that the entrepreneur can do well. Rejected ideas don't have to die but can go into a category called "purgatory." An idea can come out of purgatory later if the right conditions arise.

Answering three questions identifies the customers:

- Do customers want it?
- Are customers willing to pay for it?
- Are customers able to pay for it?

Customers might want it and they might be willing to pay for it, but if they don't have any money, the point is moot.

"Companies must visualize their customers precisely, says Merchant. "A business has not figured out its target market if it can't draw a picture of its ideal customer. For example, the target customer might be a 35-year-old male wearing a Façonnable shirt, who is trying to solve a calendar problem because he wants to stay connected. Facebook's initial target customers, for example, were bored young adults who didn't know how to exist without technology."

Question 4: What Price Will You Charge?

Is the offer competitively differentiated to target a distinct set of customers who are willing to pay? A startup should *create* a market, says Merchant, not go into an existing one:

> *When creating a market, the price must be as high as the company can possibly get away with. Most entrepreneurs fail to charge enough, but price doesn't matter because customers will make the company discount it anyway. A startup should always set the highest possible price for its products.*

> *The natural tendency is to set a low price to achieve significant sales volume. A startup company, however, won't have significant sales volume. It's counterintuitive. Product managers often miss their $2 billion product launch number because they assumed that setting a low price would drive sales.*

> *One client got no sales traction when it entered the government market with an existing commercial product. The company thought it needed to reduce the price to get traction. We talked to 50 customers but didn't ask about price.*

> *Customers never give a reliable answer about price because they buy products for other reasons. What matters to customers about the offer? What are their alternatives? What are they thinking about in the process? Who are they talking to within the company? Price is never the foremost concern in the purchasing process. The big concerns are qualitative. Price becomes a factor only after customers have already decided to buy. Then it's simply a matter of figuring out price and from whom to order.*

> *We told the client to double the price because it had not yet effectively communicated the value proposition. We got a hostile response and took it up to the CEO. Our data suggested that revenue would increase if the company raised the price. After a contentious argument, the CEO finally agreed to make a pilot offer at the increased price. In six months that price increase generated an extra $26 million in profit.*

Entrepreneurs should clearly articulate their value proposition to support the highest possible price for their products.

Question 5: How Will You Take It to Market?

How will the company connect the product to the customer? Does the company need a sales channel? Will third-party sales partners sell the product? How does a company find the right channel partners and properly motivate them if they're already selling somebody else's product?

A startup needs to understand its value proposition to the sales channel, says Merchant:

> One client thought they had a better product offer than Cisco. They planned to give their channel partner 10 points of margin when Cisco was giving the partner 30 points. That strategy was doomed because Cisco's channel already had a strong connection with the target customer base. Winning in the channel was not about the product but about outbidding Cisco by offering the channel partner more margin points.

> Creating a new market is expensive and requires choosing the appropriate tools to create market awareness. Most companies use all of the marketing tools at once. They do case studies, buy advertising, and do public relations simultaneously. Each of those tools accomplishes an entirely different result at a particular time in the sales process. If a company doesn't understand exactly where it is in the product life cycle, using these tools is a waste of money. If a company is in the awareness creation phase, it should spend money only on public relations. Spending money on anything else would be a waste.

Many companies rely exclusively on web-based tools to create market awareness, says Merchant. Internet marketing programs can be very efficient, but they don't displace all of the traditional tools:

> Startup companies should not forget basic marketing disciplines. Entrepreneurs should use public relations, which is still one of the most effective market awareness creators.

> Entrepreneurs must invest wisely on marketing programs even if they have tons of money. Venture capitalists press their portfolio companies to use cash to accelerate growth, but they don't want entrepreneurs to throw money away. If a company can grow quickly, venture capitalists will encourage it to spend money on marketing because they want a fast-growing company.

Accelerating growth is like pregnancy: getting three women pregnant won't make a baby faster because it still takes a gestation period. Entrepreneurs have to be realistic. A team with a $3 billion opportunity can't accelerate growth with marketing programs if it hasn't started selling its product. Accelerating growth comes only after sales begin. A successful company needs marketing to accelerate growth, but first it needs to crawl, then walk, then run, and then sprint. If a company tries go from crawling to sprinting, it will land on its face.

Question 6: Can You Deliver?

Is the go-to-market strategy connected to the offer? Delivery is about knowing what the company should do in-house. A startup company should do marketing only when it can add value—and outsource everything else.

Delivery is also about managing the product within the company, says Merchant. Sales compensation, for example, must be aligned with the company's objectives. Getting the compensation right is the only thing that matters to a salesperson. When compensation is properly aligned, the sales team can focus on selling.

To win the compensation negotiation with the sales team, an entrepreneur can never leave sales compensation open to interpretation and must document it clearly. The management team's roles and responsibilities must also be well documented, with the incentives aligned in the right way. It's critical to get compensation and incentives right.

Keeping the Business Model Flexible: Mike Edwards

Because change is the one constant in business, a successful business model is subject to change. Successful entrepreneurs embrace change and are not so attached to their business models that they ignore market signals to adopt a completely new strategy.

"A company will raise money based on a plan to build widgets," says Mike Edwards, director of Savvian Advisors, "but the original business plan is rarely the billion-dollar opportunity." The billion-dollar opportunity becomes visible only after building widgets for a while. A company has to build widgets to be in the right position when the billion-dollar opportunity presents itself.

Companies must remain aware of changing markets to avoid missing a left-turn opportunity that could drive a billion-dollar valuation. Making that left turn takes courage and requires selling the new opportunity to the company's investors and other stakeholders.

O&I Systems, for example, took a left turn into optical networking. The company was developing a core network product when it saw the metro-optical networking opportunity. The founder sold his venture capital directors and investors on this bigger opportunity. As a result, that company had a valuation of several billion dollars when it went public. O&I Systems got a billion-dollar outcome by changing its business model.

Summary

Successful companies have a sound business model that addresses six components:

- The offer
- The competition
- The market and the customers
- The price
- Going to market
- Delivery

A successful business model must be flexible.

Call to Action

Answer the following questions to develop your company's business model.

Offer

- What problem is your business actually solving?
- What customer pain does your business address?
- Is the pain severe enough for customers to pay for your solution?

Competition

- What is so unique about your product that no competitor can imitate it?
- Who are your company's competitors?
- Who might enter the market?

Market and Customer

- Who are your company's ideal initial customers?
- Who are *not* your company's initial customers?
- Do these customers want your product?
- Are they willing to pay for it?

Price

- How will your company price its product?
- Have you set the right price?

Going to Market

- How will your company take its product to market?
- Will you use sales channels like distributors?
- How will you motivate your channel partners?
- How will you create market awareness?
- What is your value proposition?
- What marketing program will you use to generate leads?

Delivery

- How will you manage the product within the company?
- How will you compensate your sales team to sell the product?
- What elements of the sales process will you outsource?

Chapter 3

A CLEAR VISION

A great leader knows how to tap into potential and turn it into reality.
—Chip Conley, founder and CEO, Joie de Vivre Hospitality

Does your company's vision reflect its spirit? Purpose, the process of your business model, and passion combine to create a compelling vision. A balance of purpose, process, and passion attracts other great people and keeps them motivated. The combination of purpose and process arouses and inspires an unshakeable belief that gives entrepreneurs the conviction to sustain the heroic effort required to build a business. Successful companies express the essence of purpose, process, and passion with a simple vision statement.

"To be compelling," says Roger Sanford, who ran P3M, a Silicon Valley marketing and public relations firm in the 1990s, "the vision must radiate enthusiasm that shouts, 'We're changing the world!'" It takes a vision that can have a big, positive impact to provide the emotional fuel to drive success.

A compelling vision is the key to success. The vision is the seed capital. Investors invest only if they believe in the vision. If your vision lacks a game-changing purpose, you will create a commodity business that doesn't excite anyone.

The entrepreneur must understand the difference between a vision and a mission. A *vision* is aspirational, but aspirations, like visions, are not always obtainable. *Missions,* however, are attainable. A mission is tactical: build a prototype widget by June 30. When a company accomplishes a mission, it undertakes another. Companies often create mission statements but fail to articulate a vision. A mission statement without a vision is a path to mediocrity.

Three Tests of a Compelling Vision: Roger Sanford

Test 1: Belief

Does the entrepreneur really believe in the vision when he looks in the mirror? If an entrepreneur truly believes in the vision, his passion will draw people in. A genuinely passionate entrepreneur exudes contagious, positive energy that will not only attract investors but also drive the entire organization. On the other hand, if the vision doesn't excite and inspire the founder, it won't excite and inspire anyone else. The company will never attract great employees or supportive investors. An entrepreneur who articulates a compelling vision will be amazed at the talent that will rush to his aid.

Pursuing the vision often accomplishes the entrepreneur's life work and gives his life meaning. If the entrepreneur accomplishes his life's work, he'll also make money. If he has only a clever idea to make money, the work won't be meaningful. Building a business simply to make a lot of money will not inspire lasting passion and will attract others who are motivated only to make money.

If building the business does not inspire the entrepreneur and his team to leap out of bed and rush to work for eight years, which is the average time to liquidity in a venture-backed startup, he should find something else to do. If the vision won't inspire the investors to keep investing through seven rounds of financing, the entrepreneur should get a regular job. To be successful, a business must have a purpose that is earth-shaking, game-changing, and juicy.

A compelling vision helped make Cobalt Networks enormously successful. Cobalt had all the usual startup challenges but created a megasuccess with the help of vision. Every member of the team was a true believer.

Test 2: Attracting the Best

Can the entrepreneur attract top talent and investors? If the vision can attract top talent and raise capital, it's compelling. Compelling visions are usually based on breakthrough ideas that create extraordinary value. A breakthrough idea like Cobalt's Qube attracts the best talent and investors. Something is wrong with the vision if it can't draw world-class talent. Because it's hard to turn a pickup basketball team into world champions, the entrepreneur should adjust the vision until it attracts great people.

A compelling vision will inspire the board, the investors, and the entire team to dream big. If an entrepreneur thinks small and attainable, the company will be modest and attract only people who are risk averse. The venture capitalists will think small, too. They will give well-meaning advice that the company needs to reduce its cash burn because the revenue numbers are off.

Unfortunately, entrepreneurs are often seduced by lip service into thinking they have a compelling vision. The entrepreneur should beware when an investor says, "We're not investing in your company, but you've got us believing." If the vision is truly compelling, an entrepreneur should be able to attract great people *and* raise money. If the entrepreneur has to push the vision, his business will likely fail.

Test 3: Market Fit

If customers are compelled to buy the product, the company has market fit. A company can have a half-baked team and an average product, such as Microsoft Windows, for example, but can pull the market if it has a compelling vision. Market fit is the ultimate test. A compelling vision drives commercial success by inspiring customers to buy.

3Dfx had a vision of becoming the world's leading graphics semiconductor company. 3Dfx balanced purpose, process, and passion to drive its success. Its founders saw a game-changing opportunity because the high cost of graphics-enabled computers made movie-quality graphics inaccessible to consumers. Silicon Graphics' $250,000 workstations generated the computer animation for movies like *Jurassic Park* but were prohibitively expensive to all but a small cadre of corporations and design firms. Because expensive products have a long sales cycle, Silicon Graphics could sell only a few thousand workstations per year.

Silicon Graphics' business model invited 3Dfx's founders to shift the prevailing paradigm by putting comparable graphics-rendering capabilities on a semiconductor. The founders' vision was to revolutionize computer graphics by putting a graphics semiconductor on every personal computer. Making superb computer graphics accessible to everyone gave 3Dfx a big purpose that inspired genuine enthusiasm.

The founders channeled this enthusiasm into a business model based on selling hundreds of millions of graphics chips for $30 each. 3Dfx went from a vision in 1994 to an initial public offering (IPO) at a $500 million post-offering valuation in 1997 because it balanced purpose, process, and passion to become the world's dominant graphics semiconductor company. The company had a market fit that helped make graphics-rendering technology a standard feature of every personal computer and enabled the computer gaming industry.

Keeper of the Vision:
Nilofer Merchant and Vivek Mehra

Steve DeWitt became Cobalt's best salesperson by selling Cobalt's vision of becoming the world's leading producer of affordable servers. DeWitt was at a disadvantage when he joined Cobalt before its second round of financing because he had replaced the deceased popular founder, Mark Wu, who had generated the vision. He made a bold move to own the vision to be able to compel people to support the company.

To own the vision, DeWitt personally invested $900,000 in Cobalt's second round of financing. His investment was a powerful endorsement of the vision and won the respect of everyone in the company. Mark Wu had animated Cobalt with its life force, but with his investment DeWitt became keeper of the vision.

"It's difficult to translate a compelling purpose and a viable business model into a vision," explains Nilofer Merchant.

Nobody tells a visionary entrepreneur that he has got it right because a vision is not true yet; it's still an idea. The entrepreneur must maintain the vision independently of handling the challenges of running the business. Holding the vision is a spiritual exercise because it requires deep and constant faith.

The founding CEO must maintain constant vigilance to ascertain whether or not the company is on target. Until success has validated the vision, a company must be agile. Because no business model avoids a collision with reality, the tough part is what to do when the company gets off target. Successful teams set egos aside and change course before the board of directors tells them to. Ultimately, nobody validates the vision until the company succeeds.

"The entrepreneur must own the vision," affirms Vivek Mehra, co-founder of Cobalt Networks and general partner of August Capital. "The vision should originate from the entrepreneur, who must own it and drive it. The board's responsibility is to improve the business plan. A good board can help the entrepreneur articulate the vision more clearly but won't contradict him about it. It is not the board's job to create a vision. If the board knows more than the entrepreneur, the board should be running the company. A company is broken if the board creates the vision."

Communicating the Vision

Once the founder owns the vision, he must be able to communicate it clearly so that others understand it immediately. Reducing the vision to a single sentence creates a powerful alignment tool that everyone can use to promote the company.

When the company's purpose and business model are complementary, the vision statement will naturally exude the passion behind the vision. When the sentence accurately reflects the balance among purpose, process, and passion, potential ecosystem partners will respond positively.

Cobalt and 3Dfx succinctly described their visions to facilitate alignment among stakeholders. Cobalt's vision was to become the leading producer of affordable servers by democratizing the Internet. 3Dfx's vision was to become the world's leading graphics semiconductor company by bringing movie-quality graphics to every desktop.

A successful vision statement captures the company's bigger purpose and gets people excited. In *Good to Great,* Jim Collins calls the vision statement a "Hedgehog Concept," which is a "simple, crystalline concept"[2] that guides all of a company's efforts. A good Hedgehog Concept describes how a company will make money doing something it loves while becoming the best in the world at it. A startup company with a game-changing innovation can aspire to become the best in the world by articulating a new product category and declaring itself the winner.

---

2   Collins, Jim, Good to Great: *Why Some Companies Make the Leap… and Others Don't* (New York, HarperCollins, 1994).

Companies that don't have a succinct vision statement often struggle. Woven Systems had a serious sales problem because its founders, Dan Maltbie and Bert Tanaka, could not articulate Woven's vision in plain English. They wanted to build a novel distributive Ethernet switch, but their vision statement was full of unintelligible engineering jargon that made it impossible to understand their concept. They talked to 60 different venture capital firms, but they couldn't sell the vision. Two venture capitalists even begged Woven's founders not to make them fund another Ethernet switch company.

The founders brought in a new CEO, Harry Quackenboss, to solve this fundamental sales problem. Within two weeks they developed a new vision based on a more conventional-looking Ethernet switch product. The team had a much better reception with another 60 venture capital firms, who could now understand what the company was building. The new vision helped the company raise two rounds of financing and get to revenue with the world's largest Ethernet switch.

Summary

- A compelling vision has three elements:
- A purpose
- A sound business model grounded in good financial discipline and process
- Passion founded on belief

The founder is the keeper of the vision.

The vision should be flexible.

Answering three fundamental questions helps an entrepreneur refine the vision:

- Does the company have a compelling purpose?
- Does the company have a sound business model that will be profitable?
- Does the founding team believe in the business?

The answers quickly ascertain whether the company has the proper balance among purpose, process, and passion. The vision results from a balanced combination of these three elements.

Call to Action

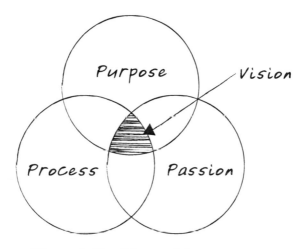

Figure 1: Drafting a vision statement

Test your vision by drawing three overlapping circles corresponding to each question (see figure 1). Using these circles, draft a vision statement similar to the sample vision statements for Cobalt and 3Dfx (see sidebar). The vision statement should capture the big purpose, the business model, and the company's aspirations.

Next, write an alternate version of the vision statement that identifies the company's new market category

Sample Vision Statements for Cobalt and 3Dfx

- Cobalt aspires to become the leading provider of affordable servers by democratizing the Internet.

- 3Dfx aspires to become the leading graphics semiconductor company by bringing movie-quality graphics to every computer.

and declares itself the winner. These vision statements will help you write the business plan in chapter 4 and articulate the verbal components of your company's marketing infrastructure in chapter 16. These statements will make it easy for you to describe your business to anyone.

Chapter 4

A WELL-WRITTEN BUSINESS PLAN

Creativity is the ability to generate original ideas that have value.

—Sir Ken Robinson, author,
Element: How Finding Your Passion Changes Everything

Writing a thorough business plan turns your company's vision into a blueprint that will guide its future. By telling the story of your business, you will align others behind the vision.

Writing a compelling business plan has two aspects: storytelling and backcasting. A good business plan tells the story of how a company will realize its vision. A great business plan also works backward from what a company will look like in the future, when it has realized its vision. The founding team can establish the quality of its working relationships and create the culture by writing the business plan together.

Cobalt's Business Plan: Vivek Mehra

"Writing the business plan helped Cobalt Networks avoid disaster and aligned the team to create our success," says Vivek Mehra.

Cobalt started without a vision but still had a $2 billion exit. Six of us started Cobalt in 1996. The founders had some half-baked ideas and a burning desire to build a company together.

37

We spent evenings brainstorming. Our first idea was a video platform for in-flight entertainment. We developed the business model, realized that too many things were out of our control, and dropped that plan. Our first idea was gone.

We got seed funding for our second idea, which was an e-mail appliance with a Java co-processor. This idea sounded pretty cool, and we had the experience to do it. When we wrote the business plan, however, we realized again that too many things were out of our control, and we abandoned that idea.

Our third idea was an all-in-one web and e-mail server. The Internet was just catching on in 1996. Business cards did not list websites or e-mail addresses. It was incredibly difficult to get an e-mail address or a website. Connecting the Internet to complex hardware is standard now, but it was a stretch back then. We knew exactly how to solve the problem by making it easy for anybody to create an Internet presence.

We never looked back after we put the idea on paper. We created an appliance so a customer could plug in and be up and running on the Internet in less than 15 minutes. It was so simple that even a venture capitalist could set it up.

All entrepreneurs should write a business plan. Entrepreneurs lead with the vision, but a vision doesn't pay the bills. Unfortunately, most entrepreneurs don't write a business plan. They take a shortcut by preparing an executive summary and a PowerPoint presentation, which are poor substitutes.

Entrepreneurs need a clear vision, a succinct "elevator pitch," and a well-written business plan. Says Mehra:

Writing a good business plan takes at least a month because it takes time to do the due diligence to affirm the vision and develop a plan to raise money. It doesn't have to be a 100-page encyclopedia, but it should be a thorough 15- to 30-page document. The founders could still be wrong, which happens often, but at least they'll have a straightforward plan.

Writing the business plan causes fallout. Cobalt's founding team, for example, shrank from six to four and eventually to three. One of Cobalt's co-founders was a software expert. The team selected an untested open-source software called Linux, but he wanted to create a proprietary Basic binary operating system for our appliance. He disagreed with our choice and quit. It was a tough decision, but we're still friends.

Then our founding CEO, Mark Wu, died in a motorcycle accident right before our Series A funding. Despite this tragedy the founding team and investor group hung together. We were committed to each other, we had a business plan, and we were determined to make it happen.

Almost everything is about the team, especially in the initial stages. Entrepreneurs should expect to spend at least 12 months figuring out who is on the team. The team should expect attrition because there's a dark side to doing a startup. Everyone talks passionately about wanting to work in one, but when it comes time to leave the big company, not everyone will be able to make the leap. Startups require long hours and incredibly hard work. Writing the business plan helps determine who is up for the challenge.

"We had a successful outcome because we executed on our business plan," says Mehra. "In 1996 investors didn't want to talk to us because we were first-time entrepreneurs.

"In 1998 Cobalt shipped its first product and did $3.5 million in revenue. The company did $25 million in 1999 and $60 million in 2000 and introduced many different products. Our rapid growth rate enabled us to go public in 1999. When Sun Microsystems bought Cobalt for $2 billion in late 2000, we had 250 employees and had shipped 100,000 servers worldwide."

Components of a Good Business Plan

A good business plan is an internal and external alignment tool. Reading the business plan gets a new team member quickly in alignment with the vision. It also brings the vision to life for investors and strategic partners.

A business plan yields a variety of written communication assets. Lawyers often use the narrative tale as the basis of a private-placement memorandum to sell securities to raise working capital. The story also provides material for the company's website. The financial projections form the basis of operation plans and annual budgets.

Writing a business plan is an excellent way for the founders to design their business with as much clarity and precision as possible. The process allows a team to begin working together collaboratively. The technologist, for example, could write the description of the company's technology and product, while the salesperson could describe the go-to-market strategy. The crucial point is that writing the business plan puts the vision into a tangible form so that the team can make it a reality, like Cobalt did.

A good business plan should contain at least eleven key elements:

- The vision statement
- The problem the company is solving
- The company's solution
- How the company will make money solving the problem
- Financial projections
- The company's unfair competitive advantage
- How the company distinguishes itself from the competition
- Biographies of the founders
- The sales and marketing strategy
- The company's development plans
- Where the company is on its roadmap

Back-Casting

> *Live as though the alternative reality had already happened.*
> —Srikumar S. Rao, author, *Are You Ready to Succeed?*

Back-casting enhances a business plan's power to shape the future. The process starts by imagining what the company will look like when it has succeeded and reverse-engineering all the tactical moves that were required to get there. By identifying the company's ideal strategic partners, for example, the team can make immediate strategic moves to develop and nurture those relationships.

Back-Casting at Cobalt Networks

Cobalt's founders dreamed the company backward from an initial public offering. The team started by understanding the financial metrics needed to become a viable public company. Then they set about designing and building the ecosystem of strategic partners, customers, and other stakeholders necessary to help Cobalt generate the requisite financial results to go public.

To rapidly generate revenue, Cobalt could not rely on sales from North America alone. Soon after entering the US market, it entered the European and Japanese markets to generate enough sales to become a viable IPO candidate two or three years after product launch.

Cobalt's strategy to enter foreign markets early in its life allowed it to increase sales exponentially. The company hired an experienced European vice president (VP) of sales, who had previously helped five other companies establish operations in Europe, and engaged a Japanese distribution partner experienced in introducing US electronic products in Japan. The European VP of sales and the Japanese partner localized Cobalt's products and drove foreign sales.

As a result of back-casting after it had confirmed and validated its business model, at the time of its IPO Cobalt realized 60 percent of its sales from Europe and Japan. Cobalt generated $60 million in revenue in its third year with the help of foreign sales. Cobalt's iconic Qube server even developed a cultlike following in Japan. Back-casting enabled Cobalt to achieve the financial strength and the market credibility to go public in 1999 in what is still one of the most successful IPOs in history.

Cobalt went public and obtained a $2 billion market capitalization because its founders shared the plan with everyone in the company. Having certainty about the financial results and the strategy required to achieve the goal of becoming a public company aligned everyone behind the founders' objectives. With awareness of the desired outcome, everyone contributed to affecting the intended result.

The business plan should envision building a company that has the financial strength to go public. Unfortunately, most entrepreneurs' minds shut down when they imagine building a successful public company like Cobalt. They buy in to the conventional wisdom that Sarbanes-Oxley makes it too difficult and too expensive and don't have a strategy to go public.

Failing to imagine becoming a public company becomes a hidden limitation. The company gets built to sell, not built to last. Investors in a built-to-sell company need to sell it to get their money out, whereas investors in a built-to-last company can sell their equity in the public market after the company has gone public. Cobalt succeeded because it dared to dream big by back-casting from an IPO.

A Back-Casting Primer: Joe Watt

Reverse-engineering successful public companies provides entrepreneurs with a much clearer picture of what their companies will need to look like to go public.

The first step is to identify a handful of admired companies in the same industry. The second step is to identify the positive qualities to emulate and the negative qualities to avoid. A startup, for example, might want to emulate the iconic and intelligent design capabilities of Apple Computer but avoid the key-man dependency that results from relying on a messianic and visionary founder like Steve Jobs for the product design.

Reading the IPO prospectuses of the admired companies calibrates expectations to reality and provides stories of how these companies built their businesses.

Back-casting starts by drawing a simple map of the company's fully developed ecosystem. The map positions the company at the center and identifies the ideal customers, strategic partners, suppliers and vendors, outsourced business process partners, and advisory board members, consultants, and directors. A complete map also includes the communities in which the company does business, the environment, and the company's employees and investors.

Identifying the optimal stakeholders makes it easier for the company to attract them. If a company foresees that Cisco will be the ideal strategic partner in two years, for example, it can invite an executive from Cisco to serve on its advisory board now. As an informal adviser, the executive will witness the company's progress and become an internal advocate at Cisco for a strategic alliance at the appropriate time. By anticipating the alliance and developing a relationship now, the company will have established itself as a credible partner for Cisco when it comes time to make the alliance.

"An entrepreneur can learn a lot from a CEO who has taken a company public," says investment banker Joe Watt, Senior Vice President of GulfStar Group:

> *Great CEOs have near-term, intermediate-term, and long-term plans when they start their businesses. They identify the attributes of the companies they want to have in seven to 10 years and work backward to determine the positioning of their products and their pathway to the future.*

> *Cavium Networks had one of the best-performing IPOs in the hardware space in the post-bubble years. Cavium had the number one position in the relatively small security microprocessor market. The company saw a much larger opportunity in the general-purpose microprocessor market and defined its now-flagship multicore multiprocessor, Octeon, back in 2001 and released it in 2006. That product defined the company when it went public in 2007. Having a long-term vision allowed Cavium to excel in the nuanced metric of design wins and drove the company's rapid growth that made going public in a difficult market a viable option.*

Figure 2 shows an example of a simple ecosystem map with the company at the center.

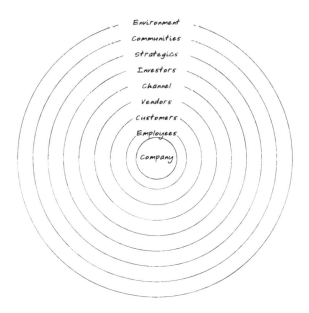

Figure 2: A simple ecosystem map with the company at the center

This technique works best as a collaborative process using the executive team's contact lists. Populating the map with names and logos, using a whiteboard or large sheets of paper, makes the future visible. A clear picture of the future helps everyone attract the ideal stakeholders to build the company.

Summary

- The business plan is the blueprint that shapes the future.
- A great business plan envisions the future through storytelling and back-casting.
- Writing the business plan collaboratively establishes the culture.

Call to Action

Write a business plan with the following elements:

- The vision statement
- The problem the company is solving
- The company's solution
- How the company will make money solving the problem
- Financial projections
- The company's unfair competitive advantage
- How the company distinguishes itself from the competition
- Biographies of the founders
- The sales and marketing strategy
- The company's development plans
- Where the company is on its roadmap

Prepare a back-casting map that models what the company will look like when it has realized the vision; include the following:

- The ideal employees
- The ideal advisory board members
- The ideal executives

- The ideal directors

- The ideal investors

- The ideal customers

- The ideal distribution partners

- The ideal vendors and suppliers

- The ideal strategic partners

- The ideal communities in which to do business

- How the company will have the most positive effect on society and the environment

Chapter 5

EFFECTIVE CORE VALUES

Being less bad is not good enough.

—Ron Pompei, principal and creative director, Pompei A.D.

Core values are the foundation of a corporate culture. Your company's values determine the rules of engagement among its employees and ecosystem partners. Are you going to intelligently design your company's culture, or are you going to let it develop by default?

Successful companies articulate their core values as a code of conduct to guide behavior. Certainty about expected behaviors promotes collaboration and teamwork. Core values that result from a collaborative process similar to writing a business plan are effective because they have buy-in from everyone. The most effective core values are well defined, with people held accountable to them. Most companies, however, have ineffective core values because employees must deduce them from the leader's behavior. This works well if the leader is charismatic, but such value systems create weak cultures and usually disappear when there is a change of leadership.

Deduced Core Values: Ken Wilcox

"Silicon Valley Bank's culture evolved by following the behavior of our CEO, Roger Smith," says Ken Wilcox.

Roger was a wild, colorful leader who was so charismatic that everyone knew exactly what it meant to be an SVB'er. The culture was 100 percent clear.

Being cheap was one of our core values. Silicon Valley Bank had the best margins of any bank in the United States because we never spent money on anything. We were legendarily cheap. A division manager spent $2,000 putting the bank's logo on fuzzy golf club covers for clients. Roger ordered the manager to recover the gifts from the clients and return them all to the vendor for a refund.

Being engaged was another core value. Every morning, Roger took attendance across his empire to ensure that we were all fully engaged at work. Roger required every employee in every office, including Boston, to attend the regular 7 a.m. daily meeting. Everybody had to sign in. The head of each office had to explain why anyone was missing. Being out sick wasn't allowed.

Roger would also call us in Boston at 5 p.m. on Friday afternoons: "Hi, Ken, how are you doing?" Of course, he was just checking to make sure we were still engaged.

Winning was another core value, says Wilcox.

We shared our wins at those morning meetings. Anybody with a new win was required to report: "XYZ Company just deposited $200,000." There would be clapping across the country. Everyone wanted to be a winner.

Roger's greeting always was, "We're winning!" At first it sounded goofy. I thought I was working for a maniac. Within a few months, however, I also greeted people by saying, "We're winning!" It felt good. We enjoyed being winners and telling each other stories about what great winners we were.

Having a solid work ethic was another core value. "We worked incredibly hard," says Wilcox. "There's an apocryphal story about Jim Rudder, who worked for free for three months until Roger decided he'd passed the trial period. During his trial period, Jim often spent the night at the office in a sleeping bag on the floor. Everyone knew that being at Silicon Valley Bank meant hard work."

Defined Core Values: Brian Fitzgerald

"Bill Campbell, the CEO of Claris, expressly defined Claris' culture by using maxims," says Brian Fitzgerald, former VP of operations at Apple, Claris, and Intuit.

> *The maxim Dissent is acceptable was the cornerstone of Claris' culture. We didn't get into fistfights. We put problems on the table and got everybody engaged to solve them quickly. Bill Campbell created a safe environment to encourage constructive dissent.*

> *No silos was another of Claris' cultural maxims. We had all come out of the silo model—separate marketing, separate sales, separate manufacturing, and separate distribution. Bill challenged us to turn these silos into an integrated whole. He got us to tie the interdependent parts of Claris' software business together with a clunking set of processes that integrated the supply chain, manufacturing, information management, and customer support.*

Following the *No silos* maxim became a competitive advantage because it enabled Claris to also become a marketing and product development business. When Bill Campbell talked to customers or distributors, he sold not only the product but also the company.

"Because we could sell the product and the company to customers," says Fitzgerald,

> *Claris had $46 million of sales in its first year. Campbell used maxims to create a collaborative culture that managed the stress of rapid growth. Great people drive growth, not processes and products; but rapid growth requires effective teamwork.*

> *Because Claris was a spin-off of Apple, we had the advantage of starting with an installed customer base. All the painful scaling issues that we'd suffered back at Apple had taught us how to organize operations to handle rapid growth. We understood the necessary core competencies and put appropriate processes in place to scale operations. All of the processes worked together exceptionally well in the collaborative culture that Bill Campbell created.*

> *A startup can lose its culture as it grows and evolves, especially if it hasn't taken the trouble to define it. To ensure that a company can grow, it must add people who buy in to the culture. Without a defined culture, people will confuse the feeling of*

a particular growth stage for corporate culture. After we grew at Apple and Claris, many people nostalgically wanted it to be the way it was. A clearly defined culture supports rapid growth and prevents it from pulling the company apart.

Hybrid Core Values: Vivek Mehra

Cobalt Network's culture was animated by a combination of core values that were both clearly articulated and deduced from management behavior. The values relating to the company's external rules of engagement with its customers and suppliers were express. Cobalt's management team modeled the internal rules. The combination of external and internal rules of engagement gave Cobalt's culture cohesion.

"Core values play a vital role in building a billion-dollar business," says Vivek Mehra.

Startups should set forth their two or three most important values because it's hard to remember more than three things. The founders need to lead by example to reinforce the core values. The CEO has to constantly model the core values throughout the organization. If a company can instill belief in those two or three values, its culture can be a powerful force.

A healthy corporate culture provides resilience. A solid culture helps a company respond when things don't happen as planned. When a company runs out of money sooner than expected because it cost more to go to market, culture determines how well a team stands back up after it falls together.

Innovation was one of Cobalt's core values. We stressed the need to innovate and measured our progress against metrics such as introducing new products every six months. Executing our goals and delivering on time were easy things to measure.

Customer satisfaction was another of Cobalt's core values but is harder to quantify. What happens when a customer has a problem? The culture determines the answer. I led by example and put my home phone number on the website. Once, a customer called me on a Sunday morning because his server went down. Leading by example is not easy.

If someone doesn't live up to the core values, the quicker a company gets rid of him, the better. It's painful, but a company will harm its culture by keeping people who don't share the values. The company should just cut them loose.

Cobalt had implicit internal rules of engagement that contributed to its big-hearted, high-spirited culture. How everyone rallied around Mark Wu's widow and three children after he died reflected the company's internal code of conduct. Cobalt's core values of generosity, teamwork, and integrity gave it a dynamic culture, says Mehra.

The company's loving response to its founder's death reflected its generosity. Cobalt accelerated the vesting of Mark's stock and hired his widow. The way everyone pitched in to support the founder's family reflected the company's commitment to teamwork. Employees bought his family a Christmas tree and took a day off work to trim it. How the company ensured his family's financial security reflected its integrity. When Cobalt went public, Mark's family was set for life.

Cobalt had an infectiously positive culture with a heart that allowed it to achieve extraordinary results. The culture might have been even more powerful if all of its core values had been expressly defined.

Defining the Company's Values

The opportune time to define a company's core values is after the founders have written the business plan. Preparing the business plan is the team's first opportunity to work together. This process often reveals shared values. Founding teams often express common values, such as integrity and respect.

A simple method of defining a company's core values starts with each person articulating his personal code of ethics. Everyone writes single sentences that define their top four personal values.

The team then lists all the values expressed in descending frequency of appearance and selects the top four. If the top four shared values are integrity, respect, teamwork, and quality, for example, the team then refines a definition for each value that reflects the company's personality. The team can either select individual definitions that resonate or collaboratively compose values with elements selected from individual definitions.

Values become a powerful force for alignment when they have buy-in from everyone. Defining the core values works best to ensure buy-in if it is a collaborative process that involves the whole team. Such values can animate a company with a powerful spirit, especially when people are held accountable to them.

Summary

- Core values are the foundation of a corporate culture.

- Core values determine the internal and external rules of engagement.

- Core values that are developed collaboratively are effective because they have buy-in.

- Core values create alignment when they are well defined and people are held accountable to them.

Call to Action

Articulate your company's core values:

- Identify the key core values.

- Choose one word that describes each value.

- Write a sentence that defines the value.

How will you apply the core values internally?

How will you apply them externally in the ecosystem?

Chapter 6
DESIGNING THE CULTURE

*Culture is the foundation. Define it with great precision so that
everyone can understand it and measure it period to period.*

—Gerry McDonough, CEO, Lead First

Core values provide the cultural foundation, but accountability makes the culture dynamic. Are you willing to hold people accountable to your company's core values? Will you have the courage to ask someone to leave if they don't act in alignment with those values? The very concept of corporate culture makes most entrepreneurs feel uncomfortable because they don't know how to create an effective one by sharing the vision and holding people accountable to the core values.

When management models the core values and has the courage to hold everyone accountable to them, culture becomes a powerful unifier. Shared values foster collaboration and create alignment because everyone knows which behaviors are expected and which are not tolerated. Accountability is the key to turning core values into a company's rules of engagement.

The best time to develop a company's culture is prior to incorporation. Most companies, however, ignore culture as infrastructure because only physical assets like computers, phone systems, and equipment show up on the balance sheet. Companies with vibrant cultures reject this limited view of infrastructure and design and nurture their culture. A values-based culture can become an extremely valuable asset that facilitates alignment, drives success, and sustains the business. On the other hand, culture can be a liability in corporations that expect employees to deduce it because it is ambiguous and unstable.

A values-based culture provides a competitive advantage because it makes the company a better place to work. Managing a company is more efficient when people know what behaviors are encouraged. Certainty enhances optimum performance. A well-defined culture creates a supportive work environment with clear rules that inspire people to deliver their best, and inspired employees are happier and more productive.

A clearly defined culture makes it easier to recruit people who share the same values—and those values provide a useful filter when selecting new employees. A values-based company won't hire a talented engineer if he's not in alignment with the values. Great companies add people who fit the culture and use their values as an objective standard to measure employee performance. Annual employee reviews, for example, can reflect whether a person's performance was in alignment with the values. Great companies preserve and protect their culture by firing people who refuse to abide by the core values.

Cobalt Networks and 3Dfx had dynamic cultures that made them great places to work. Neither company, however, expressly defined the values that determined the internal rules of engagement, and only Cobalt articulated the external rules of engagement with its ecosystem. Tragedies, not accountability, animated both companies' cultures.

Like Cobalt, 3Dfx also lost a co-founder in an accident. A drunk driver killed Alma Ribbs in a head-on collision when she was seven months pregnant with twins. Everybody rallied around the company. Ribbs's death gave 3Dfx a heart and unleashed an indefatigable win-for-Alma spirit that amplified the enthusiasm behind its vision and drove its success in the graphics semiconductor industry. Companies can animate their corporate cultures without a tragedy, of course, by articulating their core values and holding people accountable to them.

Seven Rules for Building a Culture: Ken Wilcox and Leo Quilici

"I have five rules for building a culture," says Ken Wilcox. "The first rule is talk the talk. The second one is walk the talk. The third rule is be successful.

The fourth one is celebrate success. And the fifth rule is escort the misfits out of the tribe. On the one hand, it's not that hard. On the other hand, it's incredibly difficult. I spend a lot of my time working on our culture, but I never quite succeed."

Talk the Talk

Talk the talk sounds very simple. The leader has to regularly articulate and model the core values and explain exactly what is important. He has to constantly pose leading questions: What counts? To what are we aspiring? Why are we here together? What are we trying to accomplish? He can't just sit in his office but must circulate daily to talk with his tribe. Says Wilcox:

> *To be effective the CEO must communicate from the heart. Leaders who don't communicate authentically from the heart fail to succeed. John Kerry, for example, was not elected president because he could not speak from the heart. I heard a woman ask Kerry, "I admire you greatly, but you don't speak to my heart. What are you going to do about that?"*

> *Employees are like that woman. Unfortunately, leaders are trained to be rational and believe that rationality requires them not to express emotions. Employees, however, have brains, hearts, and souls and need to be spoken to as whole human beings. Great leaders speak from their hearts. The best way to speak from the heart is to tell true stories and be truthful.*

Walk the Talk

The CEO can't just talk about the company's core values; he has to embody them. "If the CEO walks the talk, his employees will automatically follow him so long as he is not a hypocrite," says Wilcox.

> *Because Roger Smith swore constantly, everybody else at Silicon Valley Bank swore also. Every sentence contained profanity.*

> *John Dean, our second CEO, never swore. Miraculously, the swearing disappeared without any corporate edict. It just disappeared because everyone deduced that swearing was no longer an accepted cultural behavior.*

If Roger had professed clean speech as a core value but had sworn anyway, he would have caused an alignment and integrity problem. Roger walked his talk. Everything Roger professed, Roger did. Even if we were philosophically opposed to profanity, because Roger was authentic and walked his talk, we walked with him. We were proud to follow an authentic leader.

This story illustrates how most leaders subconsciously create their company's culture because employees automatically emulate their leader's behavior. "Silicon Valley Bank had a vibrant and dynamic culture that fueled our growth in the Roger Smith era," says Wilcox. "Everyone deduced the culture from Roger's charismatic behavior, but Silicon Valley Bank might have been even more successful if Roger had expressly promulgated the tenets of the culture."

Be Successful

Building a real business creates success. "Roger Smith clearly defined the metrics of success and encouraged us to meet them," says Wilcox. "He ensured that we were successful and always cheered us on. He rewarded success, and he engaged in it himself. We were winners."

Celebrate Success

Silicon Valley Bank was a successful tribe that celebrated. "Periodically," says Wilcox, "we'd put down our weapons to gather at a restaurant and have a big celebration. Celebrating brought us closer and made us feel good to be part of the bank."

Escort Misfits out of the Tribe

Wilcox's final rule for building a culture is the most difficult one to apply. "If someone doesn't fit the culture," he says, "the company must be disciplined and expel him from the tribe. If someone doesn't embrace the values, talk the talk, walk the talk, succeed, and celebrate afterward, they don't fit the culture. If you let them stay in the tribe, you will compromise the culture. When a company tolerates too many people who don't fit, it will destroy its culture. A CEO who follows the formula to create a dynamic, sustainable culture is more likely to succeed."

Drive the Culture

"The sixth rule," says Leo Quilici, Cobalt's initial chief financial officer (CFO), "is that the CEO should drive the culture intentionally." He needs to be cognizant that everything he says and does—whether or not he shows up late for meetings—flows through the company to create its culture. "It's the Roger Smith story: if the CEO swears, everybody else will swear. The CEO should not allow his culture to just happen because it will be mushy. A clearly defined culture, on the other hand, gives a sense of belonging and a clear sense of direction."

Propagate the Culture

Quilici's seventh rule is for companies that have a second or foreign location: one of its principals should work there for a year to establish the culture. "Creating a culture that spans one office is difficult enough," he says, "but it's even more challenging when a company has remote locations because the office leader there will establish the culture. Without someone in place from the home office, it will be impossible to impart the culture. Creating a successful foreign subsidiary is challenging, and having a different culture can sink it quickly."

Summary

Defining a corporate culture is a critical success factor. Every company has a culture, which can either evolve haphazardly or be driven. Smart entrepreneurs decide what kind of culture they want to create in their companies and foster it, instead of allowing it to develop by default. This gives them an advantage over competitors that expect employees to deduce the company's values from management's behavior. Organizing the cultural infrastructure creates a dynamic culture animated by inspired individuals who are aligned with the company's vision and values. Chapter 20 shows how to further strengthen a corporate culture by incorporating its elements into the foundational legal documents and elevating them to constitutional status.

Call to Action

Holding people accountable to the company's core values is crucial. These seven rules help CEOs build a culture and make it easier to hold people accountable:

- Talk the talk.
- Walk the talk.
- Be successful.
- Celebrate success.
- Escort misfits out of the tribe.
- Drive the culture.
- Seed other offices with a cultural representative from the home office.

Chapter 7

WORKING WITH A MENTOR

Get real. Teach us. Mentor us.

—Christiana Wyly, venture partner, Satori Capital

If you are serious about increasing your probability of success, engaging a mentor is one of the best moves you can make. Starting a company without experienced guidance is asking for trouble, and acquiring your leadership skills by trial and error can be fatal to the company. Who is your mentor? If you don't yet have an experienced mentor, you should engage one as soon as possible.

A clear vision and a well-crafted business plan are essential to attracting an experienced mentor. The best test of the founder's leadership ability and the power of his vision is whether he can attract an experienced executive as a mentor. An enthusiastic mentor will share his excitement with his network and attract other resources necessary for success.

The right mentor often effortlessly directs additional talent to join the company. Solaicx, a pioneer in advanced equipment to manufacture solar wafers, attracted Robert Medearis, the founder of Silicon Valley Bank, as the chairman of the board and the mentor to CEO Bob Ford. Medearis joined the board soon after incorporation and attracted Bill Yerkes, considered by many to be the father of commercial photovoltaics, as chief technology officer (CTO). Yerkes's stellar reputation enabled Solaicx to recruit a team of top engineers, which attracted venture capital investors. Medearis's experience as founder of Silicon

Valley Bank and the CEO of several companies empowered him to guide Bob Ford and manage the board. Medearis's presence as the mentor attracted the resources needed to build Solaicx into the company that MEMC Corporation acquired in May 2010 for approximately $103 million.

Qualities of an Ideal Mentor

For the founder of a startup, the ideal mentor has been the founder and the CEO of a successful business. An executive who has been in the CEO's hot seat with ultimate responsibility for meeting payroll every month knows what it takes to build and run a business. A mentor who has managed a successful business has the experience to guide his mentee to promote success and avoid failure.

The ideal mentor has nothing left to prove. His business achievements have provided him with sufficient material wealth and ego gratification that he is free from worry about survival and social status. His successes have brought a confidence that enables him to guide from the heart, not lead by the sword.

Gordon Campbell acquired deep inner confidence from building two public companies—Seeq Technology and Chips and Technologies—and inventing the fabless semiconductor industry. With nothing to prove, Campbell mentored the CEOs of Techfarm's portfolio companies from a place beyond ego. Campbell loved mentoring executives to help them develop their talents. His CEOs felt safe and supported because he made it clear that he was an ally who wanted to empower them to succeed and not a rival for their positions.

As a successful founder, Campbell knew exactly what skills are required to run a company. He knew from personal experience that first-time CEOs have the potential to become great leaders but rarely have the skills to build a successful company much less run one. Campbell built on his entrepreneurs' limited prior management experience to teach them how to build and manage their companies.

The ideal mentor shows the founding CEO the skills he needs to acquire and coaches him to cultivate his leadership abilities. Campbell pushed the executives in Techfarm's portfolio companies especially hard. As an active executive chairman of most Techfarm companies, he empowered the CEOs to lead but was not afraid to give forceful guidance.

Steve DeWitt wanted Cobalt Networks to spend more on marketing to drive revenue growth rather than become a profitable company. Contrary to what was in vogue during the Internet mania, Campbell insisted that Cobalt's financial plan included a path to profitability. DeWitt adjusted the budget so that it increased the marketing spend, but he also worked toward the goal of becoming a profitable business. As a result, when Cobalt went public it stood out as a business of substance among a crowd of Internet companies built on hype and weak financial statements.

Campbell manifested many qualities of the ideal mentor. His advice was authentic because it rang with the truth of his experience. He was fearless in speaking his truth and willing to accept the consequences, which could include losing a relationship. When 3Dfx Interactive, which was then the leading graphics semiconductor company, wanted to extend its business by buying a circuit board assembly company, Campbell was not afraid to tell the CEO and the board that they were making the mistake that ultimately destroyed the company.

Campbell had no ego-driven need to control his CEOs. His advice was authoritative but not authoritarian. He helped them avoid disasters and empowered them to succeed. He believed in his protégés and was generous with his time and advice. This belief and generosity of spirit instilled his mentees with confidence. Campbell's candor in pointing out his executives' weaknesses as opportunities for improvement prevented their confidence from developing into hubris.

To teach his executives in the trenches, Campbell often let them continue a course of action right to the brink of disaster. He and his partner Kurt Keilhacker repeatedly assured NetMind that Techfarm would provide the second round of funding. NetMind had trouble landing customers and was running low on money. With only a few weeks of operating cash remaining, Campbell and Keilhacker told Matt Freivald, NetMind's CEO and founder, that Techfarm would not fund the company unless it acquired more customers.

With the company's survival at stake, NetMind's executive team increased its sales efforts and won a 10,000-seat order for its software from Boeing. NetMind validated its business model with a big order from a Fortune 100 company and won its Series B financing. The founders learned that sales were necessary to show investors that they had a good business.

Finding a Mentor

Finding an experienced mentor like Gordon Campbell is difficult and requires patience, perseverance, and luck. It is even more difficult to get one actively involved in a startup company.

The best way to find a mentor is to articulate the profile of the ideal mentor and identify possible candidates. It often takes months of networking to find the right person. After an entrepreneur has found a mentor, it is smart to formalize the role with a position on the board of directors or advisory board or as a consultant. It is best to set up a formal meeting schedule and work with the mentor to devise a professional development plan. Issuing a stock option grant appropriate to the mentor's experience and expected contribution can help inspire his full engagement.

Some venture capital funds have general partners who have built and run successful companies and can provide experienced mentorship to founding CEOs. Because most venture capital funds have relatively few general partners like Gordon Campbell who have built and run successful companies, an entrepreneur should find himself a mentor *before* he raises venture capital. It will be an added bonus if his venture capital firm can assign a general partner who has built a successful company as a founding CEO to help mentor him.

Establishing a Foundation of Trust

The ideal mentor is motivated by love of mentoring, not money. Gordon Campbell loved being a mentor to the founders of Techfarm's portfolio companies. Campbell understood that people perform optimally in environments where they are supported and trusted. He demanded the best of his mentees but in a supportive way. He created safe environments in which his protégés could be vulnerable. They felt safe sharing their insecurities about building their companies. Campbell based his approach to mentorship on trust. As a result, the executives often emulated his approach in mentoring their employees. This created a foundation of trust that helped animate the extraordinary cultures enjoyed by Cobalt, 3Dfx, and NetMind.

Campbell's mentorship extended to the founding team of each company. He encouraged each executive team to take risks and collaborate creatively. His mentorship emboldened the founding team and laid the foundation for a trust-based culture.

Campbell generously connected his mentees to his vast network of trust-based relationships. These connections enabled the founding executives to rapidly grow their companies with the extraordinary people who had helped Campbell successfully build two public companies. Connecting his protégés to his network accelerated the attraction of the right resources.

Qualities of an Ideal Mentee

Campbell's confidence inspired the founding teams of his most successful startup companies to consistently surround themselves with people who were wiser and more experienced than they were. These teams weren't afraid to admit that they didn't know it all. Because they could admit their weaknesses and were not threatened by wiser and more experienced people, the founders of these companies repeatedly attracted great people who contributed to their companies' successes. Cobalt, 3Dfx, and NetMind succeeded largely because they consistently attracted the best people.

Experienced venture capitalists recognize when the founder's leadership skills are not yet up to the task of building a company. As a result, some offer term sheets for financing that are contingent on replacing the founder with an experienced CEO. Such venture capitalists are not malicious; they've just invested in too many failed companies led by first-time CEOs and want to prevent another losing investment caused by an inexperienced founder.

An entrepreneur often misperceives a venture capitalist's concern over his leadership skills as a veiled desire to take over. Despite this common fear, the last thing a venture capitalist wants to do is run a company. Venture capitalists like to invest in great leaders who can build successful companies that will provide their funds' limited partners with a return that exceeds the S&P 500.

Venture capitalists are efficiency experts. Their ideal investment is in a company that is so well run that all they have to do is participate in board meetings and write a glowing summary of the company in their funds' annual reports. Venture capitalists like to work smarter, not harder. Running an entrepreneur's company is not on their agenda. Entrepreneurs can enable venture capitalists to work smarter by securing effective mentorships.

Many startup companies fail because nobody tells the founder that he needs to become a great leader to remain as the CEO. To build a billion-dollar company, the founder must develop new skills to handle billion-dollar problems. Every founder must be realistic about how difficult it is to remain the leader through all the stages of a company's growth. Bill Gates of Microsoft and Steve Jobs of Apple managed to do it, but it is a rare feat; these men are exceptional leaders and businessmen. An experienced mentor challenges the founder to continue to develop his leadership skills.

Great entrepreneurs recognize that their success depends on acquiring a new set of leadership skills. To remain the leader, an entrepreneur must be as committed to developing and refining his leadership skills as a professional golfer is about improving his game. If the leader doesn't make a commitment to constant personal and professional growth, the board will likely replace him as soon as the company outgrows his existing skills. If the founder can't make this commitment, he shouldn't expect to run his company for long.

Gordon Campbell demanded an unwavering commitment to personal and professional growth from the executives of Techfarm's portfolio companies. To prepare for its IPO, Cobalt Networks hired veteran presentation coach Jerry Weissman to refine the public-speaking skills of Cobalt president Steve DeWitt and CFO Ken Chow. DeWitt and Chow created a dynamic IPO road show presentation that balanced DeWitt as the energetic visionary with Chow as the conservative and grounded CFO. Campbell also encouraged them to have fun. On the road show, DeWitt and Chow challenged each other by seeing how often they could describe Cobalt's products with phrases such as "hunk of burning love."

Mentor as Tormentor: Jim Hogan

"An entrepreneur doesn't need a yes man," says Jim Hogan, partner at Vista Ventures, "but requires someone who can fearlessly provide a seasoned second opinion. It's best not to play safe by selecting a peer or friend for a mentor."

Hogan worked for two companies, Symantec and Cadence Design Systems, that achieved billion-dollar valuations like Cobalt. Says Hogan:

When I was 36 years old, Symantec assigned a 55-year-old executive to help me manage my job. He wasn't a mentor. He was a tormentor. He was a great mentor because he took great pleasure in lovingly pushing me hard beyond my comfort zone.

Now, I push all the executives in my portfolio companies in the same way. I got involved in an Internet advertising company, Blue Lithium, where two brilliant guys in their midtwenties were the growth engine. They understood the market and created a new business model, but they needed experienced guidance. The founders made some classic mistakes before they brought in some gray-haired guys like me to mentor the executive staff. Blue Lithium spent $5 million per year on litigation that would have been simple to avoid if the company had had an experienced mentor to guide them from the start.

Blue Lithium eventually found the right balance of seasoned talent and creativity to fuel its growth. "The company went from zero to about $100 million in revenue in two years, with 60 percent gross margins," says Hogan. "That combination allowed a huge exit."

Knowing Who Is Top Dog: Chris Gill

"Almost all of the startup teams we back are first-time teams led by first-time entrepreneurs," says Chris Gill, CEO of SVForum, "but the key is to find an independent director who can mentor the CEO and help him be top dog. To remain in the job, the CEO *must* be top dog. If the CEO isn't ready, he should get an independent director to be board chair. Otherwise one of the venture capitalists will become top dog. If that happens, the CEO and the company are in big trouble."

Creating a Mentoring Culture

Your workforce expects your values and culture to self-actualize them and take them on a life path.

—Robb Smith, president, Integral Institute

Having a mentor models a commitment to personal growth that can have an enormously positive effect on corporate culture. A founder with a mentor demonstrates that it is safe for a person to be a work in progress. His example encourages the rest of the team to commit themselves to personal and professional development. A corporate culture that celebrates self-improvement has a competitive edge. A habit of making things better becomes an infectious attitude that can bring unexpected improvement to other aspects of the business.

Providing mentors for all members of the executive team fosters a culture of continuous improvement. A company's informal advisory board is a great place to engage mentors for the executives. For example, the chief technology officer could be paired with a more experienced CTO mentor serving on the advisory board. Executives serious about professional development often engage an executive coach or join an executive development organization, such as the Alliance of Chief Executives, to help them develop their skills and realize their potential.

Mentorship has many facets, but it requires a willing and receptive mentee to be effective. The relationship works best when based on trust and conducted with absolute candor. Mentorship can be one-to-one or one-to-many. Gordon Campbell, for example, often convened the executives of Techfarm's portfolio companies to group events where he could mentor them all simultaneously. Campbell also experimented with peer-to-peer and collective mentoring at the annual retreat at his ranch, where the gathered executives from Techfarm's portfolio companies helped solve problems facing one another's businesses.

A great leader aspires to create a mentoring culture that is dedicated to continuous improvement on both an individual and a collective level. He models mentoring in his relationships with his management team and inspires them to mentor those under their authority. The ultimate in mentoring is a co-mentoring culture where everyone is committed to helping everyone else develop and improve their skills. A great leader finds a mentor who can help him activate such a mentoring culture.

Every founder should think big, aim high, and get an experienced mentor like Gordon Campbell involved with his company. Ideally, a founding CEO would have two mentors: one to serve as chairman of the board and one to coach him privately as a trusted confidante. If the CEO can find only one mentor with experience comparable to Gordon Campbell's, he should have him serve as chairman to lead in the boardroom and seek other advisers to mentor him privately.

Repeat founding CEOs can also greatly benefit from having a mentor. With a mentor whose execution wisdom was acquired from having built successful businesses, a founding CEO is more likely to succeed. An entrepreneur should keep looking for an experienced mentor until he finds one. His success depends on it.

Summary

- Every entrepreneur needs an experienced mentor.

- An experienced mentor can attract experienced talent that accelerates success.

- The ideal mentor is beyond ego and has nothing to prove.

- The ideal mentor has built and run a successful company.

- The ideal mentor-protégé relationship is based on trust.

- The ideal mentor holds the founding CEO accountable and pushes him out of his comfort zone.

Call to Action

Find a mentor.

Chapter 8

CONSCIOUS LEADERSHIP

Be mindful of the power of your wake.

—Kip Tindell, co-founder and CEO, The Container Store

How are you going to earn the privilege to continue to lead your company? Do you understand that everything you do is a leadership communication? Are you prepared for everyone under your leadership, including investors and employees, to assess your every action?

Leaders who develop self-awareness to assess themselves and who welcome feedback about their leadership abilities are more likely to succeed. Venture capital investors are astute judges of an entrepreneur's leadership abilities. Venture capital funds generally invest in companies only when they have put the founder through a rigorous assessment and believe in his capacity to lead. Entrepreneurs who assess themselves with the same intense scrutiny have an advantage and are more likely to maintain the right to lead.

Assessing the Founder: Kathryn Gould

"As an early-stage investor, I am very candid about my assessment of a CEO's executive abilities," says Kathryn Gould, co-founder of Foundation Capital.

If I don't think the CEO will make it, I'll tell him up front. If I'm not sure, I'll share my doubts and set proper expectations.

I like to establish the desired performance criteria and schedule regular performance reviews. Setting expectations eliminates much of the CEO's anxiety about job security and creates an open forum for a constructive dialogue between the CEO and the board. Within a year everyone will know whether or not the CEO is up to the job.

When he's not up to the job, sometimes it's easy and sometimes it's ugly. Easy is wonderful: the CEO stays and remains productive and is honored as a founder. Ugly is awful: the CEO can't accept that he's not up to the job. Unfortunately, some founders destroy their companies rather than be replaced.

To minimize the possibility of such a disaster, Gould recommends that the CEO ask the venture capitalists directly whether they think he's right for the job:

Sometimes the CEO will have to make the investors tell him the truth. They'll often sugarcoat their assessment of his leadership abilities because they're enamored with the company's technology. They don't want to turn the CEO off and have him go to the venture capitalist down the street. If the CEO has any doubt about what the investors think of him, he should find out.

The CEO also needs to do some soul searching to understand whether his skills are what his company needs right now. It's hard for a CEO to admit that he's not perfect and may have some weaknesses. Sometimes in the development stage a technology-oriented person is the perfect CEO to lead the company to build the product. Once the product is done, however, that same person might not have the right set of skills. Building a company from an idea to a successful business requires huge changes for everybody. The CEO's skill set needs to change, too. Building a team is an upward spiral. Very rarely does the founding CEO make it the whole way.

Developing the product is the easy part, says Gould:

All companies stumble when they start selling the product. It's scary when a company starts selling and nobody is buying. Companies plow through the wall to introduce their product but don't worry about sales until sales don't happen. Then everybody sits around for months, wondering what to do. The goal is to shorten those months. It's the rare company whose sales take off when the product hits the market.

While a company is still in the development stage, the CEO needs to concentrate on what's next. The company must figure out how to sell the product as soon as possible. A company should develop its market as carefully as it develops its products.

Investors look for a team that stands out because it knows its strengths and weaknesses, says Gould. "An A-team is honest about its abilities and admits its weaknesses. The members of an A-team confront one another about problems and issues. They have appropriate domain expertise and they round each other out. They're fun and willing to take risks with one another."

"I've been extremely successful investing in first-time CEOs," Gould continues. "I gauge CEOs by certain characteristics rather than by how many times they've done it before."

Gould outlines her philosophy of the winning traits in a founding CEO:

The CEO must be the best salesman in the company. When the CEO gets in front of a customer, the company will get the deal. That kind of selling is my number one criterion. If the CEO can sell products, the CEO can raise money and recruit people. All the other kinds of selling are easy. If a founder is not that CEO, the company should probably find another chief. If a founder is that CEO but is inexperienced in other areas, he shouldn't worry but just keep selling. He'll be okay. The CEO must be the best salesman in the company and a great leader. He doesn't have to be the world's best leader, just a good one. The rest is easy after that.

I look for CEOs who embody the old adage A's hire A's, and B's hire C's. If a CEO who can sell has hired a really good team, I don't care if the team has holes. I'd rather have the nucleus of an A-team with holes than invest in mediocrity. Once a company has hired a mediocre guy, it takes a long time to get rid of him and he upsets the whole team. People are afraid to hire the junior marketing person until they have hired the vice president of marketing. Time is money. If a company finds a great person, it should hire him and not wait until it has hired the senior person.

Hiring an A-Team

Steve DeWitt was Cobalt's best salesman and united everyone behind its mission of selling servers. When Cobalt's sales took off, DeWitt managed the company to a deliberate rate of sales growth. He measured weekly sales against the desired growth rate and circulated the metrics to every employee. Everyone always knew whether Cobalt was on plan to meet its sales targets.

DeWitt installed a bronze ship's bell in the middle of Cobalt's office. The bell tolled every time the company sold a server. A large order triggered dozens of tolls of the bell. Everyone felt the excitement when the bell tolled. Even the board of directors got excited when they heard the bell during a board meeting. The sound of the bell generated infectious enthusiasm and let everyone know that the company was on track to meet its goals.

DeWitt ensured Cobalt's success by surrounding himself with A-team players and by engaging Gordon Campbell to guide him as a mentor. DeWitt recognized that his CEO role included being a coach, mentor, guide, facilitator, negotiator, and diplomat, and he developed new skills to enhance his performance. DeWitt became adept at applying the appropriate business discipline—including accounting, marketing, and operations—to address the challenge at hand.

DeWitt recruited A-level executives and board members and used Campbell to vet them. Cobalt added to the board of directors Jordan Levy, the founder of Ingram Micro, a leading electronics distributor. Levy's experience in the sales channel helped fuel Cobalt's explosive growth by providing the company with instant national distribution. Campbell was brutally honest with DeWitt about his leadership abilities and the quality of the team. As a result, Cobalt built a balanced, experienced A-team that rounded one another out.

Avoiding Founder's Disease

Steve DeWitt had the combination of confidence to take risks and humility to seek help from more-experienced people when needed. Unfortunately, many startups fail because the founder is too insecure to surround himself and his company with the best possible people.

Confidence without humility is the hubris of founder's disease. An entrepreneur with founder's disease is unlikely to work with a demanding mentor such as Gordon Campbell or ask for a candid assessment from an investor like Kathryn Gould. He will likely attract C-players and create a mediocre team.

Seasoned venture capitalists quickly recognize the pattern of founder's disease. Intuitively, venture capitalists compare a startup's founding team with those of their most successful companies. The criteria of comparison may vary, but venture capitalists look for patterns of behavior that correlate to higher probabilities of success and avoid patterns that correlate to failure. If an entrepreneur doesn't assess himself for founder's disease, the venture capitalists he pitches certainly will. If they spot the pattern, his company is unlikely to get funding; and if it does, he will likely be replaced.

Avoiding the One-Man Band and the Me-Do-It Syndrome

The one-man band is a common form of this affliction. Solitary founders rarely understand that building a company is a team sport that requires a strong executive staff. Such go-it-alone founders can sometimes use brute force to build a business, but without the support of other executives they eventually become impediments to growth.

The CEO of a semiconductor company was a classic one-man band. He was a control freak. He could not delegate and had no executive team to support him. He made every decision—from hiring new employees to buying paper clips. The 3-foot stack of paper in his in-box was also the company's accounts payable department. Vendors' invoices languished for months in his pile. His inability to surround himself with an executive team prevented his company from scaling to its full potential. Lucent Technologies eventually acquired his company, but no one was especially happy with the return.

A common symptom of founder's disease is an unbalanced allocation of equity among the founders. A legendary entrepreneur who had sold his prior company to Microsoft for about $500 million was so enamored with his new technology that he believed venture capital investors would buy stock in his latest company at a $500 million pre-money valuation. This founder allocated 90 percent of the founding equity to himself, 8 percent to a stock option pool, and 1 percent to each of two unnamed executives. Such unbalanced equity allocations often prevent founders from attracting the top talent needed to help them build their businesses. Based on his reputation and prior success, this entrepreneur raised venture capital at a much lower valuation, but his new business failed in a few years because it remained a one-man band at its core.

Some entrepreneurs with founder's disease act like three-year-olds who have just discovered their independence. Such founders are impervious to advice and believe that they can do everything themselves. They surround themselves with loyal but unchallenging yes-men who lack the experience to help build a company that scales successfully.

The cure to founder's disease is an experienced mentor. Many executives fear that having a mentor reveals vulnerability and weakness, but the opposite is true: having a mentor actually reveals confidence and strength. Even the most severely afflicted founding CEO has received the benefit of a successful mentorship. Almost everyone has had a great music teacher, golf instructor, or college professor whose mentorship inspired the acquisition of new skills. Reminding a reluctant CEO of the value of such teaching relationships is a good way to inspire him to find a mentor.

Determining whether You Are Building a Product or a Company

After raising venture capital for two successful companies, Lasso Logic and PacketTrap, and selling them before the second round of equity financing to SonicWALL and Qwest Software, respectively, Steve Goodman realized that he is not a builder of built-to-last companies. Goodman has a gift for developing software products that are extraordinarily valuable as product line extensions for public companies. Goodman's companies are the product for larger, established businesses. With clarity that the *company* is the product, Goodman is now building an incubator to generate multiple companies designed as acquisition candidates to augment the product lines of established businesses.

To avoid having agendas and motivations that conflict with those of employees and investors, an entrepreneur must determine his ultimate product: whether what he is building is a built-to-last business or a built-to sell company.

Three Steps to Creating a Culture of Contagious Spirit: Chris Melching

Steve DeWitt knew how to motivate people and keep them excited with simple techniques like ringing a bell. He surrounded his team with an ever-expanding circle of great people and created a culture of contagious spirit.

"There are three simple things that a leader can do to infuse a company with spirit to drive extraordinary performance," says Chris Melching, co-founder of Center Stage Group:

> *Model a culture of contagious spirit, keep the number one thing the number one thing, and demand authenticity. Everyone wants a great workplace. The leader should aspire to make his company the best place his employees have ever worked. Establishing a creative partnership environment makes it easier for a founding CEO to motivate his team.*

> *Leaders often think they are motivating people when they're not. Most executives schedule professional networking but don't schedule time to motivate their own teams. If executives fail to make time to motivate people, their motivational skills get out of shape. Motivating people is easy if you make it a habit, like working out at the gym. It requires constant effort and a disciplined approach.*

Model a Culture of Contagious Spirit

Take Google, for example. The "Googleplex" campus epitomizes a culture of contagious spirit. There are bicycles everywhere and groups of happy people eating. Google's culture exudes a playful energy. Creating a culture of contagious spirit starts with awareness, says Melching.

> *The leader's job is to create a great place to work. He should walk the halls to make sure it feels like a fun place to be. The leader's job is to activate a creative partnership culture by infusing it with spirit.*

> *Successful CEOs know that everything they do is a communication to the team. Effective leaders are aware that communication has verbal and nonverbal aspects, including body language. A smiling CEO sets the tone for the entire company. The leader must visit people in their cubes or take them to lunch to make them feel cared for.*

> *The leader must connect with people to make sure they are happy. A recent Gallop poll showed that having friends at work is what keeps employees actively engaged and is more important than having a good relationship with the boss. When employees have friends at work, they are happier and more actively engaged.*

The leader should find out what employees enjoy doing and what motivates them personally and professionally. A great leader inspires employees with work that pushes them in the ways they want to be challenged. Inspiring work creates a buzz and builds a workplace where people want to be.

Keep the Number One Thing the Number One Thing

The leader's job is to make everyone aware of the company's top priority. "Great leaders don't just share the vision and the strategy once a year at the annual picnic," says Melching; "they share them all the time and present them with care. There's an alignment problem if employees can't identify their company's current most important objective."

On a practical level, the leader needs to determine what everyone should be doing. If best manufacturing practices are important, the leader should get everyone focused on best practices. If reducing complexity or stopping drama are important, the leader's job is to get everyone focused on solving these problems.

Demand Authenticity

The leader's job is to create a safe environment that encourages those conversations, says Melching. "For example, the leader must ensure that there is good communication between the business development person and the software developers. He must ensure that the original founding team talks openly to new additions to prevent petty resentments from developing."

The leader must also identify the conversations that need to happen that are not happening and bring those conversations to the table. He needs to gently coax these topics out into the open and encourage everyone to speak up. "Enabling employees to have those difficult conversations transforms conflict into constructive outcomes and establishes a trust-based culture," says Melching. "A safe environment builds trust, and trust keeps everyone motivated."

A great leader not only stimulates the important conversations but also models authentic communications. How conversations are constructed is as critical as having them. The best tool for ensuring real conversations that foster a supportive workplace is the nonviolent communication framework developed by Marshall Goldberg. His approach encourages empathetic communications that promote understanding between people and reduce friction.

Nonviolent communication has four basic components. The first step is to observe what is happening objectively without judgment or criticism. The second step is to identify the feeling that the interaction evokes. The third step is to connect the feeling to an unmet need. Finally, the observer makes a clear request for help to meet the unmet need. A leader can use this approach to create a safe container for collaboration and creativity.

When a leader observes a coworker talking rudely to a customer, for example, nonviolent communication allows him to connect with the colleague to adjust the behavior. Instead of triggering a defensive reaction by labeling the employee as being rude, the executive can simply say that he is upset by the behavior because it doesn't meet the need to treat customers with respect. He can follow his non-judgmental observations and analysis of the feelings connected with the unmet need with a simple request to treat the customer well. This simple technique can greatly amplify the safety of a workplace.

Accountability: Nilofer Merchant

Great leaders hold themselves and others accountable. "Great companies develop a system to check whether or not they are on track," says Nilofer Merchant, founder and CEO of Rubicon Consulting.

> *Great teams have frequent conversations among themselves to hold themselves accountable to the corporate culture. In a healthy culture, it's totally acceptable to fail. To create a healthy culture, allow people to fail quickly and improve. Establishing the proper cultural framework early creates a system capable of making rapid adjustments.*

> *In addition to knowing the number one thing, every company should always be aware of its top 10 objectives. Cisco, for example, started identifying its top 10 objectives when it was a small company. John Chambers still creates the top 10 list. Everyone reports on those top 10, and they get bonuses for achieving them.*

Startups should follow Cisco's example and establish goals and put systems in place to align employees to accomplish the company's main objectives.

Self-Assessment

Because great businesses are built by great people, a conscious CEO cultivates a deep understanding of people and constantly assesses himself and his team. Psychology, especially the science of personality, can provide valuable insights into how to improve performance. Great companies like Agilent Technologies and Intuit, for example, use the wisdom of such tools as the Enneagram personality system and the Insights Discovery Profile to foster better interpersonal communication that promotes alignment and a more conscious, self-aware workforce.

Evaluating the team creates an invaluable habit of self-assessment that will help the company grow through the different stages of development. A team that can be brutally honest in its self-assessment will be better able to make the adjustments necessary to improve. Writing the business plan, for example, often reveals that the team is missing key players or that particular team members may not be suited for particular executive roles. An engineer, for example, may be ready to lead the product development team but might not be prepared to be the chief technology officer. Developing the habit of self-assessment early generates a culture of continuous self-improvement.

Ideally, the founder models candid self-assessment. Because future employees, customers, strategic partners, and investors will all make assessments of the entrepreneur, it's best for him to anticipate these evaluations by proactively assessing himself and his team.

Successful founders gather as much information about their strengths and weaknesses as possible because they understand the enormous influence their personalities and abilities have on the success of their businesses. Many executive coaches use tools such as the Enneagram and the Myers-Briggs assessment to provide their clients with comprehensive profiles of their aptitudes and personalities. Other resources such as the Johnson O'Connor aptitude test and Tom Rath's book *StrengthsFinder 2.0* can also provide an entrepreneur with a comprehensive assessment of his talents.

One of the shortcomings of current professional education programs is that they generally do not include the development of cognitive faculties and consciousness. We live in a time when modern developmental maps of human consciousness such as spiral dynamics and integral theory are widely available.

The current paradigm of managerial education stresses the development of professional skills and aptitudes without cultivating development along lines of cognition and consciousness. A conscious corporation requires leaders who strive to develop both their talents and their consciousness. Happily, there are assessment tools like the Values Technology Values Management Inventory and the Cook-Greuter Leadership Maturity Profile that can help a leader assess his levels of cognitive development and consciousness.

Successful entrepreneurs have the courage to learn about themselves and leverage the resulting insights to become better leaders.

Summary

- People choose their leaders.
- Everyone assesses the leader's ability to lead.
- Great leaders:
    ◊ Assess themselves
    ◊ Earn the privilege to lead
    ◊ Refine their ability to lead
    ◊ Create a culture of contagious spirit
    ◊ Establish objectives
    ◊ Hold people accountable

Call to Action

Inventory your leadership skills, including your aptitudes, personality, and leadership ability.

Aptitudes

What are your natural aptitudes?

The Johnson O'Connor aptitude tests (*www.jocrf.org*) and Tom Rath's *StrengthsFinder 2.0* (New York: Gallup Press, 2007) are excellent tools for making an inventory of a person's aptitudes.

Personality

What is your leadership style?

A basic understanding of your personality is essential to effective leadership. The Myers-Briggs personality assessment (*www.myersbriggs.org*) and the Enneagram (*www.enneagraminstitute.com*) are two of many resources that can give an entrepreneur insights about his personality and how it interacts with others.

Developmental Levels

What is your stage of personal development?

A variety of personal development models have emerged that can provide deeper insights into your development than can aptitude and personality profiles.

- Values Technology's Values Management Inventory (*www.valuestech.com*) provides insight into a leader's stage of development as reflected in his current leadership style and suggests additional skills to be cultivated.

- The Cook-Greuter Leadership Maturity Profile (*www.cook-greuter.com*) helps leaders determine where they are and where they are headed, and it suggests tools and practices to help them continue to evolve.

- Conscious Pursuits' Spiritual Intelligence Assessment (*www.consciouspursuits.com*) assesses a leader's ability to act with wisdom and compassion.

Leadership Ability

Who can provide you with honest feedback about your leadership abilities?

Identify the key advisers who can give you a candid assessment of your leadership abilities and get their feedback. Based on the inventory, create a leadership development plan. Having a mentor is essential, but consider also hiring an executive coach or joining an executive development organization such as Vistage (*www.vistage.com*) or the Alliance of Chief Executives (*www.allianceofceos.com*).

Chapter 9

A BALANCED TEAM

The best thing you can do for your employees is to surround them with people who are fantastic.

—Kip Tindell, co-founder and CEO, The Container Store

Everyone says that it's all about the team, but how can you tell if you have a good one? Are you ready to have everyone judge your company by the quality of its team?

Many veteran venture capitalists have a knack for finding founding teams that have the right stuff. Gordon Campbell, for example, picked founding teams that shared a common pattern. He intuitively selected balanced teams and helped them maintain that balance as their companies grew. Understanding what Campbell looked for gives you a framework to assess your team.

Five Archetypes

Techfarm's portfolio companies usually had three founders of particular core archetypes. Cobalt, 3Dfx, and NetMind all had three founders: a visionary, a technologist, and a salesman. Each had a visionary who saw the completed vision and knew how to integrate its parts; the visionary was the natural leader at the concept stage. The technologist had the knowledge and the technical skill to translate the vision into a product, and the salesman matched the product to an unmet customer need.

The founding trios shared common traits. The founders were friends who had worked together before. Each was senior enough in his field to see the big opportunity. Each company had a sound business model with a clear path to a profitable business. More importantly, the founding teams had the self-confidence and the humility to surround themselves with smarter and more experienced people. This combination of archetypes and traits attracted the best employees, customers, vendors and suppliers, consultants, strategic partners, and investors.

The developmental pattern contained two additional archetypes: a money person and a mentor. Each company had an office manager or finance person to provide structure by managing the details. Having someone to ground operations in sound business disciplines freed the visionary, technologist, and salesman to concentrate on building the business. In all companies, Gordon Campbell played the role of the fifth archetype, the mentor; he ensured not only the visionary's success but also the success of the entire company. Campbell kept his teams balanced by making sure that they maintained open communication and collaborated freely.

Having all five archetypes present at the beginning was not necessary for a startup to be successful. Most of Techfarm's companies started without an office manager. It's easy to fill that role because there are many good administrators who can manage the details. Cobalt Networks, for example, hired Leo Quilici as interim CFO to manage the quotidian details with financial discipline.

Campbell intuitively assessed founding teams for the three core archetypes to determine whether the team was complete. He looked for a visionary who could articulate the vision, a technologist who could turn the vision into a product, and a sales executive who could translate the product into sales. If one of these core archetypes was missing, the founding team was out of balance, and investing in it was premature.

Venture capitalists like Gordon Campbell are pattern matchers; they compare the founding team of every prospective portfolio company with the developmental pattern of their most successful company. They automatically assess a founding team for archetypal balance. It is critical for an entrepreneur to assess his team and make necessary adjustments to present potential investors with a balanced leadership team.

If a company has only a visionary and a technologist, for example, it will probably have trouble connecting its product to customers. Without sales and marketing experience, such an imbalanced, incomplete team will have a lower probability of success. Adding an experienced sales executive will improve the chances of success in both fundraising and business.

Gordon Campbell looked for teams that had worked together before and had experience in the domains of their proposed businesses. To the extent that the team had not worked in a startup, Campbell filled the gap with his experience from having built two public companies.

A team with prior startup experience understands the unique challenges of such a venture. Unless they have been in a startup before, executives from big public companies such as Pepsi rarely succeed as founders of scrappy startups because they are not used to having to play multiple roles without large staffs to support them. Industry seniority signals that a team is more likely to have the senior-level industry contacts and experience necessary to succeed.

Cobalt's founding team, for example, exhibited Campbell's ideal developmental pattern. Mark Wu was the prime mover, the visionary founding CEO and leader. Vivek Mehra was the brilliant technologist, the founding CTO. Mark Orr was the thoughtful marketing guru, the founding VP of marketing. The three founders had become friends while working together at Apple. They knew one another's strengths, tolerated one another's weaknesses, and had a good sense of humor. They were a natural team. Seniority in their domain helped them see the big, hidden opportunity in the server market. The founders' knowledge about the applicable technology enabled them to seize the opportunity.

Campbell augmented the team's strengths with his company-building acumen and served as its mentor. He leveraged his vast contact list to build powerful strategic alliances and expand Cobalt's team with trusted people.

Campbell's approach also required that the founders accept him as their mentor and as an integral member of their team. Techfarm purchased 20 percent of the founding equity of each portfolio company on the same terms as the founders. Campbell worked only with teams that recognized and welcomed his company-building prowess.

"The core team should be balanced like Cobalt's," says Vivek Mehra, "with a visionary leader, an engineer, and a marketing person. How the team works together is important. The team will grow, but it's best to keep the team small and cross-functional, with three to five people who are not all engineers or all marketing people. Cobalt's founding team was flexible and accepted new people who joined in more-senior positions or with more equity. The founders were willing to do what was best for the company by accepting the possibility of playing lesser roles."

3Dfx had a balanced founding team with domain seniority. Gary Tarolli, the CTO, is one of the world's leading authorities on the complex polygonal mathematics at the core of 3Dfx's graphics-rendering engine. Tarolli, then a professor at Massachusetts Institute of Technology, worked at the bleeding edge of 3D mathematics. With his expertise, 3Dfx had the right technical skills. Gordon Campbell's semiconductor industry experience helped co-founder Scott Sellers to translate the vision into products. Campbell led the team as a hands-on executive chairman, and co-founder Ross Q. Smith, in his role as VP of sales and marketing, connected the products to the customers with his endearing Texas drawl.

NetMind also had a balanced founding team. Matt Freivald was the visionary founder who saw the opportunity. Alan Noble was the brilliant engineer who single-handedly coded the complex software necessary to realize Freivald's vision. Mark Richards was the empathetic marketing genius whose natural warmth elicited the authentic customer feedback that enabled Noble to write winning code. NetMind's ability to harness the complementary skills of its founders enabled it to create complex synchronization software with minimal resources. Gordon Campbell and his partner Kurt Keilhacker completed the team with their experience building businesses together.

Techfarm walked the talk and modeled the same developmental pattern for its portfolio companies. Techfarm's partnership fielded a balanced team with complementary strengths. Campbell's partners at Techfarm with few exceptions were people with whom he had worked before. Nancy Dusseau, Jeff Gramer, Kurt Keilhacker, and Koji Morihiro had all worked with Campbell at Chips and Technologies. Techfarm modeled the fluid teamwork that arises from the familiarity of preexisting trust-based relationships. Techfarm's core team evolved over time, but Campbell always maintained the balance among the five archetypes.

When Techfarm raised its first venture capital fund, TechFund, in 1997, its team reflected the pattern sought in its portfolio companies. TechFund had a balanced, senior team that had worked together for years. Campbell was the visionary leader who saw the big picture, designed the investment strategy, and served as the team's mentor. Kurt Keilhacker was the skilled analyst who affirmed Campbell's nose with financial logic. Keilhacker had worked with Campbell since Chips and Technologies and was a trusted partner. Jim Whims was the marketing genius behind the Sony PlayStation, which achieved $1 billion in revenue faster than any consumer product in US history. Whims helped connect TechFund's portfolio companies to their customers to drive sales. Koji Morihiro, who was based in Japan, connected TechFund and its portfolio companies with investors and strategic partners in Asia. TechFund also had an office manager and a controller who managed the details.

Harnessing the Power of Trust

Conscious capitalism and sustainability are team sports.

—Sally Jewel, president and CEO, REI

Gordon Campbell understood the power of the bond of trust forged by prior working relationships. He used trust to build a creative, collaborative culture that accomplished great things. Techfarm's culture helped its partners work together to generate outstanding returns from the companies in its incubator from 1994 to 1997. Cobalt Networks so revolutionized the server business that it grew to $60 million of revenue and was acquired by Sun Microsystems for $2 billion four years after incorporation. 3Dfx so dominated the market for 3D graphics semiconductors that it had a $500 million market capitalization after its IPO less than four years after incorporation. NetMind created such an effective way to push selected information to mobile devices that it was acquired by Puma Technologies for approximately $750 million within four years of incorporation.

Cobalt's founders used the trust established by their prior collaboration at Apple as the foundation of a stable environment for creativity. The founders extended their trust and affection for one another to all employees to create a safe and supportive workplace that inspired everyone to unleash their creativity and share their knowledge. Because the founders were so comfortable communicating with one another and taking risks, the other employees also felt empowered to contribute their best efforts to the company.

Founder and CEO Mark Wu used his team's natural balance to build on this foundation of trust to create a dynamic, creative, and collaborative culture. Reading about Hewlett-Packard's corporate culture, the HP Way, inspired Wu to use a functional culture as the foundation of his company. His engineering background gave him the discipline to manage the details. In addition, Wu had worked in sales and understood customers. Mark Orr combined a gentle personality with a logical and structured approach to marketing. CTO Vivek Mehra contributed engineering logic to the team. He was calm and comfortable taking risks, including using the untested open-source Linux software as the operating system for Cobalt's products.

Gordon Campbell's style of mentorship expanded the safe environment for creative collaboration created by the trust among Cobalt's founding team. As the active chairman of the board, Campbell's proven execution ability took the pressure off the founders. He was authoritative and instilled confidence in the executives to work together and take risks. After Mark Wu's tragic death, Campbell steadied the team and provided interim leadership.

Steve DeWitt replaced Mark Wu as CEO. An extraordinarily gifted salesman, DeWitt had become a disciplined manager as an executive VP at Cisco. Campbell mentored him to enhance his effectiveness as Cobalt's new leader. The core executive team was flexible, confident but humble, and worked well together. The rest of the company adopted the executive team's collaborative approach to foster an extraordinary culture.

Assessing Collective Intelligence

Gordon Campbell created a collaborative environment for every group with which he was involved. Once a year he invited the two or three top executives in each portfolio company to his ranch for a weekend retreat. The group warmed up with a fun activity like having a paintball war. There was good food and ample drink, but these gatherings were serious. The collective assembled in the barn, where each company's team solicited solutions to its most pressing problems from the executives of the other companies; they accessed the collective intelligence of the assembled executives to solve their problems.

For weeks afterward the executives were animated with excitement about the business solutions from their peers. These off-sites exuded the creative, collaborative spirit of the dynamic cultures of 3Dfx, Cobalt, and NetMind. How Campbell consistently created safe environments for creative collaboration, however, was a mystery.

Imitating the Pattern

In 2002 I began selecting clients with founding teams that were inclined to match the pattern of the five archetypes and built a law firm using the pattern. I naively believed that using this archetypical pattern alone would quickly replicate the success of Techfarm's portfolio and spawn successful companies like Cobalt, 3Dfx, and NetMind.

The pattern did have a positive impact on several companies, but without my understanding the logic behind its efficacy, its effect as an accelerant of success was limited. Solaicx, for example, augmented its team with the mentor archetype and brought on as chairman Robert Medearis, who attracted the talent that ultimately drove the company's $103 million exit in 2010.

Vladimir Miloushev, the founder of 3Tera, one of the pioneers of cloud computing, used an understanding of the five archetypes. 3Tera modeled the pattern with a trust-based founding team that had worked with Miloushev before in his prior companies. He was an intuitive genius who foresaw the future of computing in the cloud. Peter Nickolov was the ingenious CTO who wrote the elegant code that realized Miloushev's vision. Krassy Nikolova, Miloushev's wife, was the CFO who managed the details of the business and nurtured the team with her big heart.

Miloushev's unexpected death in 2007 galvanized 3Tera's culture in the same way that founders' deaths catalyzed the cultures of Cobalt and 3Dfx. One of the directors, Barry Lynn, an experienced banking executive and venture capitalist, became CEO and mentored Peter Nickolov in his new role as president. The company weathered long periods of low or no pay and developed its software with little outside capital. 3Tera leveraged its balanced team to generate extraordinary value. CA, Inc., ultimately acquired 3Tera in 2010, but 3Tera might have been even more successful if it had fully understood and harnessed the complementary nature of the archetypes.

Assessing the Balance of the Founding Team

Here is a simple template to assess the balance of a founding team. The template comprises circles representing each of the five archetypes and two triangles, an equilateral triangle on top and an isosceles triangle on the bottom. The stacked triangles form a diamond, which represents the company, evoking its collective strength.

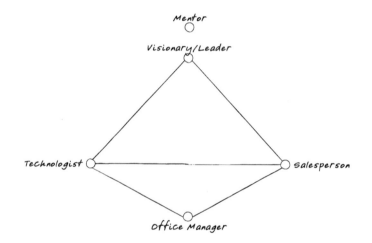

Figure 3: Assessing the balance of the founding team

An entrepreneur can use this template to analyze the completeness of his founding team. If the team is missing one of the archetypes, the entrepreneur can look for someone to fill the role. If a current team member clearly isn't up to the allotted task, the entrepreneur can find a replacement. The next chapter explains why having the three core archetypes—the visionary, the technologist, and the salesman—is so critical to accessing a company's collective intelligence.

Summary

Founding teams of technology-driven startups are balanced with five archetypes:

- A visionary

- A technologist

- A salesman

- An office manager

- A mentor

Founding teams that have worked together before have an advantage because of their preestablished trust.

Call to Action

Use the template in figure 3 to assess the balance of your founding team.

- Are any archetypical roles as yet unfilled?

- Are any team members not suited for their roles?

- Can you identify people to fill holes on your team?

Chapter 10

ACCESSING HUMAN INTELLIGENCES

Live each day with the entire brain alive and tingling with the life force.

—Matt Goldman, co-founder, Blue Man Group

How are you going to get your team to work together effectively? How are you going to maintain a collaborative culture as your company grows?

Ward Ashman, an organizational development consultant, solved the mystery of how the interaction of the archetypes enabled Techfarm's portfolio companies to animate creative, collaborative cultures.

Ashman's company, Trimergence, incorporates an understanding of the three fundamental human intelligences—logic, emotion, and intuition intelligence—to create corporate cultures that have what he calls the "evolutionary advantage." Application of the three intelligences enables creative partnership cultures that empower people to make their maximum contributions while building a successful business.

Techfarm's archetypal pattern had intuitively facilitated logic, emotion, and intuition intelligence to create a whole-brain culture that thought as one. The technologist applied logic intelligence, the salesman tapped emotion intelligence, and the visionary contributed intuition intelligence. Techfarm and many of its progeny serendipitously accessed their collective intelligence to create dynamic cultures because the core team balanced logic, emotion, and intuition intelligence.

Accessing the Three Intelligences: Ward Ashman

"Our model," says Ashman, "joins together the three primary human intelligences—logic, emotion, and intuition—and assumes that humans have all three of these intelligences." Logic intelligence is characterized as being left-brain and process oriented. Emotion intelligence is characterized as being about the heart and how things feel. Intuition intelligence is characterized as being right-brain and systems oriented. His assumption is that each of us tends to overuse one as our "primary intelligence":

The basic idea is that people have different perspectives based on their primary intelligence. These different perspectives cause people to view and interpret the same reality differently. Unfortunately, because most of us are unaware of the three intelligences, we assume that others are like us. We mistakenly assume that they perceive reality in the same way we do. Guess what—they don't!

We only have two options when we don't understand the underlying principle of three intelligences. The first is to attempt to convert others to our perspective, which encourages the king model. Trying to convert everybody into a follower tends to create a reign of terror. The other option is to kill them off, which we call the "convert-or-kill" paradigm. It's very expensive in business to kill people off by firing them just because they don't share the same perspective. An executive can never count on everybody being just like him. In fact, it's a guarantee that they won't be.

Ashman says that understanding the three intelligences helps an executive anticipate how people will respond to him. Logic determines what makes sense and the process to get things done. Emotion provides the ability to connect at a heart level with people so that they feel safe and loved. Emotion causes people to enjoy being in a work environment. Intuition provides the ability to pick up unspoken messages and to see the big picture. Says Ashman:

The value proposition is that understanding the three intelligences enables a person to make a productive connection with everybody, which promotes effective teamwork and fosters functional communication across an enterprise. Knowledge of the three intelligences can accelerate the creation of a positive and dynamic corporate culture. A corporate culture in which the value of each of the three intelligences is understood and celebrated creates synergy.

Another way to describe this synergy is "full bandwidth." If a startup company is operating at full bandwidth, the collective becomes more than the sum of its parts. Operating at full bandwidth gives a company an evolutionary advantage with three benefits: accelerated growth, diversity of personality, and ability to deliver the best decisions.

Ashman says that consciously using all three intelligences empowers a company to perform better than its competitors in an evolutionary way. It will operate on a higher level because most companies rely on a single primary intelligence and play convert-or-kill:

Many companies reflect the primary intelligence of their leader or the dominant primary intelligence of the team. Engineering- and logic-centric technology companies, for example, have logic-dominated cultures. Some great companies like Cobalt Networks accidentally unleash the diversity of the three intelligences to create success.

Using the three intelligences to transcend the convert-or-kill paradigm creates a tremendous opportunity for a breakthrough to work together. Leveraging the diversity of personality orientations is evolutionary.

Ashman gives the example of a chief operations officer (COO) in a Fortune 500 company who was overbalanced on intuition. The board considered him for CEO but questioned his ability to connect with people because he talked too fast and got angry when people couldn't follow his leaps in logic. These behaviors almost prevented him from becoming CEO.

Coaching helped him realize that he relied so much on intuition that he left people behind. He slowed down to make better connections and started accessing emotion intelligence so that people felt safer asking him questions. Answering their questions gave him the opportunity to explain himself better. Slowing down reduced his frustration because people could now understand him. Shifting his behavior enabled him to become an effective CEO. Ashman explains:

It's extraordinarily simple to understand the three intelligences because we all have them. Unfortunately, we forget that we have them and that we can use them together to get maximum throughput. Our egos can severely affect them. Understanding another person's point of view is much easier when ego is removed. Patience and active listening make it easier to use the three intelligences.

Ultimately, we exist to evolve to make our maximum contributions in life. Those who can grow quickly have an evolutionary advantage. When a company empowers all of its employees with a basic working knowledge of the three intelligences, it can activate the collective intelligence by facilitating better communication. When a startup has the evolutionary advantage on a collective level, it increases the probability that it will not only get funded but also become a billion-dollar business.

A leader can establish a culture of creative partnership by putting these concepts into action. Instead of the reign of terror caused by the convert-or-kill paradigm, his company will have a creative partnership environment where people feel safe and inspired to be their best. Ashman says that a creative partnership culture requires the CEO to facilitate and transmute conflicts into creative outcomes: "Unresolved interpersonal conflicts are often the biggest problems in a startup because they erode the team's ability to perform. Most technology-based startups employ technical people who are brilliant in the process logic of building widgets but lack the emotion intelligence to handle relationship conflicts. An effective CEO resolves these conflicts before they create dysfunction that impedes performance. The ability to quickly turn a conflict into a creative solution promotes success."

Acknowledging the Role of Feedback

Feedback is the key to creating a culture that turns conflict into creativity. Feedback from colleagues reinforces understanding that each of us has all three intelligences and enhances self-awareness. When people understand that their personalities are more flexible than their primary intelligence, they can pay more attention to how they are showing up. Supportive colleagues can let a person know when he is overusing his primary intelligence and encourage him to step out of his comfort zone to access the other two. On the other hand, in a convert-or-kill culture because feedback is not valued, it is difficult to cultivate self-awareness. Feedback encourages collaboration among colleagues and reinforces the idea that your success is my success.

A great leader provides people with an understanding of the diversity of their personalities and holds them accountable for cultivating all three intelligences. Maintaining a creative, collaborative culture encourages each person to access all three intelligences to add more value. Developing fluency in the language of each intelligence creates a culture with an evolutionary advantage over convert-or-kill cultures that overly rely on the primary intelligence of the leader or dominant group.

Techfarm and the Three Intelligences

The founding teams of Techfarm—Cobalt, 3Dfx, and NetMind—unconsciously used the three intelligences to access their companies' collective intelligence. These companies unconsciously harnessed the complementary nature of logic, emotion, and intuition intelligence to create whole-brain cultures.

Having a visionary (intuition), a technologist (logic), and a salesman (emotion) was critical to success, but the secret accelerant of success was how the primary intelligence of each archetype interacted with and complemented the others. In Cobalt, 3Dfx, and NetMind, the visionary CEO held the vision, the technologist CTO made the product, and the sales and marketing executive made the money, but it was the complementary nature of their intelligences that animated the whole-brain cultures of these companies.

The astounding thing, however, was that none of the founding teams was aware that it had accessed its company's collective intelligence. With Gordon Campbell's guidance, the founding teams of Cobalt, 3Dfx, and NetMind had unconsciously used the three intelligences to foster creative, collaborative cultures that drove their explosive growth.

Several factors enabled these companies to access their collective intelligence. Good team chemistry was critical. The founding teams had built-in bonds of trust from preexisting relationships that facilitated cooperation and collaboration. Friendships among the visionary, the technologist, and the salesman indicated that the founders had transcended convert-or-kill and had a greater facility to create a whole-brain culture that accessed its collective intelligence.

These companies' dynamic cultures turned their employees into neural nodes in a human network. Cobalt's culture, for example, functioned efficiently as a human intelligence network. Campbell and DeWitt created an environment that supported a diversity of personalities. People freely shared intelligence about the company's ecosystem. By receiving this data in DeWitt's weekly reports, people could make more intelligent decisions in response to changes in the market.

Using Logic, Emotion, and Intuition Intelligence

A founding team can apply a basic understanding of the three intelligences to intentionally create a collaborative culture like Cobalt's. Psychoanalysis is not necessary. A basic understanding can provide everyone with a decoder that facilitates functional communication among people of different primary intelligences. If the founding team promotes effective communication across the three intelligences, other team members will contribute fully to the company and animate a creative, collaborative culture.

On the other hand, the convert-or-kill paradigm generally creates unbalanced monocultures. If the leader is a left-brain logician, logic will tend to be the dominant intelligence of the culture. This explains why, for example, law, accounting, and engineering firms tend to be citadels of logic. When a company fails to access logic, emotion, and intuition intelligences together, it will generate less comprehensive solutions to problems.

If an intuitive has a logician for a boss, for example, he will experience a disconnection if he can't explain the logic to support his solution. An intuitive arrives at a solution without a formal linear or logical process; but without the logic to articulate the solution, the intuitive is at a loss. His boss will either try to "convert" the intuitive to explain his solution logically, or he will "kill" the intuitive by firing him because he can't understand the intuitive's apparent irrational impulsiveness for wanting to put a solution into action without taking the time to uncover the logic.

On the other hand, a logician who understands the complementary nature of logic and intuition will use the intuitive as a sounding board for solutions to complex problems. An intuitive can also use the logician to help him develop the logic to support the solution.

Using the Three Intelligences on the Board of Directors

To ensure access to its collective intelligence, a corporation should not only apply the three intelligences to its management team but also to its board of directors. Corporations' two-tiered management structure requires them to tap the collective intelligence of both levels of management. The directors of Techfarm's companies worked well together and cooperated to build great businesses because Campbell intuitively maintained whole-brain thinking in the boardroom so that boards focused not only on financial results but also on building the business.

Any board of directors can use the three intelligences to assess whether it is balanced with representatives of each type. A board with four logicians and one director of emotion intelligence, for example, will need to include a systematic, big-picture analysis characteristic of right-brain intuitive thinking to ensure balanced decisions.

Cultivating Diversity of Other Intelligences

Fostering a diversity of other types of intelligence also contributes to the vibrancy of a corporate culture. Gender balance is important to maintain masculine and feminine perspectives. Companies can use the diversity of gender, country of origin, and faith of their workforces to amplify the power of their collective intelligence. Companies that leverage a variety of such diverse perspectives develop better out-of-the-box solutions to complex problems.

Collective Actualization

Abraham Maslow's hierarchy of needs overlooked a level above the need for self-actualization: the need for *collective* actualization. Humans are social animals and are predisposed to be part of whole-brain collectives in our families and workplaces so that we can develop logic, emotion, and intuition intelligence. In a supportive environment, each person will step out of the comfort of his primary intelligence and cultivate the other two. Cobalt's whole-brain culture, for example, met its employees' needs for self- and collective actualization.

Balancing the Three Intelligences

To cultivate a basic understanding of the three intelligences, a founding team can use Trimergence's simple Three Intelligences Self-Assessment Tool (see appendix A) to determine each person's primary intelligence orientation among logic, emotion, and intuition intelligences.

After taking the self-assessment test, the team can use a simple model of three overlapping circles to analyze itself for balance among the three intelligences. The first circle represents logic intelligence, the second represents emotion intelligence, and the third represents intuition intelligence. Where the three circles overlap represents balance and symbolizes whole-brain thinking.

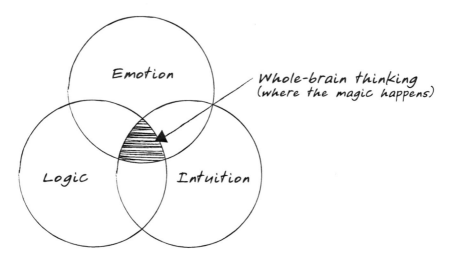

Figure 4: Balancing the three intelligences

Using this three-circle model may reveal the opportunity to add a person of complementary intelligence to the mix to improve the balance. In the high-tech environment of Silicon Valley, founding teams tend to be left-brain logic-centric and are often missing an emotion intelligence–oriented VP of sales or marketing, like Mark Orr, who can connect the company's brilliantly designed product to the customers who need it. Any company can use this simple diagnostic tool to assess whether it is balanced and to help intentionally create the nucleus of a creative, whole-brain culture. The more a team can promote the dynamic complementary nature of the three intelligences, the more likely the company will be to animate a dynamic whole-brain culture.

Summary

- Understanding the three basic human intelligences—logic, emotion, and intuition intelligence—is critical to fostering a creative, collaborative culture.

- Creative, collaborative cultures that use all three intelligences enable whole-brain thinking.

- Whole-brain cultures make better decisions because they approach problems from a wide variety of complementary perspectives.

- Whole-brain cultures have an evolutionary advantage over traditional convert-or-kill cultures.

- To be fully effective, extend the whole-brain culture into the boardroom.

Call to Action

- Have each team member determine his primary intelligence using the Three Intelligences Self-Assessment Tool in appendix A.

- Check the team for balance among the three intelligences by using the three-circle model above. If a founding team has five logic-oriented engineers, for example, it will likely need to add intuitive- and emotion-oriented members to achieve balance.

- Assess the board of directors for balance to ensure that whole-brain thinking extends to the boardroom.

- Develop a plan to create and maintain a whole-brain culture that will inspire employees to deliver their best.

Chapter 11
CULTIVATING CONSCIOUSNESS

There is nothing like the genius of human consciousness to drive human creativity.
—Patricia Aburdene, author, *Megatrends 2010: The Rise of Conscious Capitalism*

How are you going to protect your business from outside forces? What is your strategy to keep up with your market so that you can adjust your business when the market changes?

Every business has a collective consciousness, but few are aware that they have one. Consciousness is man's basic tool for success and survival in life. A *Webster's* definition of *consciousness* is "the state of being conscious," with *conscious* meaning "fully aware." Your business will have a competitive advantage if it cultivates consciousness because it will be more adept than its competitors at responding to the market.

The value proposition is that a business that cultivates its collective consciousness is more likely to survive. Conscious businesses have an edge because they are aware of what is happening not only in the market but also within their own company.

To elevate its consciousness, a business requires leaders who cultivate as high a level of consciousness as possible. Just as most companies deduce their values from the behavior of leaders like Roger Smith, a business deduces its level of consciousness from that of its leaders. Consciousness allows a business to use the perceptions of what is happening both internally within the business and externally within its ecosystem to respond appropriately and in alignment with its purpose and values.

Columbia Business School recognizes the correlation between consciousness and success. For several years it offered a class titled Creativity and Personal Mastery, which focused on creativity and personal development as a secular approach to cultivating an understanding of the development of consciousness. This course was so popular that students from across multiple disciplines as well as other schools applied to attend. Other business schools—such as the Haas School of Business at the University of California, Berkeley, and London Business School—asked the professor, Srikumar S. Rao, to teach his course to their students. When the correlation between consciousness and performance has become more widely accepted, development of consciousness will likely become a core component of professional curriculums, such as MBA programs and law schools.

This book's bibliography contains several resources about the development of consciousness. The spiral dynamics model outlined in Don Beck and Christopher Cowan's *Spiral Dynamics* provides an eight-stage map of the evolution of both individual and societal consciousnesses. On an individual level, Rao's book, *Are You Ready to Succeed?*, inspires an entrepreneur to become aware of his life purpose and provides an introduction to the development of his consciousness. Resources like these provide business leaders with tools to develop their individual consciousness and the collective consciousness of their organizations for competitive advantage.

Whole Foods, Cobalt, and Consciousness

The term *conscious capitalism* implies that companies that adhere to the tenets of conscious capitalism are more conscious than their peers and are more likely to succeed. The companies featured in *Firms of Endearment* developed a relatively high degree of collective consciousness. Whole Foods, for example, and its co-founder and co-CEO, John Mackey, have articulated the company's core values, which stress the importance of having mutually beneficial relationships with its interdependent network of customers, vendors and suppliers, employees, growers, and investors. Whole Foods recognizes that its continued success depends on having satisfied customers and maintaining good relationships with its other stakeholders. The company empowers all of its employees to uphold its core values in their relationships with all of its stakeholders. Cultivating its collective consciousness enables Whole Foods to maintain premium margins in the traditionally low-margin grocery business and provide an exceptional return to its investors.

As a part of his commitment to personal and professional growth, Mackey has developed his consciousness. He understands that continued success in a fast-moving, interdependent global economy requires that he operate at as high a level of awareness as possible. Cultivating consciousness has increased Mackey's awareness of what is happening in the totality of the business and his ability to make more appropriate responses.

Mackey has shared his personal development path on his CD set, *Passion and Purpose,* to inspire others to cultivate the development of their individual consciousnesses as part of their personal and professional development plans. He intuitively knows that the power of a business's collective consciousness is amplified when people develop their individual consciousnesses.

Developing his consciousness has also made Mackey a more authentic leader, by helping him outgrow the architecture of the ego and face the fear of the shadow. At a basic level, the ego is who we pretend to be, and the shadow is who we are afraid we are. By cultivating his consciousness, Mackey built a company with a compelling purpose in alignment with his life's purpose of providing humanity with a peaceful and sustainable future through healthy food.

Cobalt's story illustrates the correlation between consciousness and performance. The combination of an experienced mentor to guide its leaders, a whole-brain culture, and an acute awareness of its market gave Cobalt a relatively high level of collective consciousness. Gordon Campbell's mentorship helped Cobalt maintain its collaborative culture, which enabled the company to respond more effectively to market changes and customer demands. Steve DeWitt reinforced Cobalt's collective awareness by sharing critical business intelligence with everyone. This heightened awareness, coupled with its collaborative culture, gave Cobalt a competitive advantage because its elevated collective consciousness caused the company to function extraordinarily well as a holistic system.

Maintaining an Intelligence Network: Joe Watt

"CEOs of billion-dollar companies maintain active intelligence networks," says investment banker Joe Watt. "They are experts at gathering intelligence about what is going on in the market and what their competitors are doing and factoring it into their business decisions." While building their businesses, Watt says, entrepreneurs should build an ecosystem around themselves so that they're well informed: "It's a sign of good leadership when we tell the CEO in a confidential acquisition process that the name of that company for sale is XYZ and the CEO says, 'I knew about that two months ago.' It's critical for the founding CEO to maintain a broad perspective and cultivate active intelligence about his industry."

Cultivating Consciousness

As we expand our individual consciousnesses, business consciousness increases.

—Patricia Aburdene, author, *Megatrends 2010: The Rise of Conscious Capitalism*

Many tools for cultivating consciousness, including martial arts, meditation, and yoga, are available in mainstream culture. The fields of psychology and neuroscience provide models for developing consciousness. Many companies have started making these techniques available to their staff. Google, for example, offers meditation programs for its employees.

Meditative mindfulness practices develop consciousness because they cultivate a still point of awareness that enables a person to perceive his habitual cognitive and emotional patterns. Making these patterns into objects is a powerful cognitive move that enables a person to no longer be subject to them. The ability to see these reactive patterns allows a person to choose appropriate responsive behaviors rather than be victimized by them into reactive behavior. Seeing these patterns also helps a leader discern the patterns of his ego and shadow and transcend them to become more of his authentic self. A good mindfulness practice develops a stable witness that can skillfully make the subject-object shift that frees a person from unhelpful patterns.

The conscious leader strives to cultivate a 360-degree view of his personality to eliminate blind spots to prevent them from having a negative effect on his business. Unconscious behavioral patterns can cause fatal mistakes that destroy a business or cause dysfunction that impedes performance. Developing consciousness and having a candid mentor are excellent methods of illuminating unconscious patterns to enable a leader to respond more effectively to the inevitable challenges.

Cultivating mindfulness may not be enough, however, if the leader doesn't also have an effective system for taming his e-mail, voicemail and traditional in-boxes. Without a method of prioritizing, organizing and managing the constant stream of information, even the most mindful executive will quickly lapse into reactive behavior to manage his workflow. David Allen's *Getting Things Done* is an excellent guide to managing these inputs to keep a leader in control, relaxed, focused and inspired.

Befriending Fear

Fear provokes unconscious behavior that kills many companies. Most people avoid fear because it feels overwhelming and uncomfortable. As a result, fear lurks in the shadow and is buried in the unconscious. Fear is a constant in startups, however, because 80 percent of new businesses fail before their fifth anniversary. Leaders of startups are especially vulnerable to fear because their companies often operate in survival mode. Until a company achieves positive cash flow, anxiety about meeting payroll and paying the rent can overwhelm any leader.

A conscious leader does not ignore or suppress fear. Embracing it enables the leader to access the business intelligence contained in its message. His fear, for example, may be telling him to immediately start raising that next round of financing because sales are not ramping as quickly as expected. Facing the fear to receive its message may keep the business alive. An experienced mentor who has borne the responsibility for meeting payroll can help allay a founder's fear and help him develop appropriate responses.

One of the most effective techniques to manage fear and anxiety is to develop heart coherence. The human heart alternates between two characteristic modes of variation in cardiac rhythm – chaos and coherence. The Institute of HeartMath in Boulder Creek, California, has developed a portable feedback device, the emWave, which can help manage stress by measuring coherence and providing feedback that helps a person control his cardiac rhythm. When a person can control his heart rate variability, the heart's rhythm alternates rapidly and regularly between accelerating and decelerating. This creates coherence of heart rate variability.

Medical research has demonstrated that the heart reacts almost instantly to changes in emotional states. Research also shows that corporate executives who have learned to induce coherence have greatly reduced levels of stress and an enhanced ability to manage their feelings. People in corporations that have received coherence training work more harmoniously. Cultivating coherence to manage stress works especially well to complement mindfulness practices discussed in chapter 8.[3]

Allowing for Downtime: Shrinath Acharya

It is important that an entrepreneur take breaks to maintain a balanced perspective. It is easy to get overwhelmed by e-mail and voice communications and become addicted to portable devices like cell phones and BlackBerrys, which enable business to be conducted ubiquitously at all times. An executive who is always in work mode must make an effort to create downtime and be off device.

"We had monthly off-site meetings to talk about what was really going on in our business," says Shrinath Acharya, co-founder and CEO of Margi Systems, which was acquired by Harman International. "These meetings helped us step out of tactical mode and think strategically. We invited industry people, who often came up with great ideas. External feedback helped our team maintain its perspective. We often got so tactical when reacting to yelling customers that we lost perspective. We got a fresh perspective by taking a break from day-to-day business to work on the company with outside advisers."

Downtime is essential to rest the brain, maintain mental acuity, develop awareness, and avoid overload and burnout. It may seem counterintuitive, but carving out some downtime every day helps an executive be more effective. Often answers to business problems appear during downtime. Steve Dewitt, for example, is an excellent low-handicap golfer who refreshes himself by playing golf. John Mackey recharges with weeks-long backpacking trips on the

---

3   Servan-Schreiber, David. *The Instinct to Heal* (Emmaus, PA: Rodale, 2004). Chapters 3 and 4 provide an especially helpful introduction to cardiac coherence and its benefits.

Appalachian Trail. Downtime gives an executive spaciousness and perspective to respond, rather than react, to challenging situations.

Summary

- Consciousness is man's basic survival tool.

- Businesses have a collective consciousness.

- Businesses that raise their collective consciousness have a competitive edge.

- Having conscious leaders raises the collective consciousness of a business.

- Business leaders who cultivate the development of their consciousness have an advantage because they are more aware of what is going on in their business and can respond more appropriately.

- Taking breaks from working *in* the business to work *on* the business helps maintain perspective.

Call to Action

- Encourage each person to develop a plan to cultivate consciousness, including coherence, as a part of their personal and professional development.

- Encourage each person to schedule downtime to refresh and regain perspective.

- Develop a program of regular off-site meetings for the team to work on the business.

Chapter 12

ENGAGING THE BOARD OF DIRECTORS

Purpose makes alignment real.

—Nikos Mourkogiannis, author, *Purpose: The Starting Point of Great Companies*

Do you understand boardroom dynamics? Is your executive team prepared for two tiers of management and reporting to a board of directors?

To manage successfully, your team needs to adjust its behavior to fit the characteristics of each tier. The board of directors is a deliberative body that operates by consensus to guide management. On the other hand, executives are action oriented and driven by a military-style chain of command, with the CEO directing the actions of the other executives. Successful CEOs lead their executive teams but guide their directors to reach consensus in the boardroom. They also develop good board processes to enhance the board's critical guidance and oversight functions and to facilitate consensus.

A board of directors is a small, tribe-like unit. Boards generally select the strongest leader to be the chairman because tribes automatically align themselves behind the natural leader. When the strongest leader is the chairman, the board will run smoothly because there won't be a power vacuum.

Many companies fail because the founder did not understand tribal leadership dynamics. Most founding CEOs serve as the initial chairman of their board but unwittingly create a power vacuum because they are still developing leadership skills and don't understand boardroom power politics. A power vacuum on a board of directors is a disaster because it invites conflict when other directors try to fill the vacuum.

The best way for a first-time CEO to ensure that his company has a functional board of directors is to find an experienced executive like Gordon Campbell to serve as the chairman. An experienced mentor usually makes an excellent chairman. The best time to bring in an independent director to serve as chairman is long before raising venture capital.

Campbell's prior leadership experience as the founder of two successful public companies made him the natural leader in the boardroom of his portfolio companies. He was clearly the top dog. With Campbell as chairman, there was never a power vacuum. After financings, new directors instinctively aligned themselves behind him. The venture capitalists joining the board didn't have to worry about a lack of leadership. As a result, the directors of Techfarm's portfolio companies focused on developing the business instead of filling a leadership vacuum.

An independent chairman of the board with previous boardroom experience can help a first-time CEO establish a sound boardroom process and avoid a power vacuum. An experienced mentor can allay the other directors' concerns about the CEO's leadership abilities and frees them to focus their energy on building a successful company.

Campbell not only empowered founding CEOs to run their companies but also showed them how to work effectively with their board of directors. He coached the CEO and the executives in preparing for and running effective board meetings. The CEOs ran the meetings, but Campbell spoke up to keep them on track. With Campbell supporting his CEOs, the boards wasted no time filling power vacuums and squabbling over leadership. Campbell focused the directors on realizing the vision.

Encouraging Whole-Brain Thinking in the Boardroom

The boards of directors of Techfarm's portfolio companies not only had experienced leadership and a sound board process but also were whole-brain. A board of directors led by a first-time CEO as chairman often loses the capacity to access its collective intelligence when venture capitalists join the board. Without a strong leader to keep the balance, venture capitalists often redirect the focus to making a return. Not only will these directors fill any power vacuum but they will also tend to focus more on financial results than on how the business is functioning as a whole. As an intuitive, Campbell encouraged a balance of perspectives in the boardroom and prevented the board from devolving into a left-brain, spreadsheet-logic-dominated monoculture.

A company's long-term survival depends on the chairman's ability to maintain whole-brain thinking in the boardroom and keep the company focused on fulfilling the vision. When the board focuses primarily on making a financial return, the power of the company's purpose is lost. Employees feel the subtle shift and become dispirited. Meaningful employment devolves into a job, and the culture disappears. Companies die when the board allows its primary focus to shift from realizing the vision to financial engineering.

Several factors facilitate such a shift to a primary focus on financial return. First, it is easy to forget the importance of vision and culture because traditional accounting does not recognize them as assets. Second, filling a power vacuum often precipitates this shift. Third, replacing the founder with a new CEO almost guarantees this shift.

The best way to keep a company focused on realizing its vision is to get both tiers of management to buy in to the culture. Cobalt had a dynamic culture because Steve DeWitt and Gordon Campbell extended it into the boardroom. When the company booked an order during a board meeting, the board heard the bell toll. When Cobalt created a stir with its racy Seven Deadly Sins ad campaign, DeWitt played impassioned voicemails about the ads to the directors so they could feel the buzz. DeWitt made sure that the board understood and supported Cobalt's culture. Successful companies indoctrinate their boards into their culture.

Many entrepreneurs don't recognize that their startups have two distinct tiers of management that require completely different managerial behaviors because in the beginning the founders are the executive team *and* the board. After a company receives investment, however, investors and other outsiders replace members of the original management team on the board—but no one tells the founding CEO how to run crisp, well-organized meetings that inform the board so that it can properly guide management by consensus. Without a sound boardroom process, the new directors will conclude that because the founding CEO can't run an effective board meeting, he can't run and build a company. The board will ultimately fill the perceived power vacuum by replacing the founding CEO. On the other hand, outside directors who experience a well-run first board meeting will conclude that the founding CEO can also run the company.

That said, boards often do replace the founder with a CEO with a proven record of building successful companies—but they destroy the culture in the transition. Because the culture is usually deduced from the founder's behavior, it often disappears when he is replaced. If the new CEO doesn't buy in to the vision and the values, the culture will be lost and the focus will shift to making a financial return.

Cobalt maintained its culture because its replacement CEO bought in to it. DeWitt endorsed the vision by making a significant personal investment in the company. Cobalt succeeded because DeWitt became the guardian of the culture and extended it to the board.

The best way to preserve culture during a management transition is to articulate its key elements and create a succession plan that will enable the new CEO to inherit the culture and maintain it. With a succession plan, employees avoid the anxiety of deducing a new culture from the behavior of the new CEO. If the new CEO preserves the positive aspects of the established culture, he is more likely to win the support of the team and prevent the company from devolving into a financial-engineering game.

Establishing a Good Board Process: Derek Blazensky and Leo Quilici

"If venture capitalists were truly brilliant," says Derek Blazensky, co-founder of Cardinal Ventures, "they would all be entrepreneurs running companies. Venture capitalists are, however, brilliant pattern matchers who see the same issues across their portfolios of companies. A great venture capitalist recognizes these patterns and contributes his pattern-matching expertise to boards of directors."

A good board process is an essential part of infrastructure, says Blazensky: "The composition of the board of directors, the frequency of the board meetings, and the quality of the board process distinguish a smooth-running board from a problematic one."

Board Composition

Effective CEOs proactively manage the composition of the board of directors. Says Blazensky:

Until a company raises outside professional money and has fiduciary duties to the investor stockholders, a startup should have an informal advisory board instead of a formal board of directors. If the founder's relatives are directors, the company should invite them off the board before the company composes its formal board of directors. The term sheet for the Series A financing will require the company to establish a formal board.

After the Series A financing, the ideal board has five directors. Generally, the common stock has the right to elect two directors, who are usually the founder, who came up with the brilliant idea, and the CEO, who may or may not be the founder. After the Series B financing, the company will have two venture capital directors elected by the preferred stock.

To keep the board focused on building the business, says Blazensky, it is critical to have an outside, independent person as the fifth director. An independent director can prevent a board from splitting into a management side and an investor-director side. A successful CEO avoids that dysfunctional dynamic from the beginning:

An experienced independent outside director can play a pivotal role. The ideal independent director contributes management expertise from several tours of duty as a CEO. The independent director should have had operating responsibility and made the numbers for several years at a world-class company. Such an independent director can be extremely helpful on the operations side of the business but is usually less helpful in fundraising.

Someone must be the leader in the boardroom because nature abhors a vacuum. If the CEO is not the leader, the other directors will appoint one. One of the venture capital directors will temporarily fill the power vacuum until the board can replace the

CEO. The CEO who fails to lead in the boardroom or have an independent director who can lead will have difficulty guiding his company.

Frequency of Board Meetings

The best practice, says Blazensky, is to hold eight board meetings per year, including four official board meetings. Startups don't need more than four formal board meetings in a year because most of the board-level discussion is about strategy and operations. The board uses official meetings to approve stock option grants, budgets, and other major items. Here is Blazensky's recipe for an effective board process:

> *An operations review meeting should follow each of the four official board meetings. The foundation of a functional board process is having the five key directors meet four times a year in formal board meetings and four times for operations review meetings. The board should always schedule the next year's meetings well before the end of each calendar year. Monthly meetings set up the CEO for failure because it's difficult to accomplish enough between meetings. Monthly meetings distract management from running the business. If the Series A term sheet requires that the board meet monthly, however, the company should sign that term sheet and take the money. The term sheet is not the place to fight frequency of meetings.*

Conducting Effective Board Meetings

The CEO should start organizing the next board meeting two weeks ahead of time to give the management team enough time to prepare their presentations, says Leo Quilici, Cobalt's CFO:

> *The CEO will damage his credibility with the board if two executives have a violent debate in the meeting. The management team can fight all it wants beforehand, but in the meeting everybody needs to be in agreement.*

> *To strive for a "no surprises" relationship, the CEO should contact board members between meetings to keep them informed. Such contacts should have a specific purpose and discuss all significant matters, particular challenges, current activities, and issues requiring their feedback. These calls should give the directors early warning of negative events to avoid surprises at the board meeting.*

"A CEO must maintain good communication with his board," says Blazensky. "The CEO must proactively educate and pre-sell each director before every board meeting because directors hate surprises." The worst place to surprise a director, says Blazensky, is at a board meeting: "Something is terribly wrong when directors get surprised at a board meeting. It's never acceptable for directors to learn new things at a formal board meeting. It is acceptable, however, to disclose something new at an operations review meeting because there is nothing to vote on. To avoid surprises, the CEO should keep all the directors informed by sharing good and bad news between meetings and keep them aligned with the vision."

"The CEO must manage the board and not allow the directors to drive a board meeting," says Quilici. "If the CEO fails to drive the meeting, the board may conclude that the CEO is not driving the company either and may act to replace him. Finally, the CEO should never ask for direction at the board meeting because his job is to lead the company and to tell the board what the direction is. The CEO shouldn't worry if the board disagrees with the direction because it's his job to determine the direction."

Conducting effective board meetings, says Blazensky is an art:

A well-run board has already reached consensus before the meeting on all matters requiring a vote, including approval of a budget, an expense or revenue plan, or an executive hire. A CEO should never call for a vote unless he already knows the outcome. Each director should have already approved the budget or other item before the board meeting. Great CEOs ensure the desired result by proactively reaching consensus in advance.

The senior management team should attend board meetings, especially operations review meetings. The VP of sales should discuss sales, and the VP of marketing should discuss marketing. Hearing the perspective of each member of the executive team helps the board gauge performance. It's usually a bad sign if the CEO doesn't invite the management team to board meetings. On the other extreme, it's a bad sign if the CEO creates a human shield by inviting half of the company because the board will not dare to address really hard issues with 30 people in the room.

"The CEO and the executive team must deliver crisp presentations at board meetings," says Quilici. "The best board meetings are always the shortest. Long meetings kill CEO authority and credibility. The CEO must organize the agenda and should consider dry-running the meetings with the management team. Preparing for a board meeting once every month is a burden because it takes a week to prepare and a week to recover, which leaves only two weeks to be productive. It is worth the effort to be well prepared because the board meeting is the management team's chance to shine for the board."

Board Responsibilities

"Frequently, entrepreneurs, management, venture capitalists, and other board members forget who they are serving," says Blazensky, "but board responsibilities such as the duty of care and the duty of loyalty flow to all stockholders." Blazensky says that directors have the responsibility to extend the duties of care and loyalty to all stockholders:

> *Being informed helps directors speak candidly and exercise the duties of care and loyalty. A great CEO prepares each director before each board meeting so that the director can privately give feedback and guidance about the company's next moves. Directors need enough time to be thoughtful in private to come to the board meeting prepared with ideas. Directors can't speak with candor if the CEO delivers for the first time at the board meeting the bad news that the company lost its biggest customer.*

> *Thoughtfulness should never be confused with indecision. A board often acts with indecision when it hasn't had enough time to process information to make a decision. A board can't be thoughtful when it learns the news at the meeting. The wrong time to ask for advice is after the board has heard the bad news for the first time.*

The board's activities are not as clearly defined as its fiduciary responsibilities. A good board, says Blazensky, will help develop the business strategy. The CEO's job is to drive the company's strategy and guide the company. The CEO should constantly remind the directors of the vision in almost every communication and update them whenever it changes.

A great board also assists with fundraising. Says Blazensky:

> *The CEO should share his fundraising strategy and ask the board for help and input. The board should also help draft the annual budget and the revenue plan and*

design the right incentives to inspire the team to climb the mountain. Proper incentives establish the metrics by which the company's progress will be measured. Reaching the goals should allow the company to afford to make the incentive payments.

Boards usually adopt incentives too quickly and base them on financial metrics like cash on hand or the size of last year's incentives rather than true performance metrics. For example, the incentive structure should reward maintaining the largest accounts and discourage losing them. An effective board designs appropriate management incentives.

The independent director is usually the right person to lead the compensation committee because he understands the pressure that management is under in operating the business. Because he is usually not a significant investor, he doesn't want to keep salaries artificially low to make his money last longer but rather wants to keep the business on track to reach its goals. His prior executive experience is also helpful in designing effective management incentives.

The board helps attract the best available executives that the company can afford to hire. An effective board also removes the underperformers who don't fit the culture or who fail to meet the performance criteria of the incentive program.

A good board of directors also helps engineer the exit transaction, says Blazensky. "The board's responsibility is to look out for the interests of all the stockholders who invested in the company. Investors make money only when a business is sold or goes public. A good board helps the company prepare for such an exit."

To encourage honest feedback about the CEO's management skills, some boards meet occasionally without him present. The board can candidly discuss the CEO in such sessions and circle back with him to discuss any issues that are raised.

Including the Board

Fully integrating the board tier of management into the business requires a structured approach. A low-pressure approach to developing an effective board process is to start holding regular board meetings before venture capitalists join the board. Board meetings are a great forum for the CEO and the management team to step out of the day-to-day operations, review the team's progress, and hold people accountable. Having a proactive method of working with the board not only helps founding CEOs avoid a leadership vacuum that causes them to be replaced prematurely but also keeps both tiers of management aligned behind the vision. An experienced mentor can help a young company establish an effective board process.

Summary

- Understanding boardroom dynamics is critical.
- Boards of directors are tribal units that operate by consensus.
- Tribes like boards of directors align themselves behind the strongest leader.
- The founder or an experienced outside director should be the strongest leader to avoid a power vacuum.
- Having a sound boardroom process is essential.
- Getting the board to buy in to the culture is key.
- Keeping the board's primary focus on realizing the vision, not generating a financial return, is critical to success.

Call to Action

- Identify the composition of the initial board of directors.
- Who is the natural leader?
- If the founding CEO is not a natural leader, is the mentor or other experienced executive available to serve as chairman to avoid a power vacuum?
- Develop a good board process that includes a meeting schedule and structure.
- Start holding regular board meetings to dry run the process and develop good board habits.

Chapter 13

BUILDING VALUE

Profits ensue from doing the right thing.

—Rajendra Sisodia, co-founder and chair, Conscious Capitalism Institute

Do you really understand money? Do you have your personal finances sufficiently in order to have the financial stability to lead your company?

A successful entrepreneur knows exactly how long he can endure without a salary and how much personal financial risk he is willing to take.

Determining the Runway

An entrepreneur's runway is determined by dividing cash on hand and available from borrowing by total monthly expenses like mortgage payments and insurance. The level of acceptable risk adjusts the runway.

A young, unmarried entrepreneur may be more willing to risk his life savings and max out his credit cards than a married 50-year-old with three kids approaching college. Determining the runway helps an entrepreneur manage the uncertainty surrounding his company's survival. Investors and employees will assume that an entrepreneur can manage the company's runway if he can confidently manage his own. Understanding the length of each team member's runway helps the founder determine the company's runway—how long it can go without raising money.

There are four common sources of financing for companies in the start stage:

- Financing from founders, friends, and family
- Income from providing services to third parties
- Government grants
- Funding from professional investors

Most startups begin operations with money from friends and family or by bootstrapping by providing services. Getting government grants requires specialized knowledge about the grant-writing process as well as patience because grants are typically made once a year on an annual cycle.

Professional investors are unlikely sources of financing for new startups. Most venture capitalists prefer to invest after a company has a product and customers because the risks of investing in a new startup are too high. Some funds have specialized seed financing programs for start-stage companies, but sophisticated individual investors are more likely sources of financing. These investors are called "angels," but their investment process is often as rigorous as that of venture capital investors, especially those organized into formal groups to invest collectively.

Every founding team must assess its sources of funding. The founder's credibility as the leader depends on providing his team with some baseline means of financial security. People follow a founder only if they feel he can get the company funded.

Understanding his company's financial condition helps an entrepreneur make informed decisions. Understanding how the marketplace values companies helps him build the company to create value. To earn the privilege to lead, the founder must understand money.

Managing the Finances: Leo Quilici

"The CEO needs to understand financial statements to have credibility with investors, the board of directors, and the executive team," says Leo Quilici, CFO of Cobalt.

No one expects the CEO to predict revenue perfectly, but he must understand the balance sheet and basic accounting concepts. When the CFO isn't at the board meeting to identify convertible debt interest as an accrual, for example, the CEO must be able to explain the balance sheet. The ability to credibly explain financial statements will support the CEO's continued tenure.

An experienced CFO takes the financial burden off the CEO and the management team, stays out of the way, doesn't consume a lot of resources, and helps move things along. The CFO should have a voice in staff meetings so that the CEO and the rest of the team can make better decisions based on his financial input. A great CFO serves as an ombudsman for the stockholders and can avert many disasters by reminding the CEO to consider an issue from their perspective.

Quilici says that the best financial staffing model for startups uses a combination of a part-time CFO and a part-time controller/accounting manager to manage the finance function. "This approach works even better if one of the financial types can not only do the accounting but also be the office manager and answer the phones and order supplies," he says. Having a part-time CFO and a part-time controller should take care of most startups' accounting and finance needs.

Here's Quilici's job description for a startup CFO:

An experienced CFO provides the sound financial practices necessary to proactively manage a business. The CFO should prepare the annual financial plan for the CEO and update it monthly. The CFO should prepare a monthly statement comparing actual results to the original plan and create a reforecast plan for the rest of the year based on feedback from the executive team about things that affect the spending plan.

Early-stage companies are in survival mode, but venture capitalists care only about meeting the development schedule and not running out of cash. There's a spending pecking order, which runs: engineering, then marketing and sales, with operations and general and administrative tied for last. An early-stage company should focus resources on its development effort.

Product development schedules drive infrastructure in early-stage companies, says Quilici: "If the schedule starts to slip, venture capitalists begin to sweat. If a company burning $200,000 per month has a three-month slip, it will have burned more than half a million dollars and may have to raise another round of financing without any new developments to support a good valuation."

Companies should invest only in the programs they need to get from stage to stage and avoid spending money prematurely, says Quilici. Infrastructure should be added incrementally only as needed and scaled to the viability horizon, which is the cash on hand:

Starting programs whose benefit will come only after the money runs out, other than product development activities, makes no sense.

Understanding the true cost of getting a product out of engineering and into the market is critical. A company should avoid hiring salesmen as soon as the CTO lays out the product architecture. Just because the engineers have finished a product doesn't mean it's ready for sale. Undoubtedly, the company will need more time to launch. Having sales and marketing people standing by, waiting for a market-ready product, just burns cash and leaves the team bored and frustrated.

Financial operations change materially when a company transitions to revenue, says Quilici. "The transition from zero to $10 million in revenue will likely be slow for an expensive product with a long sales cycle. On the other hand, the company will have cash flow problems if it builds inventory of a low-cost, high-volume product and sales don't happen." Once sales take off, a company's biggest cash burn shifts from payroll to inventory, and the focus becomes accounts receivable on the balance sheet.

"A startup needs a rational compensation system with standards that can be applied consistently across the company," says Quilici.

A simple compensation structure helps avoid morale problems caused by paying one senior engineer $80,000 per year and another senior engineer with the same qualifications $120,000 per year simply because he went to the right school.

A complete compensation plan includes logical equity compensation guidelines for making stock option grants to employees. Venture capital investors require their portfolio companies to reserve about 20 percent of the fully diluted capitalization in a stock option plan. Such investors might not agree to replenish the option pool if a company runs out of options between financings, so it's important to have grant guidelines and an option budget that ties to the hiring plan.

Quilici also stresses the imperative of keeping records current. "The financial staff should always maintain audit-ready financial statements to be ready for the annual audit and for due diligence for the next financing or an exit transaction," he says. The ability to quickly deliver well-prepared financial statements creates the impression that a company is well run and can support its valuation.

He also recommends that a startup organize all corporate records, agreements, and legal documents in a single location. "Management can respond effortlessly to due diligence requests when important documents are organized and focus on the transaction at hand. Having preparing PDF files of important documents allows a company to respond quickly during a financing or exit transaction. Because first impressions matter, a rapid and complete response will often reassure the other party and affirm the valuation."

Understanding Valuation: Joe Watt

"Investment bankers don't determine valuations," says Joe Watt, "notwithstanding the common misconception that they do. Bankers merely provide a lens to view valuation. Understanding how Wall Street approaches valuation is fundamental to realizing a company's valuation potential during financing transactions and strategic acquisitions." Ultimately, Watt says, markets determine valuations by balancing risk and greed:

Valuations for startup companies are influenced by four stages of risk. Funding risk is about whether a company can raise money now and in the future. Venture risk is about whether a company can hire the right people and develop and sell the right product. Competitive risk is about whether a company can compete and scale in the marketplace once it has products and customers. Execution risk is about whether management can actually build a billion-dollar company.

How well a company can execute influences its valuation, says Watt, but a favorable investment environment is critical:

An investor's view of current and future economic conditions affects valuation. Changes in perceived risks beyond the control of a company's management and independent of the company's financial performance or future earnings potential adjust valuation.

Because a paradigm of risk out of its control determines a startup's valuation, attaining a premium valuation is not a reliable indicator of financial success. To create value, it's important to have realistic valuation expectations.

To create a billion dollars of value, a company must either be strategic or perform. To be strategic requires one or more competitors who really want or need to acquire the company. Attaining a billion-dollar valuation usually requires a total addressable market of at least $2 billion, yearly revenue approaching $500 million, yearly earnings of $25 million, or $50 million of operating free cash flow per year, with annual growth of at least 25 percent for the foreseeable future.

The average time from funding to IPO for a growth company is nine years. "The average company goes public with a market capitalization between $350 million and $400 million," says Watt. "Except in special situations, $200 million is the minimum valuation necessary for going public. Attaining $750 million of market capitalization is the next benchmark because that's when research coverage and institutional ownership begin for a company." To get to a billion-dollar market capitalization, says Watt, a company needs to keep growing for two to three years after going public:

Investors in startup companies have an insatiable appetite for growth. Growth is the end goal, but it is not measured by sales alone. Growth also includes all contributors to long-term value realization and risk mitigation, such as patents, products, and partnerships. To maximize valuation, a company should grow as fast as possible in the early stage of its development, and then focus on profitability when it gets ready to go public. If the goal is to become a public company, it's necessary to smooth out fluctuations in revenue on a quarter-to-quarter basis because Wall Street demands consistent performance.

Wall Street investors increasingly focus on the quality of a company's ecosystem. Wall Street loves endorsements from strategic partners and strong commercial relationships with the technology giants in the marketplace. To satisfy Wall Street, entrepreneurs should build ecosystems around their businesses and identify their key component stakeholders as they create their long-term business plans. Entrepreneurs should consider using strategic partners like OEMs [original equipment manufacturers] to enable them to minimize the capital required and scale their business more quickly.

Few companies reach a billion-dollar valuation without an acquisition strategy and acquiring other companies, says Watt. When planning the business, making return-on-investment (ROI) calculations, and figuring out where the company wants to be in eight years, entrepreneurs should factor in strategic acquisitions and develop an acquisitions strategy.

"Whether it is website hits, energy-conscious consumers per household, or broadband penetration in Africa," says Watt, "every industry has its key metrics. Smart entrepreneurs ask young investment bankers and research associates to explain the key nuanced metrics applicable to their businesses. Performing well relative to such metrics can support a premium valuation."

Creating Value: Ramkumar Jayam

"Building a billion-dollar company requires three things," says Ramkumar Jayam, co-founder of Platys Technologies. "First, the company's market must be sizeable and taking off like a wildfire. Second, the company must have the financial resources to trigger exponential growth by adding salesmen and scaling operations because only exponential revenue growth rates can create a billion-dollar valuation. Third, the company must take advantage of market transitions like Platys did with the fibre channel market.

Jayam defines three phases that a startup company undergoes:

> *Platys had completed both the initial start phase, which involves defining and developing a product, and the intermediate build phase, which involves proving the concept by getting customers to buy it. By selling Platys early, we avoided the execution risks associated with the third growth phase, which requires building an organization with sales and operations capabilities to scale. An entrepreneur must always be aware of which phase his company is in because the risks and the challenges of each phase are different.*

> *We founded Platys, got some venture capital financing, and started selling our technology right away. We quickly realized that our real product was the enterprise because Platys attracted the attention of several large companies that wanted to buy it. Soon, Platys got acquired by Adaptec for $150 million.*

The best acquisitions happen, Jayam says, when a company like Platys is *not* seeking to be acquired. If the customer's problem is real and solving it creates a sizable market, there will always be multiple vendors serving that market:

> *The best way to get acquired by a company like Hewlett-Packard [HP] or IBM is to identify its customers and serve them even better than it does. Potential acquirers will automatically line up to buy a startup when it wins their customers and gives them great support.*

> *Platys' acquisition strategy was to win the design for the new platform by getting buy-in from our new IEEE partners like HP. Once we secured the platform, when salesmen from our competitors called on those accounts they learned that Platys had already won the design. By winning the platform design, we won the market before it opened. Our acquisition started from the buy side because larger companies wanted this new market. We were not looking for a buyer, but the buyers were looking for us.*

> *Once we were in play, we weighed the advantages of selling the company against the risks of building it toward an IPO. We balanced the certainty of shareholder return in an acquisition against the risks of achieving a greater return in an IPO. We looked at our shareholder return and felt a sale to a public buyer with an established infrastructure to push the product gave the best value to the shareholders and outweighed the risks of raising another round of financing and building toward an IPO.*

Summary

- Entrepreneurs need to understand personal and corporate finance.

- Successful entrepreneurs have their personal finances in order and know exactly how long they can survive without a paycheck.

- Successful entrepreneurs always know the financial condition of their companies and how long its financial resources will last.

- Successful entrepreneurs understand valuation and maintain an awareness of their companies' enterprise values at all times.

Call to Action

- Analyze each team member's personal runway—how long they can survive without pay or on minimum wage.

- Analyze the company's runway and identify the likely sources of financing.

- Select a person to fill the CFO function.

- Develop a two-year financial plan.

Chapter 14

FLAWLESS EXECUTION

Modern management, the technology of human production,
is man's most important systemic innovation.

—Gary Hamel, director, Management Lab

Are you ready for success? Do you know what to do when sales take off?

Successful companies have an operations plan, and they know how to execute it. Many startups fail, however, because they are so focused on short-term survival that they don't plan for what happens if they actually succeed. Companies focus on producing the product, landing the first customer, or getting the venture capital investment, but they forget to prepare the operational infrastructure. Successful startup companies understand operations.

Planning for Operations: Brian Fitzgerald

"In 1978 a little startup company called Apple hired me to pack boxes because they were about to ship 400 computers," says Brian Fitzgerald, former VP of operations at Apple, Claris, and Intuit. "Apple expected the personal computer industry to develop slowly and planned to grow sales to $5 million a year. Nobody dreamed that Apple would achieve a billion dollars of annual sales in four years."

Apple didn't understand operations, says Fitzgerald:

> *Because it failed to anticipate how quickly the personal computer industry would take off, Apple spent the next four years reacting to explosive growth and the demands of a growing customer base. It was absolute chaos.*

> *We have great war stories, but reacting is not the right way to scale operations. From 1976 until 1982, Apple did its own vertically integrated manufacturing and assembled all of its printed circuit boards. This was an enormous job, which required dozens of small consignment manufacturing shops because there were no large contract manufacturing companies. Apple ran $20 million of consigned inventory per month on purchase orders before it consolidated assembly.*

Apple was so reactive, says Fitzgerald, that it couldn't plan how to keep up with demand. It got so trapped in reactive mode that it was almost impossible to break out of the cycle. "We finally consolidated manufacturing operations to become more efficient, but lack of process cost Apple money. The company was lucky to survive quality issues that reduced gross margins because it was the only game in town. Throwing things over the wall like we did 30 years ago at Apple is no way to run operations."

To respond intelligently to demand, Fitzgerald says, a startup should analyze the core operational competencies it will need to scale operations. It doesn't have to spend money to put those competencies in place, but it should develop an operations plan in anticipation of success. "It may be more appropriate to outsource some of those core competencies," he says, "but that requires defining precisely what a company needs out of its outsourcing partners. A company must build strong relationships with its outsourced partners and monitor them constantly so that they can scale to match the company's growth."

Fitzgerald also recommends that a startup company avoid processing itself to death when faced with rapid growth:

> *It's fine to evaluate standard manufacturing processes such as ISO 9000, SCORE, TQM, and Six Sigma to find one that fits the company. Process, however, should not dictate whether or not the company should take advantage of an opportunity. There's a tendency to adopt the most exact manufacturing process, but if a company tries to be too perfect, everything shuts down.*

In the early days, Apple had no manufacturing process. It hired an operations executive from Martin Marietta to deploy a disciplined process and run quality assurance. He implemented manufacturing specifications that were so exact that they immediately shut down the entire company. Apple fired the Martin Marietta guy after five days.

If your company adopts a standard manufacturing process, it could face the same issue today, says Fitzgerald:

Your operations guy might refuse to accept a $50 million purchase order because it doesn't meet his metrics. If you have a $50 million order, to hell with the metrics. Growth drives innovation, initiative, and improvisation, but implementing sound processes takes a balanced approach. It's best to continually reevaluate the manufacturing process and adjust it as a company grows.

Learning to Love the Part You Hate

"Every executive hates some part of his job," says Fitzgerald. "The hated aspect might be a process, a function, or using a challenging technology, but to be successful, the executive must learn to love what he hates to do." Almost every CEO dislikes some aspect of operations, but ignoring it can inhibit the company's success down the road. It can be a disaster if he doesn't face it:

There were a lot of smart guys at Intuit in 1994, but they hated operations. Bill Campbell asked me to run business operations because Intuit had big problems. It had great products and marketing, but it had no cash and was losing money. When I got there, it was an operation guy's worst nightmare. Intuit was a $300-million-a-year public company with thousands of customers, without any operational infrastructure.

In my first week, Scott Cook, the founder, told me, "I really hate trucks." Cook's vision was to use electronic distribution to deliver software that empowered individuals to take charge of their personal finances. At that time Intuit sold standard application software in packages shipped by truck because it had not implemented basic logistics processes. It took a couple of years to correct operations to get rid of the trucks and distribute the software electronically. We had many unhappy customers and investors while we changed course.

To avoid such pain, Fitzgerald says, have an operations plan to anticipate success.

Getting Things Done: Vivek Mehra

"A compelling vision without execution is people hallucinating," says Vivek Mehra, co-founder of Cobalt and general partner of August Capital. "An entrepreneur who can't execute has a worthless vision." The lack of execution ability causes startups to fail:

> *When we started Cobalt, we didn't know that building a company is a never-ending process. After we shipped the first product, the customers wanted more features and asked for the next version of the product. We had to get used to a never-ending stream of innovation and execution. It never got any easier.*

> *Many entrepreneurs mistakenly think that they're done when they ship the product. That's just the beginning because now the company has paying customers who expect products and services. To meet their expectations, the company must be prepared for constant execution. The only way to make it easier is to hire incredibly smart people to execute as flawlessly as possible.*

Cobalt's ability to get things done enabled its success. In four years it shipped about 30 distinct products, including four product lines, and many localized versions. "We adapted quickly to customer demands," says Mehra, "because we had a six-month product development cycle that gave us an advantage over our competitors, who had one-year product life cycles. We focused on getting products out quickly instead of predicting where the market would be in two years. The product had to be acceptable, but if it wasn't perfect, we just shipped an improved version in six months."

Developing an Operations Plan

To prepare for success, an entrepreneur should develop an operations plan and have an experienced operations person on the executive team or advisory board. A good operations plan outlines the company's entire supply chain. Thorough plans map out how the product design generates the bill of materials (BOM), which determines the vendors and the suppliers and ultimately the sales and distribution strategy. The operations plan identifies whether the company will manufacture its product or outsource its manufacturing.

Writing an operations plan identifies risks in the supply chain. The bill of materials for a complex product like Cobalt's Qube has many parts and subassemblies. Some parts are standard, off-the-shelf products that are readily available; others require custom manufacturing and have long lead times or foreign sources. A good operations plan identifies long-lead-time items and single-source supply parts and develops a strategy to address those risks. Happily, there are many good software tools available to help companies manage operations and the supply chain.

Creating an effective operations plan requires that management accept the operations organization as a strategic component of the company, not simply a cost center or a tool for tactical implementation. Brian Fitzgerald combined a value-added approach to operations with cross-functional collaboration with other business disciplines to help Scott Cook get rid of trucks. A good operations plan involves the CFO. If a company suddenly has millions of orders, for example, how will it pay for inventory? Getting the CFO involved to arrange in advance for accounts-receivable financing or lines of credit is prudent. Operations are not critical during the concept stage, but it is important to be ready with an operations plan when customer demand kicks in.

Summary

- Successful startups plan for success.
- They have an operations plan
- They have the talent and the experience to execute the plan.
- An operations plan enables a startup to meet demand when sales take off.

Call to Action

Develop an operations plan for success. It should address how the company will scale its operations in the event that sales explode like Apple's did in its first four years. A thorough operations plan answers the following questions:

- What are the elements of the supply chain?

- Who will manufacture the product?

- Who will assemble the product?

- What components go into the bill of materials?

- What single-source, foreign-source, long lead-time, and other risks can you identify with respect to the BOM?

- How are you going to address those risks?

- How will you sell and distribute the product?

- How will you finance the inventory build?

- Have you included other disciplines such as finance in building the operations plan?

- Do you have the experienced talent to pull it all together?

Chapter 15

LISTENING TO CUSTOMERS

To inspire creativity, remain curious at all times.

—Matt Goldman, co-founder, Blue Man Group

Listening to customers is a habit of successful companies. Successful startups begin listening to potential customers in the concept stage because they know exactly what an entrepreneur needs to know to succeed. Are you ready to listen to your customers? Customer feedback ensures products that customers want and need.

It's everyone's job to find out what the customers' problems are. When asked, customers will tell what features they want included in a product. Cobalt avoided costly mistakes because its engineering and marketing teams met frequently with customers to find out what they wanted. Sometimes, however, an entrepreneur must ignore customers because what they want goes against innovation. Cobalt, for example, ignored customers who asked for really small server devices because it concluded that small servers would be too unstable.

Getting the first customers is critical. The secret to making the first sale is to find customers with real-world problems. Customers who buy products from startups are either lone wolf risk-takers or small enterprises—but they buy only if the product solves a real-world problem.

Making the first few sales is a challenge because potential customers always ask for homework. Homework happens when customers ask a startup to redesign the product or add customized features. Entrepreneurs must be wary of wasting time and engineering resources with unnecessary homework, especially from big, established companies that may not admit that they never buy from startups.

The long-term goal is to turn the first few sales into a structured sales process that's repeatable with some predictability. Having a scalable sales process allows companies to achieve exponential growth.

Paying Attention to Customer Feedback: Mark Orr

"Cobalt's first challenge was to improve the Qube so that it would sell better," says Mark Orr, Cobalt's co-founder and VP of marketing. "We had immediate success in the United States and Japan when we launched in March 1998. Somebody rang a large ship's bell every time we sold a Qube. The bell rang a lot after the launch, but then it stopped ringing. For several weeks, one ring was a good day. Selling the Qube was more difficult than building it." Orr says that Cobalt had to make fundamental changes to the product to get the bell ringing again:

> *When the bell stopped ringing, we listened to our partners. Mitsui, a huge Japanese trading company and one of our strategic investors, gave feedback on everything, including a list of more than 150 product defects. They even told us that the font of our logo was one point size too small.*
>
> *It was easy to fix things with detailed feedback. The third version of the Qube was right for the Japanese market. Ultimately, Cobalt succeeded in Japan because of Mitsui's thorough feedback.*
>
> *The second challenge was to build a better product. To get sales going, we listened to our customers, who told us that they wanted a Qube that could fit in standard server racks. Happily, it was relatively simple to put the guts of the Qube into a one-rack unit device that met their needs. Because it solved an important problem, customers tolerated the Qube until we changed the product design. Within 14 months of launch, we were selling pizza-box-sized servers that fit standard server racks.*

The third challenge, says Orr, was to establish strategic relationships in the sales channel to drive sales: "We engaged Ingram and Merisel Tech Data as our distribution partners. Our sales channel partners gave us additional feedback about what customers wanted." Listening to customers and strategic partners paid off, says Orr. "Customers loved the new rack-formatted servers. The bell started ringing again. The rest of the story is history." Sales really took off, and revenue compounded at a 35 percent quarter-to-quarter growth rate on three continents for the next several years.

Finding the "We" Solution: Steve Bengston

"Successful companies recognize that their biggest problems require 'we' solutions," says Steve Bengston, director of PricewaterhouseCoopers. Cobalt's story illustrates how applying the power of the "we" can solve tough problems. Says Bengston:

> *When Cobalt's bell stopped ringing, selling more servers was a "we" problem. The solution came from asking everyone, "What do we need to do to start getting sales volume?"*

> *The CEO takes the lead in finding the solution to a big problem. The CEO has to activate the "we" to solve a problem together. Cobalt solved its sales problem as a team and involved its ecosystem partners in creating the solution. Cobalt solved its sales problem because it fearlessly disclosed it and asked everyone to help solve it.*

Cobalt made getting feedback from customers and strategic partners a habit. "Its early success in improving the Qube and redesigning it to fit in standard server racks confirmed that feedback positively affects the bottom line," says Bengston. "Cobalt's engineering and marketing teams routinely called customers to ask, 'What do you think? What did you like? What don't you like?' As a result, Cobalt consistently offered products that its customers wanted."

Letting the Customer Design the Product: Ramkumar Jayam

Ram Jayam tells how Platys Technologies listened to customers to build a winning company after launching a product that nobody wanted. "Platys almost died because we blew a million dollars building a 3094 interface product that the market no longer wanted," says Jayam.

> *We had very strange conversations with potential customers about other promising technologies. The customers were not interested in any of our technology,*

but all wanted to talk about fibre channel. We didn't know anything about fibre channel, but the customers kept asking us if we could build fibre channel products.

We hired an engineer who understood fibre channel, storage, and the Ethernet. While he generated ideas, we were out listening to customers to find out what they wanted us to build. We didn't try to sell anything for six months. We just listened to the ecosystem.

We joined the IEEE forum to redefine the fibre channel market with Internet protocol storage. We worked with Cisco and IBM to drive the new IEEE standards. This investment had no immediate return because nobody paid us for our contribution. Our investment paid off enormously, however, because our work developing the standards put us in the vanguard of a whole new market, and we developed deep relationships with all the potential acquisition partners. Getting in front of a nascent market helped Platys enormously.

After listening to the ecosystem, Jayam says, Platys created product specifications:

When we asked customers if they wanted to buy our proposed fibre channel over Ethernet [FCoE] product, they told us they wanted something entirely different. Because they knew that we had core technology, our customers helped us develop the product that solved their problem. The customers told us what the market wanted and helped us define a product bringing fibre channel out to Ethernet and addressing data storage.

We carefully orchestrated our conversations with customers because fully defining the FCoE product required several meetings. This process was counterintuitive because we just wanted to tell the customers to buy our product. When the customers know more about the market, however, a startup needs to keep listening.

Summary

- Successful companies listen to their customers.
- Customers know what products they want.
- Listening to customers is the best way to build products that customers need.

- Successful companies meet customer needs by creating feedback loops that keep them informed about what the customer wants.

Call to Action

Develop a plan to make listening to customers a habit by answering the following questions:

- Who are your potential customers?

- Do you have personal contacts at these target companies?

- How can you engage these customers in a dialogue about your product now?

- Who should be talking to these customers?

- How are you going to get marketing and engineering involved with these customers?

- Are there market forums like IEEE or conferences where you can efficiently access large numbers of potential customers?

Chapter 16

AN AUTHENTIC BRAND

Make this idea the most attractive idea in business.

—Jim Stengel, president and CEO, Jim Stengel Company LLC

Successful companies create powerful brands to shape the perception of their businesses in the marketplace. A strong brand can make a startup appear as a market leader from day one. How are you going to manage how others perceive your company in the marketplace? Does your corporate identity accurately reflect your company's persona?

An effective branding strategy reflects the power of the purpose in a company's public persona. A well-defined brand with an authentic persona elicits a positive emotional response from customers to drive sales. An effective brand starts with the company's name. The corporate identity includes the company's name, the logo design, and a branded website and other elements such as business cards, letterhead, and signage. Marketing techniques such as public relations and advertising are more effective if a company has a good corporate name and a clearly articulated identity.

Choosing a Winning Name: Susan Russell

"A verbal brand is the Swiss army knife of marketing tools," says Susan Russell, partner and co-founder of the Russell Mark Group. "The names of a company and its products create the vocabulary of a verbal brand. The tagline, corporate description, and text at the end of news releases and on the splash pages of a website contribute to a verbal brand. These language elements combine with the text of marketing collateral to create the verbal brand."

A successful verbal brand explains who the company is and what it does, to establish the company's identity in the marketplace. It also highlights the company's competitive advantages and distinguishes it from the competition. "Each element makes a different contribution to create the corporate identity," says Russell. "The name might not highlight the competitive advantage, but the tagline sets the company apart from the competition. The verbal brand should send a consistent, trusted message over time. Everyone in the company should be able to use it easily."

Five Elements of a Winning Name

Russell identifies five elements that set the gold standard for a company name.

- **It must be legally available both as a corporate name and as a trademark.** Because a winning name is worthless to you if it isn't available, this is the first thing to check. The name must be legally unencumbered. Startups often ask whether they need to change their name. That's a no-brainer if there is a legal challenge and the startup has received a cease-and-desist letter from a lawyer. In such cases companies should change the name.

- **It must be free of negative connotation.** Ensure that the name doesn't have negative meaning in English, Spanish, and French. *Nova*, the name of a Chevrolet automobile, means "it doesn't go" in Spanish.

- **It must be easy to say and spell.** *@Large Software* turned out to be a difficult name for an expense management company. It was impossible to find the company's URL on the Internet because the "@" turned up everything. The name also had negative associations with criminals at large. The new name, *Extendancy,* works better because it conveys that everyone can submit their expense reports from anywhere. McKesson's product, Supply Management Online, allowed customers to order products online, but it was very slow. When McKesson named the product with an acronym, *SMO,* customers derogatorily called it "slow" or "SHMO." Changing the name to *McKesson Connect* created a more positive product identity.

- **It must be short.** This rule has many exceptions. For the true gold standard, the ideal name has only one or two syllables. *Apple* is a good example of a two-syllable name. *Microsoft* is a well-known brand that breaks the rule with three syllables. A name with more than three syllables is asking for trouble. Shorter is always better.

- **It must be proprietary.** Make sure that no other company is using a similar name. It's common to find many uses of a name or similar names in the marketplace. Startups often subconsciously choose names that sound familiar. Using a familiar name won't be proprietary and will be what trademark attorneys call a "weak mark." Pronto Aviation, a maker of taxi jets, suffered a weak mark because the *Pronto* name was already used in the aviation industry. An airline and another aircraft maker were both called Pronto. The new name, *Eclipse Aviation*, is much more proprietary and evokes more than speed. *Eclipse* suggests not only getting ahead quickly but also casting a shadow over the competition.

The Science of Naming

Developing a name is similar to an engineering project. It is a defined process with logical steps that have a beginning and end. "A good name does not come out of the blue like a bolt of lightening," says Russell, and it is not a product of inspiration but comes from following a logical process:

A good naming process has a schedule with deadlines. Convening a small group of interested people to run the project keeps it manageable. There must be a designated decision-maker to make the final selection because people rarely agree about the name.

A well-run process keeps all key stakeholders informed to ensure their support. Many naming projects fail because the proponents forget to get buy-in from the board and key stakeholders. Informed stakeholders can also give objective feedback about whether a name change is necessary.

The next step is developing a naming brief that articulates the key communication messages and objectives. The key objective is to create brand equity and to develop a name that distinguishes the company from its competitors. The trick is to define the intended messages and objectives in the naming brief to provide a reference point against which to measure the name.

Generating the names is the mysterious part, says Russell, who emphasizes that developing a good name requires having many options to choose from because many names are not available. "The key is to accept suggestions from a lot of people because that not only yields many choices but also makes people feel like they're a part of the process. Staging a contest among employees is a time-honored approach that often yields successful names."

The project team itself can also engage in one or more brainstorming sessions to generate ideas. Consider audio-recording the session or at least have several designated note-takers. Allow the team members to brainstorm freely, calling out suggestions and associations as they come to mind. Avoid the temptation to evaluate or make value judgments, which will impede the momentum. A relaxed—and likely fun and quite noisy—session that allows for an anything-goes exchange of ideas can often yield a wealth of possibilities.

After the project team has selected four or five finalists, it needs to check if they are legally available. "The company must be prepared to be heartbroken," says Russell. "A fantastic name may already be in use or be unavailable. Check *www.USPTO.gov.* A quick Google search is also a good way to check. Having a trademark attorney do a search will determine whether the trademark is available."

A company shouldn't expect the right name to jump off the page, Russell adds. "Because names gain meaning over time, it's important to give them time to acquire that meaning. A name might be appealing because it's obvious or because it's already been used in the marketplace. Make sure the name is broad enough to give the company room to grow."

Before the project team makes its final decision, it should test the name with customers: "Customer opinions will yield a better choice and affect a smoother roll-out. An outside perspective is often a wake-up call because the market may have unanticipated problems with a prospective name." Russell continues:

> *A fundamental strategic question in developing a verbal brand is whether a company needs a separate brand for its products. Having only one name is a master-brand strategy. If the company is Zork, for example, and the products are Zork Enterprise and Zork Express, there is only one name and one brand to build. That's cheaper and faster and is usually the way to go. It's very simple and clear.*

The products easily relate to one another because they're all part of Zork. For a new company, this is a simple and elegant way to establish a brand.

If a company has multiple brands such as Smart Systems for the company and Blue Hawaiian for the products, the company name can stand for distinct attributes and the product name can suggest different qualities. A multiple-brand strategy gives a company more flexibility going forward and also avoids the stigma of an unsuccessful product. Diebold's brand, for example, which is associated with ATMs [automated teller machines] and physical security devices, was tarnished by its master-brand strategy because of faulty electronic voting equipment. To dissociate the faulty voting product from the parent company, Diebold changed its subsidiary's name from Diebold Election Systems to Premier Election Solutions.

A master-brand strategy can get undermined, too, Russell adds. "If something goes wrong with the company, all of its products can be polluted by the tarnished company brand. Tyco, whose CEO went to jail, had a master-brand strategy. All of Tyco's products were blemished by the tarnished corporate brand."

Naming Products

Product naming is complicated, says Russell, because companies usually have several product names. "Product names should support the company strategy. Good product names evoke what the company does and how the products fit together."

A company's product names need to work as a flexible system that allows the company to easily add new products or discontinue old ones, says Russell. The system should also create a coherent picture of the product line. If there are five product lines, for example, it should be clear how they fit together and relate to one another.

When to Change a Name

Companies often change their names because they have outgrown them or the names have become misleading. "Easyphone, which made software for call centers, outgrew its name after developing software for web screens," says

Russell. "The new name, *Altitude Software,* implies a bigger idea and suggests that the customer will ascend and move forward rapidly."

Regional naming issues are common, says Russell: "California Physician Service Agency was a physicians group owned by Blue Shield of California. The company outgrew its regional name when it started doing business in other states; it became CareTrust Networks."

When should a name *not* be changed? Says Russell:

> *If a name meets all the gold standard criteria but is not perfect, that's no reason to change it. People have such strong personal opinions about names that it's difficult to develop a consensus. If everybody doesn't agree that the name is ideal, that's no reason to change it. If the name doesn't violate any naming rules, is legally available, is easy to say and spell, is proprietary, and describes what the company does, the company should give it some time.*

> *A company should not change its name if it has measurable positive brand equity. A company has positive brand equity when it is known in its market and its customers associate it with its name.*

Sometimes a company wants to change its name if the Internet domain name is not available in the dot.com form. "Changing a good name simply because the perfect URL is unavailable is also not a good reason," says Russell. "Few dot.com URLs are still available. Many new companies are now using dot. biz, or they add a descriptor such as Inc. or Corporation to the end of the URL.

"Good names avoid trends," Russell says. "We talked many companies out of putting *dot.com* after their name in 1999 because it was just a trend that would go away. They all thought it would improve their stock price."

Creating a Brand That Customers Will Buy: Dan O'Brien

"Companies make products, but customers buy brands," says Dan O'Brien, partner and co-founder of Michael Patrick Partners. "Brand management is very important. Once established, a brand can be distributed globally to be recognized everywhere. The creation of a solid brand identity and the development of a communication system that promotes the brand are critical to a company's growth and success. A successful corporate identity communicates the company's personality and inspires positive customer feelings that generate sales."

Four Steps to Developing a Brand

O'Brien's method of developing a brand is a simple, commonsense process with four distinct steps.

1. **Build consensus.** It's best to assemble a small project team that is intimately familiar with the company. The team should comprise decisive people with a deep understanding of the company and its business and culture. The team should ask big, philosophical questions, such as:

   - Who are the company's customers?

   - What do the customers care about?

   - What does the company stand for?

   - What does the company inspire in its employees, customers, and partners?

A well-run process uncovers a company's essence. Answering these philosophical questions reveals the essential truths about a company. The project team should edit and refine the answers to articulate the salient points.

"The team should then document its conclusions in a creative brief that captures the company's core qualities and the elements of the desired brand essence," says O'Brien. "The brand essence should provide the perfect nugget of meaning that inspires the brand."

The creative brief should also analyze the competitive landscape to show how competitors present their brands in the marketplace. "It helps to analyze competitive brands by placing them on a matrix of attributes that might range from personal to institutional and from traditional to trendy," says O'Brien. "The matrix helps determine where to position the company's brand so that it best stands out from the attributes of competitive brands."

2. **Explore and select.** Developing the brand essence leads to designing the corporate identity. The project team should explore many options, including different colors, type fonts, and logo designs. The team should narrow the possibilities down to the best two or three and make

sure the selections still resonate. Before investing any time or money in one of the choices, the team should check with legal counsel to see if the trademark is available. The team should continue to refine and improve the corporate identity until it arrives at a solution that works.

3. **Refine and deliver.** "The brand should be bulletproof so that it works everywhere," says O'Brien. "The corporate identity needs to work in multiple media channels in a variety of different personalities— including in black-and-white, grayscale, and color—and on a variety of backgrounds, including white, midtone, and black. The company needs to anticipate all the places where it will use the logo—like being embroidered on hats, painted on trucks, or rendered in neon." Anticipating all uses creates the requisite brand consistency, says O'Brien, and when the brand always appears consistently to all stakeholders, the brand equity will constantly increase. A strong brand increases the company's ultimate enterprise value.

   A company should make the brand components accessible to everyone to accelerate the development of brand equity. "All employees should be able to download the logo file in a variety of formats, such as TIFF, PDF, and JPEG," says O'Brien. "Providing easy internal access to the brand components fosters their widespread use, which grows brand equity."

4. **Build and extend.** The goal is a brand identity that works in all applications, including business cards, presentations, literature, trade show graphics, and websites, says O'Brien. The components of the brand identity are shorthand for the brand. The two serve and complement each other.

Using Your Brand to Be a Market Leader

A great brand makes a company look like a market leader on day one, says O'Brien. "A well-designed brand defines a company with a sharp focus and presents its business well. A market-leading brand conveys a company's authentic personality to its ecosystem. Developing the brand is an investment. If a company invests well in its brand early on, it will have it forever and its equity will keep growing with its business."

It's important to complete the branding process, says O'Brien. "People are frightened of change and often have second thoughts when they get to the end of the process. The company should trust its decisions and check the final brand identity against the creative brief. It's best to trust that the company has made the correct decision and roll out the brand."

O'Brien's ideal corporate identity process assembles a comprehensive branding team, including a naming firm, a public relations firm, and some sales and marketing strategists to augment the design team:

The company should avoid treating the team members as four separate disciplines and include them in the process of developing the creative brief. Including everyone in the branding process aligns them with the same information about the company. Assembling a complementary team is less expensive because it maximizes efficiency. When it's time to engage public relations, the PR team will be up to speed, too. Before a company engages in any of these four disciplines, it should figure out where best to spend money to create demand and increase revenue.

Developing effective internal communication is critical to ensuring that everyone is operating from the same messaging script. It is important to develop crisp internal rules of communication to project a consistent corporate voice that inspires how the receptionist answers the phone, what out-of-office greeting people leave on voice-mail, what signature block people use on their e-mail, how the company is described in news releases, and how the logo is used.

The VP of marketing should enforce the consistent use of these elements to maximize brand value. If people are operating from different playbooks, the company will miss dozens of subtle opportunities to build its brand equity. Singing from the same branding songbook accelerates the development of positive brand equity.

In the end, says O'Brien, standing out in the market has three components: a crisp value proposition, a compelling ROI, and enthusiastic customers. "Show someone why they should care and that other people care and have paid money for it. All of a company's marketing programs should work together to set the company apart from the competition."

Cobalt's Brand

Steve DeWitt was a master of perception because he used Cobalt's brand to create the impression that the young company was big, established, and credible. Cobalt's brand helped DeWitt be his company's best salesperson and enabled everyone to effortlessly sell its servers.

Cobalt's branding strategy drove its success. Facing tough competition from established public server manufacturers like Sun Microsystems and well-funded startups like Whistle, Cobalt developed a memorable brand that stood above its competitors.

Cobalt designed its server to be so cool that it would sell itself. The Qube sparked the question "What the hell is that?" when somebody saw one across the room. Cobalt extended its brand into a jaw-dropping, iconic cobalt blue server that drew customers to the product like a magnet. As a small startup company, Cobalt discovered that developing its brand was the best way to buy attention.

Cobalt produced a series of black-and-white posters depicting the Qube in full cobalt blue as the object of each of the seven deadly sins. The poster "Lust," for example, featured a beautiful woman seductively cradling the Qube. Cobalt's branding efforts created a positive buzz in the market that enabled the company to compete successfully against its larger and better-funded rivals.

Developing the Elements of Brand

Going through the collaborative process of writing the business plan and developing the core values gives a founding team a good sense of the company's personality. The next step is to create a brand that reflects that personality by developing the elements of the verbal brand and the corporate identity. The name, logo, website, and other elements of brand complement one another to reinforce the brand.

Use a collaborative process like Susan Russell's gold standard to come up with the company name. Once the name is settled, work with a corporate identity firm to develop a logo, website, and other trade collateral like business cards and a letterhead that reflect the essence of the company's personality. The business plan and the core values will help the branding firm create a corporate identity that reflects the spirit of the business.

While the corporate identity is being created, the founding team can work in parallel to develop a tagline that captures the spirit of the vision statement, a two- or three-sentence "elevator pitch" that expands on the vision statement, and a cover paragraph for use in e-mails and other communications that summarizes the essence of the business plan. The team should also distill the business plan into a one-page executive summary that includes financial projections and biographical information about the team. Developing a PowerPoint presentation for investors (covered in chapters 22 and 23) is premature at this point and can wait.

The elements of a brand create a pyramid, with the smallest element—the name—at the top and the largest and most public element—the website—at the bottom. Figure 5 provides a simple model for visualizing how the key elements work together to create a brand.

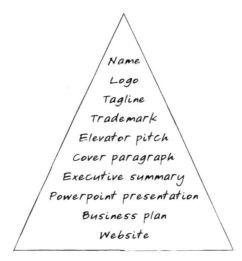

Figure 5: The elements of a brand

Summary

Successful companies build powerful brands with two components: the verbal brand and the corporate identity.

- The verbal brand is the corporate name and the language elements. A successful verbal brand explains who the company is and what it does, to establish the company's identity in the marketplace. It should send a consistent, trusted message over time.

- The corporate identity includes the logo, website, and other elements of trade dress like the letterhead and business cards that reflect the essence of the company's personality.

- The elements of the verbal brand and the corporate identity complement and reinforce one another to create a powerful brand.

- A powerful brand leverages an authentic personality to connect with the customer to drive sales.

Call to Action

Use Susan Russell's gold standard naming process to develop a winning company name. Involve as many people as possible to develop as many suggestions as possible. Using a collaborative process to arrive at the name forms a feedback loop that reinforces a company's ability to listen.

Designate a team to develop the corporate identity using Dan O'Brien's system. At the same time, work collaboratively to develop the other elements of the verbal brand such as the tagline and the executive summary. Share these elements with your branding firm; they will enable it to develop a crisper identity, and the firm will likely have ideas about how to use them to reinforce the brand.

Chapter 17

DYNAMIC PUBLIC RELATIONS

Always remember the power of one.

—Tim Sanders, author, *Saving the World at Work*

A company's stories bring its brand to life. Humans love good stories. The purpose of public relations (PR) is to tell a company's best stories so that its stakeholders love it. An authentic story provides a competitive advantage because customers prefer buying from companies with a true story that comes from the heart. People love stories where the hero overcomes adversity to succeed. Cobalt, 3Dfx, and 3Tera had powerful stories because each overcame the death of a founder. These companies also had compelling stories because they offered game-changing technology. Their tragedies fostered an endearing vulnerability that enabled them to tell their stories from the heart. How are you going to tell your company's story? Are you ready to share it?

Smart companies use public relations to amplify their brand. Effective public relations uses stories to project a company's unique personality into its marketplace to enhance its corporate identity. The story might be how the founders got the idea for the company. Cobalt's founders, for example, decided to build a company together over coffee at a Parisian café while on a business trip for Apple.

Accelerating Growth with Public Relations: Ross Perich

"The job of public relations is to accelerate a company's growth," says Ross Perich, Vice President of Trainer Communications. "The company pays a PR agency to place stories about it in publications. Published stories generate the credibility that all startups need. Startups' customers worry about whether the company will still be in business tomorrow. Good public relations creates powerful third-party credibility. Says Perich:

> *Public relations is a distinctly different discipline from advertising. With advertising, a company pays a fortune to a publisher to create a glossy, full-page advertisement that appears in a publication like* Forbes*. Advertising is appropriate for an established company to enhance its brand by telling the subliminal part of the brain to "Buy Oracle Enterprise now." Advertising in publications like Forbes, however, is not appropriate for early-stage startups.*

> *Most startups spend the majority of their marketing budgets on public relations. It's more effective to create awareness by pitching Mossberg to write about a company than to pay big bucks for an ad in the* Wall Street Journal*. As the company matures, advertising enters the mix. Because public relations and advertising are expensive, a company has to be very focused to get the best return on investment.*

Perich offers the following five tips for maximizing the return on your public relations efforts.

Timing Is Everything

"A company has one chance to make it and needs to get it right out of the gate," says Perich. "Everybody may be fired up and excited, but a company shouldn't jump the gun. The entrepreneur with the Stanford MBA may be ready to tell the world about the shiny thing the company has built in the garage, but it's better not to go out at all than to go out too early. If the company uses public relations too early, it will have the wrong message. The brand won't develop any equity."

Perich says a company should know who its customers are before it engages public relations: "If a company can't sing to the right audience, it might as well not sing at all because ultimately the right customers will pay to keep the company in business. In fact, singing to the wrong audience can hurt more; the company is better off doing nothing."

Using Public Relations Correctly

Even though cash is always tight in startups, public relations is not a place to skimp because you get what you pay for, says Perich:

> *The VP of marketing needs to manage the CEO's expectations and get his buy-in on any PR program. If the CEO has one idea of success and the marketing executive and the public relations agency have another, the program is doomed.*

> *If the CEO has a big ego and wants an article in the New York Times, the VP of marketing is in trouble if he places a story in Automotive News, which is what all the factory floor guys who buy the product are reading. If the VP has done his homework, he sets the CEO's expectations about the target publications so that he, the CEO, and the agency will all be in alignment.*

It's important to remember that the customer is king, says Perich. Companies can't forget to learn what the customer wants and why they are buying their products. "Customer focus groups are a great way to get to know them and their needs," Perich says. "Everyone needs to understand the customer because a public relations program will never take off if customers have a relationship only with the vice president of sales."

Good public relations can raise awareness among investors as well. Startups often engage public relations, says Perich, because they need some visibility to attract investors: "Startups need to excite the investor community to raise a round of funding, but if no one knows about a company, chances are Sequoia and Mayfield will not know about it either. Sales are everything, but public relations can drive sales only if the company has a pipeline of the right prospects."

Public relations can also help a growing company with recruiting. "It's a challenge to retain and recruit talent when Google and the competitor down the street have more money and are wooing away the employees," says Perich. "Good publicity can reinforce the impression that a company is a cool place to work."

Public relations can increase visibility for a company with a rock star CEO and management team. Perich says an experienced management team from Cisco, Juniper, Microsoft, and IBM, for example, is an asset worth touting: "Good public relations can help a relatively unknown startup leverage human capital to attract customers and employees and grow revenue."

Good Stories Make the Best PR

Simplicity is best. Stories about the company and its investors often make the best public relations. Says Perich:

> If Noname.com is selling into the enterprise market, its prospects will all ask, 'Your product is great, but are you guys going to be around in six or 12 months? Who are your venture capitalists?" Pointing to an article that touts the company's $12 million round from Sequoia and discusses the pending second round with Mayfield brings credibility with a company's prospects.
>
> Off-the-wall stories are the best PR assets. The lead story in Forbes or the local paper always has a human element. WhereNet, for example, had developed a wireless real-time location system using RFID [radio-frequency identification] for heavy industrial uses. An amusement park in Denver put WhereNet's chip in a wristwatch so that parents could find lost children. WhereNet didn't recognize the PR opportunity because the amusement park application was outside the core business.
>
> When WhereNet demonstrated the technology at Highland Hills Water Park in Denver with a Girl Scout troop, the results were gaudy. WhereNet got a two-page story in the New York Times and had more than a hundred instances of print coverage and 150 broadcast hits. Chron4 TV in the San Francisco Bay Area delivered the story to every NBC affiliate across the country. That story put WhereNet on the map and launched its brand. Every company should look for similar human-interest stories within its four walls.

The ideal PR story explains why businesses should care about the product and how they will get a compelling return on investment in nine to 12 months, says Perich. "Effective public relations requires that the company let go of the product because customers buy on ROI and a compelling business case. No one wants to hear the founder bragging about the product; people want to hear how the product will help their businesses, not why the underlying algorithms or software make the product the coolest thing ever."

When to Use Public Relations

Business is all about customers. Great public relations leverages the customer, but it can feel like a Catch-22, says Perich. "How can a company leverage customers if it doesn't have any? That's why a company should launch a PR campaign only after it has at least one beta customer who can talk positively about it.

Customers provide a whole spectrum of PR possibilities, says Perich: "One customer might be willing only to contribute a quote for a news release but might give five phone interviews to the media if the company can give him a boondoggle to Las Vegas. Providing the customer's CEO with a speaking engagement at the next Vegas trade show, for example, might inspire him to take a reference call from a prospective customer."

Smart companies get commitments from their customers to generate good public relations. "A PR expert can help the sales team build rapport with customers to acquire raving fans," says Perich. "In exchange for a $50,000 discount in the contract or purchase order, for example, a customer might agree to give three press interviews over the next six months."

Effective PR campaigns start within a six-month window before product launch, when companies have names, brands, and beta customers who can provide good third-party endorsements, says Perich. "They still have money. Startups should never start public relations unless they are starting to generate revenue from beta customers and have at least six months of cash runway. That approach puts too much pressure on the sales team. Six months later the company might not have revenue and will have to pull the plug."

Getting the Best Bang for Your PR Buck

Good marketing programs won't sell the product if the product doesn't solve the customer's pain. "To demonstrate ROI for marketing dollars," says Perich, "a good program evaluates each sales and marketing component and fixes what's not working. Is there a problem with the product? Does the product have the wrong price or value proposition? Is it lacking key features?"

The threshold requirement for engaging a PR firm is having customers willing to go to bat for the company, says Perich:

> *Understanding the competitive landscape is also critical because the first question the media will ask an entrepreneur is, "Who are your competitors?" The media won't believe the entrepreneur if he says that there aren't any.*
>
> *Identifying the competitors is the easiest way to help the media understand a company. The media wants to put a startup in a tiny bucket. Tell the reporter that Cisco is the main competitor, for example, but show how the company plans to beat Cisco in one tiny segment of the market.*

To get the best results, says Perich, startups should get experienced PR executives who have managed corporate communications for sophisticated enterprise customers like Oracle to commit to working on the account. "Bait-and-switch is commonplace in big PR agencies," he says. "Senior people will work on the account for 60 days and then turn it over to the kids just out of college to learn on the company's time. Bait-and-switch doesn't work for startups."

An entrepreneur needs a nimble PR team with experience in startups because the first mover often has the advantage and startups have limited financial resources. "Companies should clearly establish their PR objectives and use deadlines to hold the agency accountable for hitting the numbers," says Perich. "Public relations is measurable by length and type of articles, quality of publications and conferences, and quantity of placements. If the PR agency doesn't provide the desired results in a timely manner, a company should find another firm that can deliver the goods."

Summary

- Every company has interesting stories.
- The stories combine with the verbal brand and the corporate identity to bring the brand to life.
- The stories may be about the people or the business. The job of public relations is to tell the company's stories so that customers love the company.
- The market loves authentic stories with a human element.

Call to Action

Gather the company's best stories to be prepared for public relations. The best stories often answer interesting questions:

- Who are the founders?

- Where did the vision come from?

- How did the founders meet?

- What made them decide to work together?

- Why did they decide to build this company?

- Where did they all come from?

- What interesting things do they like to do?

- What adversity did they overcome in their lives?

- What is special about the company?

- Develop a strategy to get stories from your customers:

- How are you going to create raving fans?

- Why is your product important to customers?

- What problem does it solve?

- How does it save them money?

- What is the return on investment?

Chapter 18

PROTECTING
INTELLECTUAL PROPERTY

Leverage your culture to drive innovation.
—Terri Kelly, President and CEO, W. L. Gore & Associates

Successful startups develop a system to protect and manage their intellectual property (IP) assets from the beginning. To the extent that the founders have preexisting intellectual property, they need to assign ownership of those assets to their company, together with any IP rights such as patents and trademarks. How is your company going to protect its intellectual property assets?

Startups should require all employees to sign an assignment of inventions agreement that gives ownership to the company of all inventions made during the course of employment. Similarly, a startup should require all independent contractors and other consultants, including informal advisory board members, to sign formal consulting agreements that assign all inventions to the company as "work for hire." Failure to have employees and consultants assign ownership of inventions to the company can destroy the value of intellectual property because it clouds the title.

Innovative startups work closely with patent counsel to determine which inventions are patentable. Patents build enterprise value by giving a company a legal competitive advantage because they prevent competitors from using a particular invention for 20 years from the time of filing. Having a legal monopoly in a particular field can be extremely valuable. To the extent an invention is patentable, it is important to file a patent application before disclosing the existence of the invention to anyone outside of the company because disclosure can preclude filing a patent. Trademarks also build enterprise value by creating brand equity.

It is also important to guard trade secrets—every proprietary invention that may not be patentable but which is extremely valuable. Coca-Cola's formula, for example, is a closely guarded trade secret known by only a handful of people. Guarding the recipe prevents competitors from copying the beverage.

Patent counsel can also help entrepreneurs develop a coherent patent strategy that includes foreign markets. Entrepreneurs should consider seeking patents and trademarks in the European Union and in countries with large markets like China and Japan. Entrepreneurs who see how the technology will evolve in their field can secure the future market by filing patent applications with claims that anticipate these developments.

Creating an Intellectual Property Strategy: Ron Laurie

"Successful startups adopt formal strategies to make intellectual property part of their infrastructure," says Ron Laurie, co-founder and president of Inflexion Point, an IP investment bank. "Having a coherent intellectual property strategy helps a company maximize its enterprise value. As a potential acquisition target, every company should maximize the value of IP assets in an exit transaction as part of its strategic plan.

Protecting Intellectual Property

To maximize the value of its IP assets, a startup must focus on protecting them from the very earliest stage. "Intellectual property is perishable because its protection is subject to numerous time limits and filing deadlines," says Laurie. "Disclosure of unprotected intellectual property can prevent a company from protecting it in certain cases. Failure to protect intellectual property early can result in an irretrievable loss of critical assets that will make a company less valuable to an acquirer. If a company doesn't protect intellectual property on or before its Series A financing, there may be nothing left to protect."

Startup companies develop their patent portfolios by filing patent applications with the United States Patent and Trademark Office (USPTO) or by buying patent assets from third parties. "Creating a patent portfolio from scratch takes a long time," says Laurie. "The process starts with filing a provisional patent application, which must be followed within a year by a nonprovisional patent application. It usually takes three or four years for the USPTO to comment on an application with an office action, and several more years after responding to the office action to actually get a patent. Buying existing patents eliminates the filing tasks and creates an immediate portfolio."

How Investors Value Intellectual Property

Venture capitalists generally resist spending money on patent portfolio development for three reasons, says Laurie:

> *First, with the decline of IPOs, most startups get acquired before patents will issue. Second, patents may be perceived to be of little value in a particular field of technology. Third, the return on acquiring patent rights from third parties may not be apparent.*

> *Patents usually issue too far in the future to be of value to venture capital investors seeking exits in a five-to-seven-year time frame. Venture capitalists are reluctant to invest what they perceive as marginal dollars that will not affect their targeted rate of return in the allotted time horizon. If the goal is to build a viable, sustainable billion-dollar business, however, their resistance should not prevent a company from investing in developing its intellectual property portfolio.*

Laurie says that acquiring a portfolio of existing intellectual property is an effective valuation maximization strategy, which may be more cost-effective than building one from scratch. "A company can build a portfolio over seven to 10 years with unpredictable results or purchase a dominant intellectual property position. Venture capitalists are often reluctant to have their portfolio companies purchase patent portfolios because there's not enough data to show that such an investment will help produce their target rate of return. It may be easier to convince a venture capital director to support the acquisition of a patent portfolio for a technology company or a company in a complex field."

The field of technology determines whether or not early-stage venture capital investors value IP assets, says Laurie:

> *There is a scale of technology that ranges from biotechnology to materials and nanotechnology; to semiconductors, computers, and telecom; to software; and finally to Internet and e-commerce. Generally, IP assets are most valuable at the biotechnology end of the range and decline in value across the scale to have only marginal value in e-commerce.*
>
> *A venture capital investor will generally support developing IP assets in the biotechnology or pharmaceutical fields because intellectual property is absolutely critical. In the life sciences, for example, the relationship between the product and the intellectual property is intimate and well established. The product can't be separated from the intellectual property, especially in the pharmaceutical industry. It's a huge event when a drug goes off patent, because everybody copies the drug.*

The value of an IP asset depends on uncertainty risk of whether an invention is patentable, says Laurie:

> *More-complex fields of technology, such as pharmaceuticals, generally have less uncertainty risk than less complex fields like e-commerce. It's obvious when a pharmaceutical company invents a new molecule. Everybody in the world can copy it unless it is protected by a patent. On the other hand, if a company invents a new network management software algorithm, no one knows whether or not it's really new and therefore patentable. The company will never know whether its algorithm is novel until it gets to litigation and spends half a million dollars having lawyers look through the archives of MIT PhD dissertations and attics full of source code that nobody has seen for 10 years.*

Until legally validated in litigation, says Laurie, a patent is basically an option. Whether it's a pending application or an issued patent, the value is in the probability that it will hold up under legal challenge. Value is just a matter of degree of whether it's a pending or an issued patent.

How the Business Model Affects Valuation

The kind of company also determines the value of intellectual property. "Valuation depends on whether a business is a services company, a product company, a technology company, or an IP licensing company," says Laurie. "The transitions between these business model distinctions are fuzzy, but intellectual property is more valuable in technology and IP licensing companies. A venture capital investor will be more inclined to invest in developing intellectual property in those companies."

A technology company doesn't have a tangible product like a software platform, says Laurie, but provides its product to companies that use it as the basis for their products. "A technology company that has someone else make the product for the end user is a good business model. A technology company isn't a product company that hasn't yet taken its product to market but rather provides the building blocks for somebody else's product. Intel, for example, lets its customers manufacture devices that use its semiconductors."

Intellectual property licensing companies take the technology company model one step further, Laurie continues, by deriving their revenue primarily from licensing:

Qualcomm, for example, is essentially an intellectual property licensing company. Recently, Qualcomm got 90 percent of its revenue from product sales and 90 percent of its profit from IP licensing. Successful business is all about healthy margins. The margins on intellectual property are so unbelievably good that many companies start out with the intention of being IP licensing companies. In the intellectual property domain, this is the analogue of fabless semiconductor companies. Because the value in semiconductors is in the design, not in the manufacture, to maximize value, an IP licensing company is a design company that lets its licensees worry about the manufacturing.

Having an Acquisition Strategy

An effective IP strategy prepares for a successful exit, which will likely be an acquisition. It's helpful to identify the top three potential acquirers in the market, says Laurie:

A company should develop its IP strategy around those potential buyers not only by protecting the product and its unique qualities but also by protecting more broadly to give an acquirer a competitive advantage against its competitors. If a patent portfolio provides a competitive edge, it maximizes its attractiveness to the acquirer.

For a networking company, for example, the top acquirer is Cisco. Intellectual property is often a deal driver for Cisco. If Cisco has three target companies in a particular technology area and one of them has a killer patent portfolio, the one with the killer patents will be the leading acquisition candidate.

In the mergers and acquisitions world, the intellectual property often gets dragged along for free because nobody knows how to value it. "That's great for the acquirers to get the intellectual property for nothing," says Laurie, "but it's not so great for the target. Targets leave money on the table because nobody understands the value of intellectual property."

Large companies often approach small and mid-sized ones for acquisition. "The big company does its EBITDA [earnings before interest, taxes, depreciation and amortization] analysis and tells the small one what it is worth. The smaller company tells the big one it's worth much more because of its wonderful intellectual property. The big one responds, 'The intellectual property is nice, but here is what your company is worth according to the standard valuation metrics.'"

An effective strategy to force big companies to properly value the intellectual property, says Laurie, is to move it out of the startup company and into an independent holding company and retain a nonexclusive license to it:

The holding company has to be independent so that it doesn't get sucked along as a subsidiary when the parent company gets acquired. The nonexclusive license allows a company to grow its business with defensible IP rights; but without holding exclusive rights to the intellectual property, it lacks the ability to offensively assert its rights against competitors. The license is purely defensive. An acquirer will get very interested in the intellectual property when it realizes it's not getting all of it. This can be an effective method to force an acquirer to fairly value the IP assets.

If a business fails, a well-developed intellectual property portfolio may provide a safety net for the investors because it may be the only valuable asset. "There is now a healthy market for IP assets, especially patents," says Laurie. "Bankruptcy trustees used to circulate Notices of Intent to Abandon Assets with lists of 25 pending patent applications and issued patents; often they just flushed these assets because there was no market and no established method of monetizing them. Now there is an active market in trading, buying, and selling patents."

Preparing for an Exit

Even if a potential merger or acquisition exit is five years off, Laurie recommends that a company create a virtual data room from the beginning because this forces it to be organized about its intellectual property, licensing agreements, and corporate documents. When the phone rings, the company will be ready. Having well-organized data supports the exit valuation by confirming that the company is well run and worthy of being acquired. Says Laurie:

> *An early-stage entrepreneur should get a copy of a typical acquisition agreement and carefully review the seller's representations and warranties about the intellectual property because the company will have to make similar representations when it gets acquired. It's best to prepare to make those representations and warranties from the beginning. To the extent that a company can't make particular representations and has exceptions on the disclosure schedule, the overall valuation may decrease. It's prudent to start from day one and build a defensible IP position that will allow the company to make those representations without exceptions.*

Demonstrating the Value of Intellectual Property

It's critical to be ready to demonstrate the IP component of the enterprise value. "Intellectual property valuation firms can provide estimates of value," says Laurie. "Following the IP brokerage market can provide an indication of value with the sale prices of comparable portfolios. *Comparable* has to be taken with a grain of salt because one patent is never exactly the same as another. Comparable portfolios can give a good sense of value that prepares a company to respond when an acquirer refuses to pay for the intellectual property. Finally, hiring a CIPO [chief intellectual property officer] as an employee or a consultant can help a company develop its intellectual property strategy to maximize its ultimate value."

Summary

- Successful companies protect their intellectual property with patents and trademarks and by guarding their trade secrets.

- Successful companies protect their intellectual property from the beginning by ensuring that all employees and contractors assign to the company any inventions they create in the course of their employment or consulting.

- Successful companies make sure that the founders assign their intellectual property to the company.

- Successful companies have a strategy to protect their intellectual property.

Call to Action

Develop your company's IP strategy and include the following elements:

- Identify any intellectual property that the founders need to assign to the company.

- Prepare an assignment of inventions agreement for employees to sign.

- Prepare a consulting agreement that assigns inventions to the company as work for hire.

- Get recommendations for patent and trademark counsel.

- Identify inventions that should be patented.

- File trademark applications for the names.

- Determine the foreign markets in which it may be appropriate to file patents and trademarks.

- Anticipate where the technology in your market is going and file patent applications that include claims for inventions that anticipate such direction.

Chapter 19

ALLOCATING THE EQUITY

What you stand for is more important than what you sell.

—Roy Spence, author, *It's Not What You Sell, It's What You Stand For*

How is your company going to do the right thing—such as allocating the equity fairly among the founders? How are you going to make decisions that balance short-term financial considerations with the long-term viability of the business? It will be difficult for your corporation to do the right thing because it doesn't have a formal internal conscience. The common-law fiduciary duties of management to stockholders impose a limited corporate conscience from the outside.

Testing the Corporate Conscience

The first test of a corporation's conscience happens during the concept stage, when entrepreneurs allocate stock ownership among the founding team. There is no magic formula or capitalization algorithm that can easily allocate the equity. A team must keep tinkering until each member can put his stock purchase agreement in a drawer without any further concern. Some teams take more than a year to complete the allocation of equity. It has to feel right.

How a team solves the equity equation not only indicates how it will respond to other problems but also predicts future success or failure. Teams that take the socialist approach and allocate equity equally among the founders are delusional. These teams are more likely to fail because they generally have avoided conflict by shirking frank and often-painful discussions about experience, relative worth, and expected contribution. Such teams will waste enormous amounts of organizational energy when they have to reengineer the company's capitalization upon realizing that the founders don't make equal contributions. Such teams generally avoid conflict, which can quickly prove fatal as the inevitable challenges arise.

The other extreme is the team that sees the majority of the equity allocated to one founder. This is usually a sign of a one-man band and a leader with founder's disease (see chapter 8). Such an allocation of equity might be appropriate if the founder had previously built three successful public companies or is reserving equity for future peer-level executives, but generally such an allocation indicates a weak and unbalanced team that will likely fail.

Venture capital investors recognize when a team has arrived at the right allocation and expect it to have gotten it right. If the founding team is courageously honest about assessing its members, some founders may fall off the team. Properly done, allocating the equity stress-tests the team in a positive way. Cobalt Network's founding team of six, for example, shrank to three. Such attrition is a normal part of the shakedown cruise inherent in the incorporation process.

Allocating the equity is also the perfect time for the founders to tap their collective intelligence and practice using the company's core values to exercise a conscience. Allocating the equity requires whole-brain thinking because the proper distribution must not only be logically based on a variety of metrics like experience and relative contribution but also be balanced and fair so that it makes sense to investors and future team members.

Vesting and transfer restriction issues compound the difficulty of allocating the relative percentages of equity ownership. Vesting is a mechanism that allows the company to repurchase unvested shares, usually at cost, when a person leaves its employ. Venture capitalists generally require that the founders of their portfolio companies subject their stock to vesting, usually over a four-year period, to ensure that the founders have incentive to stay and build the company. Vesting also protects the founding team members themselves by ensuring that a founder who owns 20 percent of the company can't quit after a week and enjoy the fruits of the labor of the other founders who toil for many more years to make the equity valuable.

Vesting has many subtle nuances, including whether some or all of the unvested shares will become vested upon a sale or other change of control of the company or upon the termination of a founder's employment without cause or for a constructive termination. For example, a team may have spent a year in the concept phase before incorporating their company and might decide to purchase their stock with 25 percent vested and the balance vesting monthly over three years.

Many entrepreneurs are tempted to purchase fully vested stock to postpone the vesting discussion. Deferring this discussion until the company has raised venture capital is a bad idea because it signals to sophisticated investors that the team doesn't have its act together. Venture capitalists will be reluctant to give a founding team any vesting credit and will ask for standard four-year vesting commencing from the date of funding.

Sometimes it makes sense to stage the incorporation process to allow the founding team to get the allocation of equity right. Founders can incorporate a company and designate the initial officers and directors while postponing the allocation of equity. This two-step approach allows a company to open bank accounts, file trademarks, receive assignments of intellectual property, and enter into contracts.

Using Core Values as Ethical Guidelines

The founders can use the corporation's core values to help them allocate the equity as well as make other important decisions. The core values provide ethical guidelines for a company's internal and external rules of engagement. They also provide the structure that supports the exercise of a conscience by setting the expectations of ideal norms of behavior. Applying the core values makes doing the right thing clearer and can help solve the equity equation to cultivate a holistic conscience.

If your board of directors makes the tough decisions based solely on its fiduciary duties to stockholders, it will ignore the consequences of corporate action on other stakeholders. This prevailing ethical paradigm makes some decisions easier, but ignoring the effects of a proposed action on all stakeholders is risky. Actions that harm stakeholders can cause them to stop supporting the business and can ultimately damage the company by tarnishing its reputation, driving away its customers, demoralizing its employees, and devaluing its stock. This paradigm is acceptable so long as management has high integrity; but when it has no or low integrity, a corporation will often act unconscionably if it doesn't have a more developed conscience to regulate its behavior.

Google famously adopted the informal motto "Don't be evil," which is said to recognize that large corporations often subordinate the greater good in the quest for short-term profits. By adopting that motto, the company established a baseline for honest decision-making that considers the impact of its actions on all stakeholders and not just the financial bottom line.

Whole Foods uses its core values as an internal moral compass to guide corporate decisions. Making decisions in alignment with core values augments fiduciary duties to create a holistic conscience that considers the interests of all stakeholders. This approach enhances corporate governance, reduces catastrophic risk, and preserves and enhances stockholder value. Considering all stakeholders also enables a corporation to exhibit moral consistency to retain conscientious employees.

Cobalt Networks acted with moral consistency that inspired its employees because its board of directors consistently did the right thing even when not legally required to. When founder Mark Wu died on the eve of the company's first equity round of financing, Gordon Campbell and Kip Meyers, a general partner at Vanguard Fund, honored their funds' commitments to finance the company. The board accelerated the vesting of some of Mark's shares to support his family. The integrity of its directors gave Cobalt an expanded conscience.

Exercising the Corporate Conscience

Having each level of management use the corporation's core values as its moral compass expands the corporate conscience. Activating a holistic conscience requires the coordinated efforts of the CEO, management, and the board of directors. Having a conscience does not make the tough decisions any easier, but it does ensure that the decisions are less likely to harm the corporation and its ecosystem and more likely to preserve stockholder value.

Almost all directors are ethical people whose conscience guides their actions within their families and communities. A moral compass governs their private lives, but in the boardroom they feel compelled to subordinate the board's collective conscience to its fiduciary duty to stockholders.

A board of directors that exercises a conscience that considers the potential adverse consequences of corporate behavior is supported by law. Under the business judgment rule, Delaware courts, for example, will not question rational judgments about how promoting nonstockholder interests ultimately promotes stockholder value so long as the directors act within a range of reasonableness. Exercising a conscience that avoids actions that harm the business, its reputation, and its market capitalization is not only prudent but also promotes the value of the corporation for its stockholders.

The US Supreme Court, which is the de facto conscience of the federal government and, ultimately, the people of the United States, modeled how a board of directors can exercise its collective conscience in its recent *Citizens United v. Federal Election Commission* decision. This controversial case overturned federal campaign finance laws that prevented corporations from making donations to political campaigns on the grounds that such laws violated corporations' constitutional right to freedom of speech under the First Amendment. The depth of the opinions rendered in the case reflects a comprehensive approach to exercising a collective conscience.

The sheer volume of the opinion demonstrates the scope of the court's examination of the key issues in the case. The five-justice majority opinion is 57 pages, with 29 pages of concurring opinion; the four-justice minority opinion is 90 pages. In reaching their decision, the justices' opinion exhaustively examines the facts of the case, the legal and social history, and the legal precedents. Although the court was sharply divided, all justices exercised their individual consciences in rendering a split 5-to-4 decision on all but one of the case's key points.

Boards of directors that act with the same degree of care as the US Supreme Court in *Citizens United* will have corporations with effective consciences that promote and protect stockholder value. The next chapter suggests simple changes to standard charter documents that support a corporate conscience.

Summary

- Corporations lack a formal conscience to provide a moral compass.

- The fiduciary duty of management to stockholders is the default moral compass in most corporations.

- Fiduciary duty of management to stockholders can create a blind spot when management overlooks the interests of all stakeholders.

- Corporations can use their core values as a moral compass to guide their behavior.

- Using the core values to consider corporate actions helps a company make better decisions and avoid action that damages the company's reputation, business, and market value.

Call to Action

- Allocate the ownership percentages and the corresponding capital stock among the members of the founding team to practice using the collective conscience.

- Use the core values to access the team's collective conscience. If the core values are integrity, teamwork, and respect, for example, view the proposed equity allocation through the lens of integrity. If the definition of *integrity* is "to do the right thing in every situation," does the allocation feel correct?

- The equity allocations should also consider vesting considerations. Is some stock already vested to reflect work already done? Is it appropriate to have acceleration of vesting in the event of a change of control? Should there be some acceleration of vesting if a person is fired without cause?

Chapter 20

BUILDING A SOLID
LEGAL FOUNDATION

The corporation is the most effective system of social cooperation ever invented.
—R. Edward Freeman, author, *Strategic Management: A Stakeholder Approach*

If you treat the incorporation process as a necessary but perfunctory step and rush to get it over with as quickly and cheaply as possible, you will miss the opportunity to amplify the power of your company's compelling purpose and core values by incorporating them into the charter documents. Including the purpose and the values in the bylaws and the articles of incorporation helps define the corporate culture with precision and emphasizes its importance as an asset.

This approach also provides a succession plan that preserves your company's investment in its culture. Integrating the core values into the charter documents along with mechanisms to hold people accountable to them gives a company a formal internal conscience to guide behavior and create a conscientious culture—both of which are powerful agents of alignment.

Such an approach ensures that a corporation's culture becomes an enduring asset that provides continuity when management changes. Unfortunately, the standard approach to forming a corporation misses the best opportunity to customize the formation documents to reinforce the company's compelling purpose and create unique rules of engagement to support its culture. How are you going to protect and preserve the elements of your company's culture? How is your company going to maintain its dynamic culture when the founder is no longer there to drive it?

Hewlett-Packard's values-based culture, known affectionately as "the HP Way," was an ephemeral asset vulnerable to destruction because the founders did not codify its elements into the foundation documents. Frugality was one of the core values of the HP Way. Executives modeled the core value of frugality, for example, by traveling by commercial airline or by shuttles between plants. After the founders retired, the company hastened the demise of the HP Way when it bought a corporate jet for the use of a successor president. Without a formal legal structure to protect it, the HP Way has declined as a cultural unifier; and for many loyal career HP employees, working at the company has devolved into a job.

The law provides every startup's institutional framework, but few entrepreneurs know that it also empowers them to modify the standard bylaws and articles of incorporation to include customized rules of engagement. In the United States, state codes establish corporations' basic rules of governance, which are reflected in standard bylaws and articles of incorporation that contain the minimum of required governance. These foundation documents, for example, determine the duties of officers and directors as well as the procedures for holding stockholder meetings. The best time to customize the charter documents is before a company is incorporated.

Including the Purpose

The first step in customizing a company's legal infrastructure is to include its purpose in its articles of incorporation. Corporations codes empower companies to pursue an almost unlimited variety of purposes, with a few proscribed exceptions; and standard articles of incorporation authorize a corporation to do anything permitted by the applicable code. While this approach provides unlimited flexibility, it misses the opportunity to celebrate a corporation's unique vision by giving its purpose prominence in the articles of incorporation.

Including the compelling purpose in the articles of incorporation can inspire people by demonstrating the company's commitment to realizing its vision. This certificate of incorporation of a wind- and water-power turbine company, for example, clearly defines its purpose and amplifies the enthusiasm contained in the vision without limiting the potential scope of its business:

> *ARTICLE III. The nature of the business or purpose of the Corporation is to engage in any lawful act or activity for which corporations may be organized under the General Corporation Law of the State of Delaware, including developing and delivering products and technologies that remove technological barriers and bring economies of scale to the wind and run-of-river electrical power generation industries.*[4]

Incorporating the Core Values

A corporation can demonstrate its commitment to its core values by incorporating them into its charter documents. Integrating the values also ensures the continuity of the culture when management changes.

Core values are as varied and unique as the corporations that articulate them. Expressly defining the company's core values and integrating them into the bylaws elevates them to a code of conduct that promotes alignment among stakeholders. The code of conduct becomes a permanent code of ethics and determines the rules of engagement both within the corporation and externally with its ecosystem. Here are the core values from the bylaws of another Delaware corporation:

> *Integrity.* We strive to do the right thing in every situation: for each other, for our customers, and for all of our stakeholders. We make ethics, fairness, honesty, and integrity the cornerstones of our business.

> *Respect.* We strive to create a safe environment, both internally and externally, based on mutual respect for each other, our customers, and all of our stakeholders. We treat others as we would like to be treated ourselves, and we treat the environment with reverence and respect.

> *Quality.* We are committed to excellence in the results we achieve for our customers, and we are continually growing and improving our business. We encourage our clients and ourselves to strive to be the best we can be. We strive to attract, develop, and inspire the best people.

---

4   This and the other excerpts in this chapter from Delaware corporation charter documents are reprinted with permission.

Teamwork. Working together to achieve common goals is the foundation of our success.

Generosity. We are generous with our time and resources not only to support the personal growth and the professional development of our team members but also to support nonprofit organizations that build sustainable communities and organizations.

Defining the Ecosystem and the Stakeholders

A corporation's bylaws invite creativity to customize other attributes of its culture and preserve them as assets. Conscious capitalism, for example, recognizes that each corporation has an ecosystem with its own unique set of component stakeholders. To promote awareness of the interests of everyone on whom the corporation has an impact, a company could add to its bylaws a definition of the term *stakeholder* to encourage management to consider the effect of corporate actions on all stakeholders:

> (6) The term *stakeholder* shall be broadly constructed and shall include, without limitation, the corporation's employees, stockholders, vendors and suppliers, strategic partners, creditors, the communities in which the corporation does business, customers, the environment, the commons, and the general business ecosystem in which the corporation does business.

Establishing a Corporate Governance Committee

Corporations can authorize the creation of a corporate governance committee of the board of directors to provide a formal internal conscience mechanism that supplements the fiduciary duties owed by the board of directors to stockholders. A corporation can modify its bylaws to expressly authorize such a committee to work with the executive leadership to promulgate its core values and ensure that management runs the company in accordance with them. A sample governance committee charter is included herein as Appendix B.

Here is a sample provision from the bylaws of a Delaware company, authorizing the formation of a corporate governance committee to serve as the ombudsman of the corporate conscience:

Corporate Governance Committee. The Board of Directors shall appoint a Corporate Governance Committee, to consist of one or more members of the Board of Directors, which shall have such powers and perform such duties as may be prescribed by the resolution or resolutions creating such committee, but in no event shall any such committee have the powers denied to the Executive Committee in these Bylaws.

The Corporate Governance Committee shall work with the officers of the corporation to promulgate a set of corporate core values to be adopted by the Board of Directors and the Corporation as the core values by which the Corporation shall conduct and manage its business. The Corporate Governance Committee shall meet at least once per year to review the effectiveness of the corporation's core values with its officers and consider and adopt any necessary revisions to the core values. Such core values shall be adopted by the Board of Directors and affixed as Exhibit A to these Bylaws.

Just as financial experts serve on the boards of directors of public companies and head their audit committees, an ethicist could chair the governance committee to provide seasoned ethical and moral guidance. Having a director designated as the guardian of the corporation's conscience could help ensure that corporate decisions and actions are aligned with the core values and support the company's long-term sustainability.

A formal conscience works best if it includes both levels of management—the board of directors and the executive team. Just as a corporate governance committee can serve as the ombudsman of the conscience, the CEO can be empowered as the agent of the conscience at the executive level. A corporation can expand the traditional duties of the president or CEO in the bylaws to provide that this officer shall manage in accordance with the core values. Exercising the corporate conscience is more effective with the coordinated effort of the CEO, management, and the board of directors.

Promoting Whole-Brain Thinking

There are infinite ways that companies can modify their charter documents to support their cultures. The scope of the charter of the corporate governance committee, for example, could be expanded to ensure that management promotes an understanding of the three intelligences (see chapter 10) to harness their complementary power to promote a whole-brain culture. A company could include the three intelligences in its core values and incorporate them into the bylaws by modifying the core value of "Teamwork" from the sample values given earlier in this chapter:

> *Teamwork.* Working together to achieve common goals is the foundation of our success. We apply knowledge of the three human intelligences— logic, emotion, and intuition—to access the collective intelligence of our employees to create a whole-brain, creative, and collaborative culture that empowers our team members to be their best.

Committing to Sustainability

Companies can modify their charter documents to reflect their commitment to environmentally sound business principles. If being "green" is one of its core values, for example, a company could articulate its own definition of sustainability:

> *Sustainability.* We are committed to being a sustainable business that (i) does not use renewable resources faster than they can regenerate, (ii) does not emit pollution and waste faster than natural processes can render them harmless, and (iii) does not use nonrenewable resources faster than renewable substitutes can be introduced.[5]

Protecting the Culture

To protect the cultural provisions, corporations can require a supermajority vote to amend or replace them. Such supermajority voting thresholds signal that a corporation is seriously committed to its culture by elevating its elements to protected constitutional status. This Delaware corporation's bylaws, for example, require a 75 percent majority vote to amend the cultural elements:

> Section 45. Amendments. Subject to paragraph (h) of Section 43 of the Bylaws, these Bylaws may be amended or repealed and new Bylaws adopted by the stockholders entitled to vote; provided, however, that any repeal or modification of (i) the second sentence of Article IV, Section 16, (ii) Article IV, Section 25(b), (iii) Article X, Section 43(j)

5   Professor John Sterman of the Massachusetts Institute of Technology inspired this definition. Professor Sterman credits these three criteria to the ecological economist Herman Daly.

(6) of these Bylaws, and (iv) once adopted as contemplated by Article IV, Section 25(b), the corporation's corporate core values set forth on Exhibit A shall require the affirmative approval of holders of at least 75 percent of the corporation's issued and outstanding capital stock, on an as converted to Common Stock basis.

A formal conscience helps management keep the needs of all stakeholders in balance. The simple changes to standard charter documents suggested here can enhance and preserve stockholder value by providing a formal mechanism to help a corporation properly consider the consequences of its behavior to avoid action that damages the business. Exercising a holistic conscience that considers the interests of all stakeholders promotes stockholder value by protecting the ecosystem.

Exercising Good Business Judgment

The business judgment rule generally protects boards of directors that consider the interests of all their corporation's stakeholders. Delaware, for example, protects directors with the presumption that, whenever stockholders challenge their decisions, they "acted on an informed basis, in good faith, and in the honest belief that the action taken was in the best interests of the company."[6] In an interdependent world where ignoring the interests of one or more of a corporation's stakeholders can be harmful or fatal, the business judgment rule alone should protect directors who consider the welfare of stakeholders.

In addition, the standard of judicial review for business judgment is deferential, and a court "will not substitute its judgment for that of the board if the decision can be attributed to any rational business purpose."[7] The exercise of a conscience that ensures that corporate actions have considered the interests of all stakeholders so as not to harm the corporation and, ultimately, the stockholders, is certainly attributable to a rational business purpose. In fact, one could argue that directors would be breaching their fiduciary duties to stockholders if they do not consider these interests.

---

6   *eBay Domestic Holdings, Inc. v. Craig Newmark and James Buckmaster* ___A 2nd ____, 65 (Del. 2010) (quoting *Unitrin, Inc. v. Am. Gen. Corp.*, 651 A 2nd 1361, 1373 (Del. 1995) and *Aronson v. Lewis*, 473 A 2nd 805, 811 (Del. 1984).

7   *eBay Domestic Holdings, Inc. v. Craig Newmark and James Buckmaster* ___A 2nd ____, 65 (Del. 2010) (quoting *Unitrin, Inc. v. Am. Gen. Corp.*, 651 A 2nd 1361, 1373 (Del. 1995) and *Unocal Corp. v. Mega Petroleum Co.*, 493 A 2nd 946, 954 (Del. 1985).

More than 30 states such as Nevada have amended their corporation codes to expressly allow directors to consider the interests of all the company's stakeholders in the exercise of business judgment. California and New York recently became the sixth and seventh states to adopt benefit corporation legislation, joining Virginia, New Jersey, Maryland, Vermont and Hawaii. Such legislation authorizes directors to consider stakeholder interests in determining whether or not their actions are in the interests of the corporation. A California benefit corporation, for example, encourages the development of a holistic corporate conscience by requiring the company to simultaneously provide a material positive impact on society and the environment while optimizing profits.

Corporations can adopt charter documents that expressly empower their directors to consider the interests of all stakeholders in the exercise of their business judgment. Such consideration can be permissive or mandatory. Here is a provision from the bylaws of a Delaware company that has a mandatory consideration provision:

> Section 16. Powers. The powers of the corporation shall be exercised, its business conducted, and its property controlled by the Board of Directors, except as may be otherwise provided by statute or by the Certificate of Incorporation. In exercising business judgment, a director shall consider the interests of all of the corporation's stakeholders to the maximum extent permitted by law.

Such an approach does not impede stockholder rights because considering the interests of other stakeholders does not give them standing to sue the corporation. B Lab, a not-for-profit organization that promotes the development of more-transparent and socially responsible corporations, provides a comprehensive approach to the business judgment rule with sample language for insertion into articles of incorporation. This language expressly states that expansion of the business judgment rule does not give rights or causes of action to other stakeholders:

> *In discharging his or her duties, and in determining what is in the best interests of the Company and its shareholders, a Director shall consider such factors as the Director seems relevant, including, but not limited to, the long-term prospects and interests of the Company and its shareholders, and the social, economic, legal, or*

other effects of any action on the current and retired employees, the suppliers and customers of the Company or its subsidiaries, and the communities and society in which the Company or its subsidiaries operate (collectively, with the shareholders, the "Stakeholders"), together with the short-term, as well as long-term interests of its shareholders and the effect of the Company's operations (and its subsidiaries' operations) on society and the economy of the state, the region, and the nation.

Nothing in this Article, express or implied, is intended to create or shall create or grant any right in or for any person or any cause of action by or for any person.

Corporations can amend their bylaws and articles of incorporation to expressly authorize directors to consider the welfare of the commons and the interests of all the corporation's stakeholders in the exercise of their fiduciary duties to the maximum extent permissible under applicable law. Such extension of fiduciary duties can be mandatory or permissive and can expressly provide that such stakeholders have no standing to sue if the directors fail to consider their interests. Here is a sample provision from the certificate of incorporation of a Delaware company that adopted the definition of *stakeholder* given earlier in this chapter:

In their exercise of fiduciary duty, the directors of the Corporation shall consider the welfare of the commons and the interests of all the Corporation's stakeholders to the maximum extent permitted by the General Corporation Law of the State of Delaware.

B Lab also provides language that would authorize directors facing competing cash bids to acquire their company to exercise their business judgment and accept the lower bid if it would be in the best interest (as defined above) of the stockholders:

Notwithstanding the foregoing, any Director is entitled to rely on the definition of "best interests" as set forth above in enforcing his or her rights hereunder, and under state law and such reliance shall not, absent another breach, be construed as a breach of a Director's fiduciary duty of care, even in the context of a Change in Control Transaction where, as a result of weighing other Stakeholders' interests, a Director determines to accept an offer, between two competing offers, with a lower price per share.

This approach provides an alternative to a line of Delaware cases that requires directors of a corporation that has received competing cash takeover bids to accept the higher bid out if its fiduciary duty to its stockholders. Because such an approach has not yet been upheld by a Delaware court, entrepreneurs wishing to empower their boards in this way should consult corporate counsel.

Using the bylaws and the articles of incorporation to turn the core values into the corporation's rules of engagement empowers the board of directors and the executives to strategically manage the corporation with a conscience that protects its stockholder value by guarding the health of its overall ecosystem. Such conscience complements the fiduciary duty of management to stockholders, which remains intact as an important safeguard to prevent abuse of stockholders' investment. A formal conscience provides a framework to ensure that the corporation's actions are not harmful so that its stakeholders will continue to support and sustain the corporation's long-term business for the benefit not only of its stockholders but all of its stakeholders.

Summary

Corporations codes authorize the formation of corporations and establish their basic rules of governance.

Standard bylaws and articles of incorporation provide a corporation's basic rules of procedure.

Entrepreneurs can modify standard bylaws and articles of incorporation to intelligently design their corporations.

Entrepreneurs can customize the charter documents to include:

- The company's purpose
- The core values as a code of conduct
- Authorization of a corporate governance committee of the board of directors to serve as the ombudsman of the corporation's conscience
- Customized definitions of terms such as *stakeholder*
- Supermajority provisions to include a succession plan and to ensure that the corporate culture is preserved as an asset
- Provisions that promote whole-brain thinking

- Provisions that extend the business judgment rule to require directors to consider the interests of all stakeholders

- The best time to intelligently design a corporation's rules of engagement is before it has been incorporated.

Call to Action

Select an experienced corporate counsel to help chose the appropriate corporate entity and state of incorporation. Incorporating as a benefit corporation or in a state with a constituency statute that empowers directors to consider all the company's stakeholders might be the right choice. Your attorney can help you incorporate the company and draft bylaws and articles of incorporation that reflect the desired culture. Such counsel can use the suggestions in this chapter to modify standard charter documents to include the purpose and the core values previously developed. Now is a good time to incorporate the company and approve the sale of stock to the founders pursuant to the allocations determined in chapter 19.

Chapter 21

UNDERSTANDING INVESTORS

Separate the pretenders from the contenders.

—Jeffrey Cherry, managing director, Concinnity Group

Your company needs the smartest money possible from helpful investors who are excited about the vision and in alignment with the culture. Because your investors will be an integral part of your company for years, you need to put as much care into selecting them as they will put into due diligence about your company. If you understand their motives, you won't get stuck with misaligned investors with conflicting agendas. There is harmony when the entrepreneurs and the investors have the same agendas. Do you understand money? Do you know the right kind of investment capital for your company?

Many startups fail because the entrepreneur and the investors have different ultimate agendas. The conflict arises when the entrepreneur is focused primarily on building a great company that realizes the vision and the investors are focused on making a financial return. The entrepreneur's job is to keep everyone focused on realizing the vision because that is the best way to meet the investors' need for a financial return.

On an absolute level, money is a commodity. In the world of startups, money is the rocket fuel necessary to launch a business. On a relative level, however, investment capital is imbued with the intention behind it and comes with the needs of the investor attached.

Venture capital investors are under enormous pressure from their limited partners to provide a rate of return superior to the S&P 500. This pressure is constant and can easily divert the focus from building a great company to maximizing the bottom line.

Several factors exacerbate this pressure. Venture capital funds have a 10-year life. This means that the general partners must return invested capital to their limited partners within 10 years. Most funds, however, provide that the general partners may extend the life of the fund by up to two years.

When an entrepreneur contemplates an investment from a venture capital fund, it is essential that he understand where the fund is in its term. If the investment will be the first outlay of a new fund, then there will be less time pressure on the entrepreneur to engineer an exit transaction to generate a return. On the other hand, if the fund is in its sixth year, there will be tremendous pressure to provide a return within the remaining four years of the fund. With the average time to liquidity in excess of eight years, the pressure to provide a financial return for venture capital investors often shifts a company's primary focus.

Each general partner is also under tremendous pressure to perform. Limited partners are now analyzing the financial performance of individual general partners because the venture capital industry as an asset class has provided a negative return for the past decade. Venture capitalists need to invest in great companies that can provide their investors with a return.

A venture capital fund assigns a partner to each portfolio company. If the investment is significant, the fund will request that the partner serve on the board of directors. An entrepreneur considering a venture capital investment should assess that partner carefully to gauge how much pressure he is under. A partner who has had several successful investments will be under less pressure than a partner who has yet to invest in a successful company. In addition, an experienced general partner with multiple successes will face less pressure than a junior venture partner making his first investment. The best way for an entrepreneur to manage this pressure is to consistently meet or exceed the company's objectives. To be successful at fundraising, an entrepreneur has to show how an investment in his company will solve the venture capitalist's big problem by providing him with a return.

First-time venture capital funds are themselves unproven startups. It will take years for a new fund that invests in early-stage startups to prove that it has a successful investment approach. As a result, general partners in such funds are under extra pressure.

Entrepreneurs should encourage their venture capital investors to form an investment syndicate with other venture capital funds to spread the risk and optimize the human capital. An ideal $5 million first round of funding might include $2 million from the lead investor and $1.5 million from each of the other two funds. The lead investor would get the board seat but would be inclined to cooperate with the other two funds because together they own more stock and could outvote his fund on matters of governance. The company would have access to the collective wisdom of all three funds. Having a syndicate also makes it easier to raise the next round of financing because there are more investors to help the company find a lead investor for the next round.

Choosing the Right Investors: Vivek Mehra

"Entrepreneurs must pick their venture capital partners carefully," says Vivek Mehra, co-founder of Cobalt Networks and general partner of August Capital. "Entrepreneurs must spend time with the venture capitalists to develop a good relationship before letting them invest in their companies. Developing a good relationship takes time. When a potential portfolio company tells August Capital that it needs our investment decision in two weeks, we'll say, 'Thanks but no thanks.' We cannot get to know a company well enough in two weeks to make a sound investment decision."

The first question to ask a venture capital firm, says Mehra, is "What advantages do you bring to the table?" If it's a hundred-million-dollar fund, the second question to ask is "How much have you already invested, and how much is kept in reserve for future rounds?" Because a startup will be around for five or six years, it's critical to get an investment from a fund at the right stage in the funding cycle:

> *A fund that has already invested $90 million and is at the tail end of its fund often pressures its portfolio companies to exit too soon and won't have adequate capital to invest in subsequent rounds of funding.*

Entrepreneurs need to make sure that the venture capitalists are people they'd want to work with because they will be on board for seven to 10 years. Venture capitalists always ask entrepreneurs for their references and check them one by one, but it's shocking how few entrepreneurs ask the venture capitalists for references. To get a variety of perspectives, entrepreneurs should ask for references and talk to the CEOs of companies that the fund and the partner have funded. Other venture capitalists and attorneys can provide additional references.

Because each venture capital firm and each individual partner has a different style, says Mehra, startups should be comfortable with both the firm and the individual before they accept an investment:

Choosing the right partner within a venture capital firm is important. Sometimes a fund will pull a bait-and-switch and lead with the senior partner but assign a junior venture partner to the company. The questions venture capitalists ask often provide insight into their character and motives.

Choose strategic partners carefully. Initially, startups have a small group of partners, including venture capital investors, advisers, and attorneys. The right partners can be incredibly helpful in providing guidance. Cobalt would not have been successful but for Techfarm's support as the incubator. Gordon Campbell stood by us in tough times. Most venture capitalists would have walked away if the CEO died a week before the financing, but Gordon and Kip Meyers of Vanguard stood firm. They honored the investment terms without any changes.

Getting funding is not a proxy for success, warns Mehra: "Many entrepreneurs mistakenly think that once they get venture capital funding, it's done. No! That's just the beginning! Many startups fail because they receive too much money and spend it on stupid things. Techfarm invested Cobalt's first $500,000 in monthly increments. Drip-feeding was good because it kept the company focused. The fear of running out of money sharpens an entrepreneur's focus. Smart venture capitalists never invest too much money in a company because it risks losing the focus."

Understanding Investors' Expectations: Kathryn Gould

It's critical to understand an investor's expectations about the rate of return on his investment. Understanding the expected rate of return and market valuation enables an entrepreneur to project the financial results required to satisfy the investor. This understanding and knowledge of where a firm is in its investment cycle enables an entrepreneur to assess whether his financial model will build a big enough company to have a viable option of going public before the pressure to provide a return forces an early sale-of-company transaction.

"I use the investment targets from old-school venture capitalists from the 1980s and 1990s and aim for 10 times rates of return," says Kathryn Gould, co-founder of Foundation Capital. "I'm a 10x investor. Both of Foundation Capital's first funds had 8x rates of return, mostly from investing in first-time CEOs."

Understanding Corporate Venture Capital: Tom Marchok

Steve DeWitt understood that investors have needs. He knew that his job was not only to get Cobalt funded but also to provide an investment opportunity that met the investors' need for a return and their particular strategic objectives. DeWitt attracted Intel as an investor by demonstrating that Cobalt's servers would consume millions of Intel semiconductors. Selling Intel as an investor accelerated Cobalt's success. Intel not only provided a strategic commercial partnership but also added cachet and credibility to the company's IPO. Intel was happy with the strategic and fiscal return on its investment.

"A corporate venture capital firm will invest in a startup company only if it meets its strategic goals," says Tom Marchok, vice president of Intel Capital. "Many entrepreneurs make the mistake of thinking that corporate venture capital groups have the same objectives as traditional venture capital firms and are interested only in a financial return. Most corporate venture capital programs are part of a company's business development group, which has the goal of growing revenues and profits. Making strategic equity investments is one tool that corporations use to increase revenues and profits."

Intel answers two questions before it makes an investment, says Marchok: *Is this company strategic?* and *If the company succeeds, how will it help Intel's business?*

Intel invests in companies that will drive sales of its products or develop technologies that support technologies and products that Intel is developing. To be relevant to a corporate venture capital program, a startup must be strategically positioned to help the parent company's business. Without a clear path to helping the parent company, it is unlikely that the startup will get capital from the corporate venture capital firm. If a startup can help the larger company, it's probably relevant and might be a good candidate for investment. Intel tends to invest in ecosystems around its own products.

If there is a good business case for Intel, then Intel answers the same set of questions that any other venture capital investor has to answer. This second set of questions includes: *How are we going to make money on this investment?*

Often a corporate venture capital firm can provide its portfolio companies with technology development assistance and access to marketing and sales channels, says Marchok: "Intel tends to invest in ecosystems around its own products. Intel plugs its portfolio companies into its global sales channels. Intel also helps them with technology development by providing direct access to engineers."

Twelve Myths of Investing: Kathryn Coffey

To succeed at fundraising, it is critical to understand how venture capital investors think. Kathryn Coffey, the placement agent for Cobalt's last round of private financing, provides insight into twelve myths surrounding venture capital investing.

Myth 1: The opportunity is so great that anyone would jump at the chance to invest. "All investors have specific investment criteria," says Coffey. "The entrepreneur must do his homework before meeting an investor to determine how his company fits those criteria. It's easy to understand what they like to invest in by reviewing the portfolio companies on their website. The entrepreneur must be ready to discuss how his company matches their investment criteria."

Myth 2: The investors will be well prepared for the meeting. "The entrepreneur should never assume that investors know anything about his company," says Coffey. "The investors will probably have done nothing more than glance at the website or look at the projections and the biographies in the executive summary. Entrepreneurs should hand out the executive summary at the meeting."

Myth 3: The investors are reviewing the opportunity. After the third and fourth Mondays come and go and the investors haven't returned an entrepreneur's calls, two things apply: they're probably not interested, and they're just rude for not having responded. "Don't dwell on their lack of response," says Coffey. "Move on and look for other investors who might be interested."

Myth 4: The investors will be really interested in the technology. "Investors might like the technology," says Coffey, "but they will be more interested in the business proposition. They want to understand the business opportunity and know how the entrepreneur will create significant value."

Myth 5: The investors will love the complex technology schematics. "Complicated charts distract investors because they can't follow them without a struggle," says Coffey. "Good presentations about technology are short, simple, and easy to follow. If investors have questions or want to dig deeper into the technology, let them follow their curiosity and allow the presentation to flow where they want to take it." The entrepreneur should never force the agenda back to what he wants to talk about, she adds, because the meeting is for the investors.

Myth 6: The investors will believe whatever the entrepreneur says. "If an entrepreneur says that he's a 'highly entrepreneurial CEO,' the investors will probably think that he's uncontrollable and perhaps even maniacal," says Coffey. "When an entrepreneur says that the company has a 'niche strategy,' investors will conclude that the addressable market is too small. Telling investors that the projections are 'conservative' probably means they are completely unrealistic. The entrepreneur must carefully manage perceptions about the projections by telling investors that they have been built from the bottom up."

Telling investors that a company is "ahead of plan," she adds, usually means that it is beating the recently revised downward projections. "Because investors will drill down into the financial statements and look at earlier sets of projections, the entrepreneur must be impeccable about what he says and how he presents it."

Myth 7: Showing upside projections will generate a higher valuation. "Showing upside projections will likely yield a huge valuation discount when investors run their own projections," says Coffey. Realistic projections will also be discounted, but an entrepreneur will gain credibility and receive a higher valuation than by presenting upside projections in the first place:

> *Three financial statements are necessary to create projections. Some entrepreneurs think they can get by with only an income statement, but normal businesses have income statements, balance sheets, and statements of cash flows. Startups need to prepare projections with all three statements that clearly set forth the financial assumptions. The financial statements should be simple, however, to avoid overwhelming investors with pages of complex financial data.*
>
> *Companies often prefer to send a PDF file of the projections, but it's better to send investors clean and well-constructed Excel spreadsheets in unlocked files. Because investors like to play with spreadsheets, it's thoughtful to give them the files so that they don't get frustrated trying to create their own. Their projections will be a lot lower if they have to create them from scratch.*

Myth 8: The entrepreneur should not provide customer references, to avoid bombarding them with diligence calls. "A company's customers are its fan base," says Coffey. "If a company doesn't provide the names and the telephone numbers of members of its fan club, investors can't possibly make a positive investment decision. The investors will call their own references, such as competitors, and the company is guaranteed to get a bad reference. Companies should proactively manage customer diligence by offering to provide selected customer references once the investors have signed a term sheet."

Myth 9: The investors will value the company based on a comparable company that has the absolute highest sales multiple. Entrepreneurs believing this myth expect that they will enjoy a valuation based on the same multiple of sales that Google enjoyed when it went public. Says Coffey:

> *Investors don't think that way because they have very specific return criteria. Investors typically work backward by imaging a company's potential exit value after a particular period of time and calculating the present valuation necessary to yield the desired rate of return based on the expected exit value. For example, if the exit valuation is $150 million in three years and the investors' objective is to achieve a*

10 times return, the post-money valuation can be only $15 million without factoring in the effect of future rounds of capital on the rate of return. If the company is raising $5 million, there's a limit to the pre-money valuation. Valuation is based on recent investments, not on some complex internal-rate-of-return model extrapolated from the ecosystem.

Myth 10: The investors want only a low valuation. "If an entrepreneur has convinced investors that they should invest in his company," says Coffey, "they want the company in their portfolio. They will pay a higher valuation if there are competing term sheets or if it's the only way to secure the investment. A higher valuation, however, often comes with tougher terms. A lower valuation will generally come with middle-of-the-road governance, liquidation preference, redemption, and other related terms.

Myth 11: The company will have a financing only with strategic corporate investors. Strategic rounds are rare, says Coffey, because strategic investors rarely lead financings. "Counting on getting a strategic investor means the financing will never happen. When strategic investors invest, they usually want venture capitalists to lead the round because it helps them justify the investment with their investment committees. Because strategic investors move slowly, having a venture capitalist as the lead investor will move a strategic investor along."

Startups shouldn't waste their time pursuing an investment from a hedge fund, she adds. "Hedge funds generally don't invest in illiquid private companies. Hedge funds will selectively invest in late-stage companies that are well funded, well backed, and well run, with an exit in view within six to 18 months."

Myth 12: The financing is done when the term sheet is signed. The entrepreneur cannot relax once the term sheet is signed because no financing is done until the money's in the bank. "I've had financings where the money was wired and sitting in escrow, and one of the partners at the venture fund asked to get the money back," says Coffey:

Startups should be prepared for investors to change their minds and keep pitching them until the deal is done. All kinds of legitimate issues come up. Projections are missed, legal structuring issues arise, and lawsuits pop up. Many things can happen to prevent a financing from closing.

The harsh reality is that valuation will not go up if good things happen once the term sheet has been signed. A company can get a great new customer, but the valuation will not increase.

Entrepreneurs should always remember that the purpose of the first meeting is to get the second meeting. "A good meeting is when the conversation is so lively that the entrepreneur doesn't even open up the PowerPoint presentation," says Coffey. "A bad meeting is when the entrepreneur flips through his slide deck and gives a lecture. An entrepreneur can tell in the first 10 minutes if it is a good meeting or a bad one."

Entrepreneurs should not play their cards too close to the vest, Coffey advises:

> *Entrepreneurs often keep information tight because they're afraid it's going to leak out. If an entrepreneur makes it hard for a venture capitalist to make an investment decision by withholding information, it will be even easier for the investor to say no. Entrepreneurs often want investors to sign nondisclosure agreements, but venture capitalists won't sign them. If an entrepreneur requires that an investor sign a confidentiality agreement, the investor will tell him to go find money from somebody else. If an entrepreneur is not willing to tell a venture capital investor what he's doing, he shouldn't waste the investor's time, but go seek funding elsewhere.*

Coffey offers one closing rule for entrepreneurs: "When they're passing the cookies, take them. This means that an entrepreneur should not micromanage the term sheet. Generally, if an entrepreneur gets a term sheet, he should sign it because he's fortunate to get an investment proposal from a venture capital investor. When negotiating the term sheet, it's best to focus on the few important issues and move on because getting the money to advance the company is what's important."

Summary

- Money is a commodity, but it carries the investors' intentions.
- Entrepreneurs need to understand the needs of their investors.
- These needs include the desired rate of return and the exit horizon.

- Entrepreneurs need to keep everyone, including investors, focused on building a great company.

- Entrepreneurs should do due diligence on venture capital investors by checking references and talking to executives in their portfolio companies.

- Entrepreneurs seeking investment from strategic investors must understand their strategic requirements.

Call to Action

It is important to have an organized approach to the fundraising process. It is best to develop a tracking system that identifies each investor with complete contact information, the person responsible for contacting the investor, the status of discussions, and a schedule of all meetings. Raising venture capital is a sales process that works best with a disciplined approach regardless of the type of investor. Excel spreadsheets or Google Docs can be used to create a simple tracking tool to manage the sales process. The executive team should frequently update the tracking sheet and apply this approach whether it is raising a seed round from angel investors, founders, friends and family or from venture capital investors.

- Identify all potential investors.

- Develop a process to track them.

- Create a tracking sheet.

- Circulate the tracking sheet to the company's allies to identify other potential investors.

- Assign responsibilities.

- Identify people in the network who can make personal introductions to potential investors who are not known to the entrepreneur.

- Ask potential investors who turn you down to make introductions to potential investors in their trusted networks.

Chapter 22

APPROACHING VENTURE CAPITAL

You can make a difference building companies that matter with investors that care.

—Sunny Vanderbeck, co-founder and principal, Satori Capital

Are you ready to approach venture capital investors? You will get only one chance to tell your story. If your story doesn't captivate the investor, you will be unlikely to get another meeting. You will be more likely to interest venture capital investors if you approach them after you have designed your company.

Successful entrepreneurs don't try to raise venture capital until they have assembled an all-star team, built the product, and lined up customers. The truth is that most startups raise the initial seed capital to build their product and land their first customer from the founders, friends, and family. This poses a challenge in capital-intensive industries like clean technology and semiconductors, where building the product can cost tens of millions of dollars, because it's difficult to raise more than a couple of million dollars from these "angel" investors. The best way for entrepreneurs to approach the fundraising process is to do their homework and design their companies as intelligently as possible.

Unfortunately, entrepreneurs often approach venture capital investors before they have done their homework. The typical entrepreneur gets a good idea, assembles a team, incorporates a company without preparing a business plan, and gets his friends to introduce him to every venture capitalist they know.

This approach is usually a waste of good introductions because venture capitalists are often too polite to tell the entrepreneur that the company isn't fundable. A venture capitalist will often say "maybe" by telling the entrepreneur to come back when he has three Fortune 100 customers. To avoid being sent on a knight-errant's quest to land those Fortune 100 customers, it's better to wait to approach venture capital investors until the investment opportunity for them is clear and compelling.

There is, however, no one-size-fits-all approach to raising venture capital. This chapter and the one that follows suggest a variety of approaches. Ultimately, the entrepreneur will have to design an approach that is appropriate for his company and its unique personality and value proposition.

Being Authentic: Dan Sapp

"The secret to the perfect venture capital pitch is to not pitch," says executive coach Dan Sapp, CEO and founder of Dan Sapp & Associates. "I recalibrate entrepreneurs' thinking and get them to stop giving presentations. The entrepreneur's job is not to present his company or to educate anybody about what he or his company does but to raise capital by selling someone a big chunk of his company." Sapp continues:

I want entrepreneurs to stop thinking about PowerPoint presentations. PowerPoint has ruined the US economy. An entrepreneur ruins his strategic thinking when his investor presentations are driven by a piece of software that comes preloaded on everybody's laptop. PowerPoint is not a differentiating technology. How an entrepreneur manages his potential investors' perceptions of his company is the only real differentiation.

An entrepreneur must pass an investor's primary due diligence test, which is much like an audition. Investors assess the quality of a team by looking at and listening to the entrepreneur. His posture, the energy of his presentation, and the authority of his voice add to or detract from the equity of the business. To pass the test, an entrepreneur must not only speak well but also position himself physically with body language that says, "I belong here. I know what I'm saying. You can trust that my ideas are valuable and useful." The quality of the entrepreneur's delivery is vital because the elements of a great presentation are also the elements of a great company.

Investors also read the team's body language and listen to the sound of their voices. How the team sits in the conference room often reflects its habits, manners, and work ethic, which affect how investors perceive and value the company.

The entrepreneur's primary job, says Sapp, is to get the investor interested in a business about which he knows little or nothing:

The investor's nephew, for example, might have asked him to meet a really nice guy he went to school with. Personal introductions lead to great meetings. The introduction to an investor should not be electronic. It is more effective to start a relationship with a phone call because the entrepreneur can use the enthusiasm in his voice to leave the impression that he is somebody the investor needs to talk to.

Most entrepreneurs want to know the 10 key points to put into their PowerPoint presentations. Although I've coached hundreds of early-stage companies and general partners of venture capital firms, I have absolutely no idea what should be in an entrepreneur's PowerPoint presentation. The crucial point is to develop a relationship with an investor and move it forward to increase the likelihood that he will buy a big piece of the business.

Regardless of how he got the first meeting, the entrepreneur's goal is to take the investor from knowing nothing about his business to knowing enough to want a second meeting. "The first meeting is not about getting investors to write a check but about convincing them that the entrepreneur is building something great," says Sapp.

All the entrepreneur has to do is convince them that it's possible for him to build a billion-dollar company so that they take another meeting.

My pitch to entrepreneurs is: don't pitch, don't educate, and don't inform. The entrepreneur's job is to convince and to influence. The more an investor knows about an entrepreneur and his history of success, the easier getting the next meeting becomes. If an entrepreneur is starting from scratch, he has half an hour to go from zero to 60 to get the investor excited about the business.

An entrepreneur should not go in to lead a business meeting without a particular result in mind, says Sapp. "If an entrepreneur approaches meetings with venture capitalists as business meetings and not as pitches, he'll be ahead of the game. His job is to facilitate the meeting to the desired outcome."

The first step in delivering an effective business communication is knowing the desired outcome. "The outcome communication doesn't start with the content but from an understanding of who the audience is, what drives them, and what they are most likely to respond to. A great business communicator knows exactly what he wants out of a meeting and prepares for it, knowing exactly what he wants people to do and what's going to be different about them when he's done with them," says Sapp.

Sapp has additional advice for entrepreneurs about that first meeting:

> *I want a T-shirt that says, "No data dumps." Most entrepreneurs give investors data dumps and flood them with information, especially when they start with a PowerPoint presentation. They cram as much information as they can into the 10 slides and talk as quickly as possible. They deliver as much information as they can in 45 minutes and hope the investor will hang on to something useful. Data dumps don't work.*
>
> *If an entrepreneur starts a meeting by telling the investor about himself and his company, he's likely to miss the purpose of the meeting. When what's driving the entrepreneur is what he knows the most about, what he's the most comfortable with, and what he's the most excited about, he's not likely to get the result he wants from the meeting. An entrepreneur will not get a second meeting if he drops everything he knows about his business on the investor's head in the allotted 15 minutes.*

Entrepreneurs must also avoid the old approach of "I'm going to tell you what I'm going to tell you, then I'm going to tell you, and finally I'm going to tell you what I told you," says Sapp. "That is a prescription for a triple data dump." The important thing is not whether the investor remembers anything but whether the entrepreneur got another meeting. "It's far more effective to start an investor meeting from an awareness of the desired outcome. Building a relationship with an investor requires a discrete set of steps. The entrepreneur's job is to lead the potential investor from one step to the next in a logical sequence without rushing the process."

Most investors will require that an entrepreneur make a presentation. "The presentation must demonstrate that the entrepreneur understands the investors and their needs, and it must provide them with a solution to their biggest problem, which is how to create value for their investors. To inspire them to start due diligence and offer a term sheet, the entrepreneur must show how his company can help the investors deliver the desired returns to their limited partners," says Sapp.

The entrepreneur needs to convince the initial audience that the idea is sound and that he and the team can make it happen. He must convince them that his business will make them look great to the rest of their partners. Ultimately, the entrepreneur must convince all the partners to buy a big chunk of the business because it will help them give their investors a good return.

The entrepreneur's job is to connect with investors to get them to invest by respecting their needs and moving them along a path that he's established for them. The meeting is the opportunity to convince them that the business should be their next portfolio company.

To meet potential investors' needs, the entrepreneur also must do some due diligence about what companies they have invested in historically and what businesses they think are hot, says Sapp. "It's smart to talk to executives from companies that they've invested in to find out what they're like to work with. It's also prudent to talk to companies that they *didn't* invest in to find out what they didn't like about those business plans."

Because each venture capital firm has a different approach, the entrepreneur should customize the presentation to fit each firm's particular needs. "An entrepreneur must do his homework before he meets with investors, or he will just be wasting their time dumping data," says Sapp.

Finally, says Sapp, entrepreneurs shouldn't finish meetings by thanking investors for their time. "Entrepreneurs don't want the investors' time; they want their money. The entrepreneur should always suggest an action that will move the relationship forward. Venture capitalists probably won't respond to a straight sales pitch, but many entrepreneurs fail to move things forward out of politeness. If the meeting went well, the entrepreneur should gently suggest an appropriate next step."

Getting the Dogs to Eat the Food: Guy Kawasaki

Guy Kawasaki, co-founder of Garage Technology Ventures, offers the following six tips for entrepreneurs seeking venture capital investors.

Tip 1: Do Something Worth Funding

"The threshold issue for every entrepreneur is whether or not he has a venture capital type of deal," says Kawasaki. "A fundable company is a viable business, but a viable business is not necessarily fundable. Many entrepreneurs have very fundable businesses and will raise venture capital. Many entrepreneurs have very viable businesses but will never raise venture capital. Entrepreneurs often confuse *viable* and *fundable*." Kawasaki continues:

> *If an entrepreneur wants to raise venture capital, his company must be worth funding, which sounds obvious. This means that an entrepreneur must believe that his company can be doing $75 million or $100 million in revenue in three or four years. This eliminates a lot of businesses, such as consultancies, service firms, restaurants, and retail stores. Many entrepreneurs just can't accept this reality because they read in the San Jose Mercury News about all the companies that received venture capital. They believe that their restaurant should also be a venture fundable deal. They're delusional because it's unimaginable that they will ever do $100 million a year in revenue.*

An entrepreneur must create a business that's worth funding by venture capitalists. "Venture capital is a very select game with only about 3,000 companies a year getting funded," says Kawasaki. "Approximately 30 million new businesses are funded every year in other ways."

Tip 2: Explain It in 15 Seconds

Kawasaki likens fundraising for venture capital to online dating. "Dating websites are personified by two extremes. On one extreme is Hot or Not, which helps find the dream girl. At Hot or Not, there's a picture of a woman or a man. You decide—hot or not? That's it. At the other extreme, there's eHarmony, which is what all parents want their children to use. At eHarmony the user creates a psychographic about how he likes to take long walks on the beach, is interested in the environment, drives a Prius, and really likes to get to know a person. That's the other extreme." Kawasaki continues:

Venture capital is Hot or Not. Investors decide in the first 10 to 15 seconds. They decide because of an entrepreneur's looks, his accent, his mood, and whether he wastes the first 15 minutes explaining his background or immediately telling what his company does. The decision to put a company into the investment process is made roughly at Hot or Not speeds. It is a dating game.

Many companies come to Garage Technology Ventures and spend the first 15 minutes explaining the founders' backgrounds. Until I hear what the founders do, I could care less about their backgrounds. If John Chambers wants to talk about his background and why he's fundable, that's okay, but he doesn't need to raise money.

The fact that an entrepreneur attended all the dot-net classes offered by Microsoft at its Mountain View campus doesn't prove he knows anything. The fact that an entrepreneur works for Home Depot doesn't prove that he understands commerce. An entrepreneur has roughly 15 seconds. A company is either hot or not; the process is not eHarmony, where we're trying to become friends.

Tip 3: Have a Clean Deal

Entrepreneurs need to present a clean deal. "Venture capitalists are always looking at dozens of deals," says Kawasaki.

A clean deal has no pending lawsuits about the intellectual property or over sexual harassment. The entrepreneur hasn't hired her husband as the chief financial officer or his wife as the chief marketing officer, and there are no relatives in the company. The entrepreneur is not working at a disk drive company during the day and creating a disk drive company at night, guaranteeing that someone is going to be pissed off that he took the technology. The entrepreneur's uncle, the divorce lawyer, is not drafting the incorporation papers. The entrepreneur has to use a good corporate law firm and present an absolutely clean deal.

Obviously, not every company is a clean deal. "In the second meeting," says Kawasaki, "the entrepreneur should admit where the deal is not clean by disclosing that there's a pending lawsuit or that in a moment of stupidity he hired his brother-in-law as chief technology officer. All dirty secrets will come out in due diligence. It's better to tell the investors than have them discover that there's a pending lawsuit. An entrepreneur needs a clean deal or he should fess up right away if he doesn't have one."

Tip 4: Use the 10-20-30 Rule

"Contrary to what Dan Sapp said, PowerPoint is the standard," says Kawasaki. "Not using PowerPoint would be like going to a haiku contest and declaring that you're not going to be limited by 5-7-5. If an entrepreneur is going to pitch to a venture capitalist, he needs to use PowerPoint. Some founders have told me they don't need PowerPoint. They think they're being bold, dynamic, and different, but they still give a piece-of-shit presentation. At least with PowerPoint, when an entrepreneur gives a piece-of-shit presentation, it has some structure so the venture capitalist knows what shit is coming." Kawasaki continues:

> *An entrepreneur must keep it simple and use the 10-20-30 rule of PowerPoint. The optimal PowerPoint presentation is 10 slides, which must be presentable in 20 minutes in 30-point type. An entrepreneur may have a 60-minute meeting, but since 95 percent of entrepreneurs use Windows, he will need 40 minutes just to hook up the projector. Most pitches, however, have 60 slides for a 60-minute meeting. There's no better way to lose a venture capitalist's interest than to cram 60 slides into a 60minute presentation.*

> *The rule is 10 slides, 20 minutes, and a 30-point font. Thirty points is the smallest font to use because it forces an entrepreneur to put only the essence of what he wants to say on the slide. Using a smaller 10- or 12-point font invites too much text, which is a sign that the entrepreneur has not rehearsed enough. When an entrepreneur starts reading his text, the audience concludes at the first slide that he is a bozo.*

If the 30-point-font rule is too dogmatic, says Kawasaki, a good rule of thumb is to find out the age of the oldest venture capitalist in the room, and divide his or her age by 2: "Since entrepreneurs mostly pitch to 60-year-old venture capitalists, 60 divided by 2 is 30. This is the logic behind the 30-point-font rule. Venture capitalists are getting younger and younger. If an entrepreneur finds himself pitching to a 16-year-old, he should use an 8-point font, but until then, he should stick with 30-point."

What follows is Kawasaki's prescription for the perfect 10-slide PowerPoint presentation.

Slide #1: The title. Most people make a big mistake in the first slide because they showcase the company name but forget their own names, email addresses, phone numbers, and mailing address, says Kawasaki. If investors are really interested in a company but there's no contact information in the PowerPoint presentation, it's game over. If the investors can't find the entrepreneur, they will lose interest and move on to the next deal.

Slide #2: The problem. The second slide should highlight the problem the company is solving.

Slide #3: The solution. The third slide should demonstrate how the company is solving the identified problem.

Slide #4: The business model. The fourth slide should describe the business model, which shows how the company will make money solving the problem. The problem the company is solving has to be real and cause real pain. The solution has to relieve that pain and be so compelling that customers will pay for it.

Slide #5: The underlying magic. "Magic is what makes a company unique and gives it a competitive advantage," says Kawasaki. "Most people get this wrong because they claim something unproven. They boast about having a patent-pending, curb-jumping, paradigm-shifting, new way to use Google to optimize the placement of banner ads, which is usually bullshit. The underlying magic doesn't have to be new technology. The magic might be that an entrepreneur is quitting his job as the VP of sales at Oracle to start an enterprise database company. The immediate incredible database in his head of people who bought Oracle databases could be the underlying magic."

Slide #6: The sales strategy. The sixth slide should describe the sales and marketing strategy, which tells exactly how the company will go to market. Most people blow this slide, too, Kawasaki says. "They say something like, 'We're going to be viral and use word of mouth.' Going viral is not a viable sales and marketing strategy. That approach destroys an entrepreneur's credibility because virality and word-of mouth-sales are primarily based on luck. When an entrepreneur says his company is going viral because he heard Steve Jurvetson talk about going viral on a panel, he's basically saying, 'We have no clue.' This slide needs more substance than 'We have no clue.'"

Slide #7: The competition. The seventh slide should describe the company's chief competitors. "Most companies create a matrix that lists all the competition," says Kawasaki. "Their companies have all the good qualities. Their columns are the ones with all the good qualities checked off. No investor will believe this matrix because everybody does it that way. A simpler, much better approach is to create a slide that shows both what the company can do that its competitors cannot do and what the company cannot do that the competition can do."

It's important to include the second section to admit holes and weaknesses to show that you're honest, Kawasaki says. It's important to present an honest appraisal of the business to avoid being caught in a lie. When investors feel that an entrepreneur is an honest person, they are more inclined to believe him when he says that he has something. If the company doesn't have a particular quality, it's best to tell the truth and admit it doesn't have it. To create the impression that the company is honest, it should be honest. The competition slide should herald the strengths and admit the weaknesses.

Slide #8: The team. The eighth slide should describe the entrepreneur's team. "Most venture capitalists say they invest in teams, but that's bullshit," says Kawasaki.

> *The only way investors know that a team is great is when it declares victory in five years. The way the venture capital business works is that a fund makes 20 investments. If a company is lucky, it will become a Google, a Yahoo!, a Cisco, or an Apple. Then the investor tells everyone, "I knew Larry and Sergei were a great team and that Eric Schmidt would step up as CEO. I knew that Pierre Odymar would hire Meg Whitman. I knew eBay had great technology and that enabling people to bid for broken HP printers on the Internet was a great business model."*
>
> *Then, somebody will ask the venture capitalist, "If you knew that Google and eBay were going to be huge successes, why did you invest in WebVan? Why did you believe that people would spend 20 bucks to have a can of orange juice delivered to their house?" That's when the venture capitalist answers, "I didn't want to do that deal. That was my partners."*

The reality, says Kawasaki, is that most starting teams are not very strong. In fact, the most interesting companies had totally unproven teams. When they first raised money, Google, Cisco, Yahoo!, Apple, and eBay had unproven teams. Perhaps a semiconductor company might have a proven starting team because people generally don't wake up one morning and decide to design a chip. In most businesses, however, the unproven team, not the proven one, is the one that succeeds.

Slide #9: The financial projections. The underlying metrics are the most important part of the financial projections, not the numbers or dollar amount, because they show how the company arrived at its projections. "If a company projects doing $100 million in year 5 because 10 percent of the people in China will be using its service, no one will believe it," says Kawasaki. "If a company projects doing $25 million in the first year because 10 percent of the Fortune 500 will be its customers, no investor will believe it." The projections must be grounded in reality.

"When I look at an entrepreneur's projections," says Kawasaki, "I add a year to the shipping date and divide the revenue projections by a hundred. That formula always yields a number closer to the actual numbers. Add a year and divide by a hundred—it's a good rule of thumb to check the projections."

Slide #10: The status and timeline. The tenth slide should present the company's status and timeline. "Many entrepreneurs pitch as if they had already won market share and achieved critical mass," says Kawasaki. "An entrepreneur will lose credibility if he doesn't provide a real status report that shows where the company really is in its product development schedule. This slide should never speculate that if the company is successful, this is where it will be."

Tip 5: Drill a Lot of Holes

Finding a venture capital investor is a numbers game, says Kawasaki. "An entrepreneur is probably delusional if he thinks that Michael Moritz of Sequoia Capital is the perfect investor because about 10,000 companies a year believe that he is the perfect investor for them. A company has to drill a lot of holes because, at the end of the day, it either got the money or it didn't. Kleiner Perkins's money is arguably better than anybody else's, but at the end of the day, money is a commodity. All money is green."

Tip 6: Get the Dogs to Eat the Food

Kawasaki's sixth point trumps all other points: If an entrepreneur can tell a venture capital firm, "Using our credit cards and our family's money, we've invested $100,000. We created this site and launched a business. In the first month, we had 10,000 registrations. In the second month, we had 20,000. In the third month, we had 80,000. We need money to scale operations to meet the demand. We need to hire an ad force because we have more demand for banner ads than we can handle right now. We have excess advertising inventory. We're doing so well that we really need capital to grow." All bullshit ends there. Kawasaki explains:

> *With a real business like that, an entrepreneur can ignore all the rules. He can have a 60-slide PowerPoint presentation and take an hour to explain what he does. The company can have all kinds of lawsuits pending. None of those things matters if an entrepreneur shows a company where the dogs are already eating the food. That's what every venture capitalist is looking for. Everybody fantasizes about being the next Google, but venture capitalists want an entrepreneur to say, "We need money to buy thousands of Linux boxes because the number of searches is doubling every day."*

Every venture capitalist dreams of funding a company that is scaling too fast, says Kawasaki. Every venture capitalist is dying to hear, "We need more money to scale," instead of the usual, "We need more money because we're behind schedule, but this time we'll really finish on time." If an entrepreneur can show that the dogs are eating the food, nothing else matters. Getting the dogs to eat the food proves that an entrepreneur already has a viable and fundable company.

Summary

- Successful venture capital investors raise venture capital after they have designed their companies.

- Most companies today raise the initial funds for their startup companies from the founders, friends, and family.

- Venture capital investors usually don't invest unless a company has a compelling vision, a team that can execute, finished products, and existing customers.

- Entrepreneurs need to manage investors' perceptions.

- Entrepreneurs need to demonstrate how an investment in their company will provide the desired rate of return.

- Entrepreneurs need to understand whether their company is fundable.

- Entrepreneurs need to be able to explain their company in 15 seconds.

- Entrepreneurs must present a clean investment opportunity.

- Entrepreneurs should consider presentations that use no more than 10 slides, use no type smaller than 30-point, and last no longer than 20 minutes.

Call to Action

- Use Guy Kawasaki's 10-20-30 rule to create a 10-slide presentation using PowerPoint.

- Practice the presentation with as many friendly critics as possible before meeting with a potential investor.

- To get feedback on adjusting the presentation, do a dry run with a professional investor who is unlikely to invest.

Chapter 23

MAKING MONEY TOGETHER

Fill the other guy's basket to the brim.

—Andrew Carnegie

How are your company and its investors going to make money together? You need to understand that venture capital investors make money only when a portfolio company gets bought or when they can sell a portfolio company's stock after it goes public. If you are interested primarily in building an enduring independent company that realizes the vision and ultimately goes public, this approach may not be timely enough to meet your investors' needs to make money. The key to having a successful long-term relationship with venture capital investors is to ensure that there is always agreement about how you are making money together. Ideally, the shared objective is to build a successful company.

Taking a Cue from Techfarm

Techfarm and its portfolio companies always agreed about how to make money together. The incubator partnered with promising teams of entrepreneurs to co-found companies, and it owned 20 percent of each portfolio company by purchasing common stock on the same terms as the founders. To meet its overhead, Techfarm charged each portfolio company a management fee of $5,000 per month and designated a partner to serve as an active executive chairman of the board.

The interests of Techfarm and its portfolio companies were perfectly aligned because no one made any money unless they built a successful company. Without the usual management fee income stream of a traditional venture capital fund, Techfarm was extremely motivated to make its portfolio companies successful. The $5,000-per-month management fee barely met the overhead because the portfolio companies often could not afford to pay it.

Techfarm was also motivated to build the portfolio companies as quickly and as capital-efficiently as possible because it owned common stock. Venture capitalists customarily purchase preferred stock, which has a liquidation preference over the common stock purchased by the founders. This means that in a sale-of-company transaction, the holders of preferred stock get their purchase price paid first before the holders of common stock see a dime. Building companies quickly and capital-efficiently meant that Techfarm and its entrepreneurs had less liquidation preference sitting before their common stock.

Because it owned only common stock, entrepreneurs felt like Techfarm was one of them. To raise capital, Techfarm called its network of high-net-worth Silicon Valley executives, who were trusted people with whom Gordon Campbell had worked before, such as Don Bell, founder of Bell Microproducts. Techfarm raised small amounts of capital for portfolio companies like Cobalt by selling promissory notes to these investors to achieve particular milestones.

Techfarm's network of individual investors also appreciated the model because they had access to investment opportunities in hot startup companies without having to pay Techfarm a management fee or carried interest. Many private investors helped the portfolio companies. The alignment of interests coupled with Campbell's leadership on the board of directors enabled Techfarm's portfolio companies to focus single-mindedly on realizing the vision.

When a company had demonstrated that it had a viable business, Techfarm would use its network to raise several million dollars. In the early days of the incubator, companies like 3Dfx raised their first round entirely from individual investors. As Techfarm's business matured, it attracted leading venture capital firms like US Venture Partners, Venrock, and Norwest to participate in the Series A financing.

Techfarm broke this business model when it raised its first traditional venture capital fund in 1997. Not only did Techfarm keep purchasing a 20 percent ownership position in its portfolio companies but it also received a management fee on the capital raised in its fund and a carried interest on fund profits. The entrepreneurs and other venture capital investors were uncomfortable because this new fee structure provided potential returns that felt excessive. Techfarm's new business model disturbed entrepreneurs and venture capital investors and created subtle conflict that reduced Techfarm's attractiveness as a partner. Techfarm had far better results as an incubator when its interests were aligned with the entrepreneurs'.

Seeing the Future: Howard Hartenbaum

"A company an investor likes may be 'hot or not,'" says Howard Hartenbaum, a general partner at August Capital, "but that doesn't necessarily lead to a date. To get to an investment, the venture capitalist looks to see whether the entrepreneur looks presentable, smart, well dressed, and healthy. Appearances trigger immediate conclusions like, 'This guy looks like a used-car dealer.' The venture capitalist decides right away that he doesn't want to deal with an entrepreneur who is trying too hard to sell something." Hartenbaum continues:

> An entrepreneur has to remember that I need to decide quickly. For me the threshold question is: *Do I like this person, or do I want to get the hell out of the room as fast as possible?*
>
> An entrepreneur's appearance and confidence level are very important. Some entrepreneurs have jokingly arrived at early-morning pitches in their pajamas. Some entrepreneurs show up in shorts and flip-flops and still get their funding. The majority of entrepreneurs, however, dress appropriately for the meeting.

Venture capitalists look for entrepreneurs who can explain their businesses in plain English and quickly answer the key questions, says Hartenbaum. "The secret to a winning presentation is to make a positive impression in the first few minutes. The rest is just supporting documentation so that the venture capitalist can walk into the partner meeting the following Monday and say without hesitation, 'I met this company called ABC. Here is what they're doing and why I think it's a big opportunity. The founder seemed credible. I called a reference. It looks like a good business. Here are some of the holes. We should all meet them to see what you think.'"

If an entrepreneur's presentation is too complex, convoluted, and difficult to listen to, he'll lose the venture capitalist's attention, says Hartenbaum. "When the investor leaves the room, he'll think to himself, *I really don't want to present that to my partners because it was so complex that I'll screw it up. Then I'll look like an idiot because I don't really understand what they do.*"

When dating, says Hartenbaum, the most important thing to find out is whether the other person is spending his life running around in circles. "The worst phrase an entrepreneur can use in his presentation is 'I'm a serial entrepreneur.' Every time I hear that, I think to myself, *Are you a serial murderer too?* The term *serial entrepreneur* implies that an entrepreneur doesn't know what he's doing. Trying over and over again without succeeding is one definition of insanity." Hartenbaum continues:

> *The first thing a venture capitalist wants to hear in a presentation is, 'I have a vision and I see the future.' If an entrepreneur is correct and can see the future, the entrepreneur may be able to build a big company behind that vision. If the entrepreneur can't see the future and can't even tell the venture capitalist what's going to happen next week, the entrepreneur is probably incapable of building a big company.*

> *When an entrepreneur claims he sees the future, his vision is either a brave-new-world model or a faster-better-cheaper model. An entrepreneur can never have both because those are completely different visions. The brave-new-world model is flying cars. Faster-better-cheaper is making a router that's 100 times faster. The entrepreneur must be very clear and specific about which model of vision he is creating.*

Keeping the Presentation to Five Slides

Guy Kawasaki explained how to make a presentation in 10 slides, but Hartenbaum likes to reduce it to five, saying, "A good presentation resolves the future first."

Slide #1: The vision and the problem. The first slide establishes the vision by defining a problem in the market. A presentation is over the moment the investor doesn't believe in the entrepreneur's vision. Unfortunately, most technology companies are looking for a market that doesn't exist or are looking to solve a problem that doesn't exist.

"Many entrepreneurs make the mistake of inventing a problem to solve," says Hartenbaum. "They're often bright, senior people in great companies like Microsoft or Google. Their technology may be really cool, but it doesn't solve any real problems. Those companies usually don't make it. The ones that make it solve a real problem using the great technologies that the entrepreneurs have mastered or created."

Slide #2: The solution. If an entrepreneur has a vision to see the future and identifies a real problem, the second slide should present the solution and briefly show how the problem is solved. "The quality of the solution is very important because a venture capitalist will not invest in a company that solved the problem by creating a consulting service or by writing a simple script for Excel," says Hartenbaum. "Venture capitalists want a solution that's hard to build and copy and that uses defensible intellectual property that doesn't infringe on other people's patents. The solution slide shows that the problem is solved so that the potential investor asks how solving it will make money.

Slide #3: The opportunity. The third slide should present the market opportunity instead of stating the business model. The opportunity slide should show how the company and the investor will make money together. "Many entrepreneurs present great companies that are bad investments," says Hartenbaum. "Statistics show that fewer than one in five technologies can be properly demonstrated. If a venture capital fund has to finance five of those companies for hundreds of millions of dollars and only one of them makes it, the fund will not make money. An entrepreneur may have a great company, but if it's a bad investment because it's going to take $75 million and eight rounds of financing just to show that the prototype works, the venture capitalists will not invest."

Slide #4: The financial projections. The fourth slide presents financial projections that say, "Let's make money together." "This slide shows the venture capitalist that if he invests the minimum amount of money to achieve the next milestone, the value of the company will increase as a result," says Hartenbaum. "If that amount is hundreds of thousands of dollars, that's good. If it's a few million dollars, that's a maybe. If it's $10 million to get a prototype out the door, it's no way. A venture capitalist would rather invest $10 million in 10 different companies at a million dollars apiece and hope that one or two of them make it than gamble it all on one deal. The odds are against startups anyway, but $10 million to build a prototype is just a bad investment."

"Let's make money together" also says that there's a big market opportunity out there. "A venture capitalist will not believe an entrepreneur who says that the company will capture 70 percent of a $700 million market growing 30 percent per year," says Hartenbaum. "An entrepreneur will be more credible if he says that the company will capture 0.5 percent of a growing $4 billion market over several years. Shrinking markets are a much more difficult proposition even if a company has better technology. Expanding, big markets and small amounts of investment required say, 'Let's make money together.'"

Slide #5: The team. "I disagree with Guy Kawasaki about proven entrepreneurs," says Hartenbaum, "because money often finds them before they come looking for the money. A venture capitalist will often invest in an entrepreneur that he's invested in before. For example, I invested in the Skype founders again when they founded another company called Juiced." Hartenbaum continues:

> *Venture capitalists generally look for entrepreneurs that are well educated, have technology backgrounds, have worked at great companies, and have domain expertise. A team with three guys out of Seybold who worked together before indicates there won't be infighting. If those three guys start a consumer Internet company, however, their lack of domain expertise is bad and undermines the value of the team chemistry.*

> *A venture capitalist assesses the quality of the team, but in the end he's gambling. The Google founders were an interesting team because they knew each other well and had promising technology. Their smarts and Stanford graduate program pedigrees made them a good gamble, but the Google team went up and down Sand Hill Road and pitched almost 50 venture capitalists who all said no. When the venture capitalists finally said yes, it was only after Google had taken off like a rocket. By then the venture capitalists fought to get into the deal.*

Avoiding the Red Flags

Venture capitalists are constantly engaged in a filtering process. "We see hundreds or thousands of potential investments per year, but our job, unfortunately, is to say yes to only two or three of them," says Hartenbaum. "Usually, we're saying no. An entrepreneur will get a no if he refuses to answer a question because he wants to follow the PowerPoint presentation. Stubbornly sticking to the presentation is a red flag. The venture capitalist has generally reviewed the PowerPoint presentation in advance and probably wouldn't be in the meeting if he didn't understand it." Hartenbaum continues:

> *If a venture capitalist asks how much money an entrepreneur is raising, the entrepreneur risks losing the sale if he ignores the question and explains the next slide. "When an entrepreneur ignores my question and insists on continuing with his presentation, I say, 'Stop.' The answer to your investment is zero. It's zero unless the entrepreneur answers my questions. If an entrepreneur is so inflexible that he can't let go of his presentation to answer my questions, he won't answer his customers' questions, either. His customers will just say, "No. There's the door."*

Very young companies often tell the venture capitalist exactly how they will spend a million-dollar investment, says Hartenbaum, but the investor prefers to hear how spending the money will benefit *him*. "The investor knows that the company will spend the money, but he wants to know that the company has accomplished something when the money is gone. An interesting investment is one that makes the investor money. To receive a venture capitalist's money, the company has to tell him how it's going to become worth more in the future."

Hartenbaum advises against cold-calling venture capitalists because they are generally overwhelmed by entrepreneurs approaching them. The best approach, he says, is to have somebody make an introduction.

> *If the first trick is to get in the door and the second trick is to get the venture capitalists interested, an entrepreneur shouldn't blow his chance on the first trick by sending an anonymous email. Venture capitalists get anonymous group e-mails all the time. Every other day I get an e-mail that says, "Dear Potential Venture Capital Investor," and hundreds of my closest friends are copied on the Cc: line. Those e-mails get automatically deleted.*

> *E-mails that make it obvious that the sender hasn't looked at what the venture firm invests in also get deleted. For example, such an e-mail might request mezzanine financing—$35 million at a $100 million pre-money valuation—without realizing the obvious: that the fund is an early-stage firm. If the sender*

clearly hasn't looked at the website, the e-mail gets deleted. The best way to get a meeting with a particular venture capitalist is to have somebody who knows that partner directly make an introduction.

Entrepreneurs who won't share information generally won't get financed. "It's fine for entrepreneurs to be paranoid," says Hartenbaum, "but they are wasting our time if they won't tell us who their customers or potential employees are. If we have to spend time pulling information out of the entrepreneur, we will probably have a terrible relationship over the next five years."

To get money from venture capitalists, the entrepreneur must trust them and they've got to trust the entrepreneur. "A relationship without trust won't work," says Hartenbaum. "Any credible, longstanding venture capitalist will be trustworthy with information because if he is not, entrepreneurs won't go to him anymore. If, however, a venture capitalist is on the board of a direct competitor, it might be prudent not to tell him everything because it's hard to keep such things separate."

Many entrepreneurs mistakenly think that the goal is to raise venture capital. "They feel validated once they've raised the money," says Hartenbaum. "Raising venture capital, however, is just one step in building a business. The goal is to build a successful business. Venture capitalists make two kinds of investments: money-losing ventures and real companies. Half—the ones that become real companies—are great. We walk away from the money-losing ventures because we make our money on the real businesses. Startups should strive to be in the right half and focus on building real businesses."

Having an Opening Gambit: Tom Barsi

"Guy Kawasaki and Howard Hartenbaum both told you that investors make a judgment about an entrepreneur in the first 15 seconds," says Tom Barsi, a repeat CEO who has raised venture capital from firms like Sequoia and Accel for companies such as Tidal Networks. "Those few seconds are the time to deliver the opening gambit, which is: *What's in it for the investor?* The opening gambit is straightforward. The investors want to know that the entrepreneur has a big opportunity. They want to know that the entrepreneur can execute his plan to make a difference to their portfolio." Barsi continues:

I recently worked with a company that had a great opening gambit because it had a $4 billion opportunity to enable collaboration between mobile devices. The company had a great customer base, had sold more than 100,000 seats, and had eliminated the technology and market risks without raising any money. With those accomplishments the company looked like a Series B stage investment, but its opening gambit was raising $5 million at a Series A valuation. This value proposition quickly got investors' attention.

When the venture capitalists start asking about a company's valuation, be careful: It's a trap. When venture capitalists ask, "What's the valuation?" the entrepreneur's answer should always be, "You set the valuation, not me." A company's valuation is like a stock price. The market always dictates the price of the company. Hopefully, a company has built the case for a good valuation because it has an enormous opportunity and a team that can execute against it. It's not for a startup to set the valuation; that's the venture capitalists' job. The best way to get a healthy valuation is to get multiple term sheets from several venture capital firms.

Finally, says Barsi, entrepreneurs should always remember that greed and fear are what motivate investors. "Venture capitalists are either afraid of missing a great opportunity or greedy because they see a capital-efficient deal where they can make a lot of money. A good investor presentation manages these emotions. Everything else goes by the wayside because, ultimately, the investment decision is based on these emotions. The entrepreneur's job is to present an opportunity that investors can love."

Summary

- Entrepreneurs must keep their investors aligned behind realizing the vision.

- Entrepreneurs and their investors must agree about how they are making money together.

- Entrepreneurs should consider using a compact five-slide investor presentation that addresses the vision and the problem, the solution, the market opportunity, the financial projections, and the team.

- Entrepreneurs should have an opening gambit that establishes in the first 15 seconds what's in it for the investors.

- Entrepreneurs should let venture capital investors suggest the valuation.

Call to Action

- Use Howard Hartenbaum's guide to create a five-slide investor presentation using PowerPoint. If you already prepared a 10-slide presentation using Guy Kawasaki's model in chapter 22, preparing a five-slide one will help you distill your business to its essence.

- Dry run the presentation with as many friendly critics as possible before meeting with a potential investor.

- To get feedback on adjusting the presentation, do a dry run with a professional investor who is unlikely to invest.

EPILOGUE

Corporations have no consciences, no beliefs, no feelings, no thoughts, no desires. Corporations help structure and facilitate the activities of human beings, to be sure, and their "personhood" often serves as a useful legal fiction. But they are not themselves members of "We the People" by whom and for whom our Constitution was established.

—John Stevens, US Supreme Court justice,
Citizens United v. Federal Election Commission

The global economic system nearly collapsed while I was writing this book. Although it is tempting to blame the wizards of Wall Street for this calamity, all of us must bear some responsibility because we have created a global economy that is populated by corporations that operate without consciences. Free-market economists have lulled those of us who make our livings in corporations into abdicating our moral responsibilities by blindly trusting that Adam Smith's invisible hand will miraculously protect the public good from our corporations. The stark truth is that external regulation is not enough to protect society from the unconscionable behavior of corporations.

The modern corporation has no conscience, and you invite disaster if you operate your business without a conscience in today's massively interdependent global economy because you won't have an ethical framework to help your company make the tough choices. Having a conscience will help your company avoid decisions that make economic sense but destroy the goodwill of the business. Without a conscience, for example, you may decide to fire 300 people and move manufacturing to a distant communist country to improve your margins, but in so doing you would demoralize your remaining employees, damage your company's culture, and destroy your relationships with strategic partners, suppliers, and the communities that have sustained your business. A conscience helps your company make the right choices.

In addition, you are doing business in a glass house. If your corporation acts unconscionably, as Toyota is perceived to have done recently by selling vehicles with dangerous accelerator problems, the world will hear about it instantly. Unless you proactively design a conscience, bloggers and websites like Twitter and Avaaz.org will be your corporation's default conscience. If you rely on the retroactive conscience of public approbation, you risk destroying the goodwill of your business if it fails to act in good conscience. British Petroleum, for example, damaged its reputation and caused its stockholders to suffer billions of dollars of lost stock value when its decision to cut corners to prematurely activate an undersea oil well in the Gulf of Mexico led to a massive oil spill.

Once upon a time, the corporation had a conscience, but it disappeared over the centuries. You can, however, design your company with a sophisticated conscience that can help you make the tough decisions. First, it is helpful to understand how the corporation lost its conscience. If you plan to form a corporation, you will actually be doing business in an entity that was designed for commerce in the Middle Ages. The amazing thing about the corporation is that it is such a brilliant agent of commerce that its original form has endured for centuries. Unfortunately, that form lacks an internal conscience that is suitable for doing business in the interconnected world of the twenty-first century.

The Corporation in the Age of Exploration

The corporation began its existence in medieval Europe with an external conscience provided by the king. In those days, kings granted charters to corporations with royal monopolies to pursue particular commercial purposes. The corporation enabled a king to extend his power beyond the limited resources of the treasury by allowing a group of individuals to raise capital for a commercial venture that also advanced the political and economic interests of the monarchy.

During the Age of Exploration from the fifteenth to the eighteenth century, the corporation served European monarchies as the agent of global exploration and territorial conquest. Canada's Hudson's Bay Company, for example, received its charter from the king of England in 1670 with a monopoly to exploit the valuable fur trade in the Hudson Bay watershed. The company helped the British monarchy extend the reach of its empire. At one time the Hudson's Bay Company controlled 15 percent of the landmass of North America.

To control the corporation, the king ruled it from the outside. If the corporation were a person, the king was the head and the corporation was the body. Separating the corporate body from its head ensured that it would not threaten the king's power.

If a corporation behaved unconscionably, the king could simply revoke its charter. Because the threat of revocation served as an external conscience, the corporation was created without an internal one. Because the king was the ultimate authority under the Divine Right of Kings, a doctrine that held that a monarch derived his right to rule from God, the corporation's external conscience, in theory, was the highest conscience on the planet.

The Corporation in the Age of Enlightenment

The corporation lost its supreme external conscience during the Age of Enlightenment in the eighteenth century. Reason debunked the legitimacy of the Divine Right of Kings, and Europe diffused the power of its monarchs into executive, legislative, and judicial branches of government. The external conscience function served by the king passed to these new entities. Creating a corporation no longer required that the king approve the charter.

As a holder of the lineage of English common law, the United States inherited the corporate architecture that separated the corporation from its conscience, but the doctrine of separation of church and state diminished the power of that conscience because the state was no longer the moral authority. In the early years of the republic, state legislatures exercised the conscience function formerly exercised by the king. Forming a corporation required formal legislation to approve the charter. Legislatures authorized corporations as quasi-public monopolies designed to serve a social function, like building a toll road, and closely supervised them to ensure that their behaviors didn't vary from the proscribed purposes set forth in their charters. Often the legislature limited the lifetime of a corporation to a term of 10 to 20 years. These checks and balances provided the functional equivalent of the conscience of the king.[8]

The Corporation in the Age of Industry

After 1800 legislatures shifted from approving corporations with inherent state-granted monopolies to allow for free incorporation under general laws. Free incorporation released corporations from the cumbersome process of having state legislatures approve their charters, and it reduced legislatures' external conscience function.

During the nineteenth century, the US Supreme Court further diminished the corporation's external conscience by reducing the power of state legislatures to revoke or alter a corporation's charter.[9] The application of the principle of limited liability in the mid-1800s eliminated another aspect of the corporation's conscience. Before limited liability, a corporation's stockholders faced unlimited liability for its debts, and its directors and officers bore personal responsibility for its actions. Courts also granted corporations some of the constitutional rights of individual citizens.[10] These developments, coupled with the freedom of incorporation, made it much easier for corporations to raise capital and proliferated their adoption as agents of the Age of Industry in the nineteenth and twentieth centuries.

Without legislatures to hold them in check and an internal conscience to guide them, corporations increasingly behaved in ways that harmed society. As a result, the external conscience function provided by legislatures shifted to being reactive. Legislatures responded to corporate transgressions by imposing external regulations on them. Abusive monopolies, for example, fostered antitrust laws, and pollution fostered laws that protect the environment. This has been an expensive and inefficient approach because it is harder to correct damage after it has occurred than to prevent it in the first place.

In response to management transgressions, courts imposed fiduciary duties on directors of corporations to ensure that corporate actions considered the interests of stockholders. Fiduciary responsibilities, like the duty of care and

8   *See Citizens United v. Federal Election Commission*, 558 US _____ (2010), minority opinion of
      Justice Stevens, pages 121 to 125 for an overview of the early history of the corporation in
      America. http://www.supremecourt.gov/opinions/09pdf/08-205.pdf.
9   *See Trustees of Dartmouth College v. Woodward*, 17 US 518 (1819).
10   *See Santa Clara County v. Southern Pacific Railroad Co.*, 118 US 394 (1886).

the duty of loyalty, formed a primitive code of conduct to guide the board of directors to exercise the corporation's conscience. This internal conscience is a default conscience, however, because it is implied by common-law precedent rather than expressly required by statute.

Some companies discovered that having a conscience was good business. Johnson & Johnson adopted its famous credo[11] in 1943 shortly before it became a public company. The credo recognizes that the company's responsibilities extend not only to its stockholders but also to its employees, its customers, its suppliers and distributors, the community in which it does business, and the world. The credo has served as Johnson & Johnson's moral compass by defining the values by which it conducts business with its multiple stakeholders. Having the credo enabled Johnson & Johnson to preserve its enterprise value by doing the right thing by recalling every bottle of Tylenol after a tampering scare in 1982.

The Corporation in the Twenty-First Century

You are asking for trouble if you rely exclusively on the fiduciary duties of the board of directors to stockholders as your corporation's conscience. That's like using the temperature gauge to operate your car. Just as your car's range of mobility is restricted when its radiator is about to boil over, your corporation's range of strategic options will be limited if you rely on only your fiduciary duties to stockholders to dictate your actions. Your company will tend to focus on short-term financial results and ignore the long-term effects of its behavior on its other stakeholders.

Many companies now recognize that the fiduciary duties of management to stockholders are only a subset of a code of conduct and a system of values that extends to all stakeholders. In the early 2000s, a movement called *conscious capitalism* emerged to evolve a more enlightened form of capitalism. At the core of this movement is the recognition that a corporation is not the traditional duality of the Age of Industry—a corporation and its stockholders—but rather a complex, interdependent ecosystem comprising the corporation and all of its stakeholders. Companies that follow the tenets of conscious capitalism, like

---

11 http://www.jnj.com/wps/wcm/connect/c7933f004f5563df9e22be1bb31559c7/ourcredo.pdf?MOD=AJPERES.

Whole Foods Market, have made the value systems by which they conduct their business with all their stakeholders the core driver of their being.

You will have a competitive advantage if you design your corporation to have a sophisticated internal conscience to supplement the fiduciary duties of directors to stockholders. To succeed in an economic system that understands the limits of its natural resources and recognizes the need to protect the environment will require you to anticipate the consequences of your company's actions like never before. You'll have to make very tough decisions that will require a strong moral compass.

This book shows how you can articulate your corporation's core values to serve as the code of conduct for management to use to exercise the company's conscience. You can internalize the conscience of the king to endow your corporation with a sophisticated internal probity—the highest form of conscience on the planet—to help you preserve and protect the extraordinary value that you will create.

KEY THEMES AND TERMS

To present the concepts in this book in plain, user-friendly English, I have eliminated defined terms and jargon. This brief glossary includes a few key themes, concepts, and terms used throughout the book.

alignment   *To align* means to bring the parts into proper coordination to create a unified whole. One of the founder's roles is to create alignment among his employees. Many of the book's ideas enhance alignment and facilitate the founder's role as an agent of it. Alignment provides a unifying force that amplifies a corporation's vitality.

collective   A corporation is generally a team of people working together as one. I use the term *collective* to mean the whole created by the individuals working together as a corporation. As a living organism, the corporation also expresses collective qualities like intelligence. Cobalt, 3Dfx, and NetMind, for example, achieved extraordinary results by accessing their employees' collective intelligence. I often use the term *collective* in this context. Accessing collective qualities like intelligence also tends to increase alignment.

corporation as a life form   This book often uses biological terms such as *ecosystem* metaphorically. Living organisms do not exist in isolation but depend on complex ecosystems for survival. As a living organism, the corporation operates within a complex system of interdependent relationships with customers, suppliers, and other stakeholders. This book often uses the metaphor of the corporation as a living entity existing in an ecosystem of stakeholders. Living organisms have DNA, which expresses genes that influence how they behave. Corporations have the equivalent of DNA in the form of corporations codes, bylaws, and articles of incorporation, which are the default rules of engagement that determine much of a corporation's behavior. Entrepreneurs can alter this legal DNA to customize rules of engagement to support the desired culture. Living organisms also have a life force that animates them. A company's culture is commonly considered the equivalent of its life force. Because people deduce the culture from his behavior, one of the founder's roles is to animate the culture. If a company is animated by a culture with a positive spirit, culture can become a driver of success.

cultural infrastructure   Aspects of a company's culture form important components of its infrastructure. Infrastructure is not just the tangible assets that show up on a balance sheet, such as equipment and furniture, but include purpose, core values, culture, and other intangibles. When developed, these assets become powerful agents of alignment and provide a cultural foundation to facilitate growth.

founders and entrepreneurs   I use the terms *founder* and *entrepreneur* interchangeably with one important distinction: During the concept stage, the *founder* is the leader among the *entrepreneurs* on the founding team. The founder is the prime mover among the startup team and is usually the initial CEO.

whole-brain   This book uses a simple model of human intelligence with three components: logic, emotion, and intuition intelligence. The term *whole-brain* refers to an individual or, on a collective level, a corporation that is able to access the best attributes of all three intelligences.

BIBLIOGRAPHY AND
ADDITIONAL RESOURCES

Aburdene, Patricia. *Megatrends 2010: The Rise of Conscious Capitalism.* Charlottesville, NC: Hampton Roads, 2007. This book provides an excellent introduction to conscious capitalism.

Adams, Rob. *A Good Hard Kick in the Ass: Basic Training for Entrepreneurs.* New York: Crown Business, 2002. The author, a seasoned venture capitalist, is brutally honest and direct about what it takes to succeed as an entrepreneur.

Allen, David. *Getting Things Done: The Art of Stress-Free Productivity.* New York: Viking Penguin, 2001. This book provides a definitive guide to being organized, which is the unspoken basis of an entrepreneur's ability to build a successful company.

Ante, Spencer E. *Creative Capital: Georges Doriot and the Birth of Venture Capital.* Boston: Harvard Business School Press, 2008. This book traces the history of venture capital in America and is required reading for anyone seeking venture capital or working in the venture capital business.

Bakan, Joel. *The Corporation: The Pathological Pursuit of Profit and Power.* New York: Free Press, 2004. This book analyzes the history of corporations and explores why they are prone to sociopathic behaviors.

Beck, Don Edward, and Christopher C. Cowen. *Spiral Dynamics: Mastering Values, Leadership, and Change.* Malden, MA: Blackwell, 1996. This book provides a map with eight stages of development of human consciousness on both individual and societal levels.

Beckwith, Harry. *What Clients Love: A Field Guide to Growing Your Business.* New York: Warner Books, 2003. This book is an invaluable guide to developing authentic sales and marketing techniques that accelerate sales.

Blanchard, Ken, and Sheldon Bowles. *Raving Fans: A Revolutionary Approach to Customer Service.* New York: William Morrow, 1993. This book explains how to turn a corporation's stakeholders into raving fans.

Blank, Steven Gary. *The Four Steps to the Epiphany: Successful Strategies for Products That Win.* Cafepress.com, 2005. This book is an essential guide to developing winning products.

Bragdon, Joseph H. *Profit for Life: How Capitalism Excels.* Cambridge, MA: Society for Organizational Learning, 2006. This book highlights an emergent model of the corporation as an organic living system whose primary means of growth are living assets (people and natural resources). The public companies profiled emphasize stewardship of living assets and provide a better rate of return than their peers.

Campbell, Joseph. *The Hero with a Thousand Faces.* Novato, CA: New World Library, 2008. This book can place the process of building a company in the context of the classic hero's journey.

Collins, Jim. *Good to Great: Why Some Companies Make the Leap . . . and Others Don't.* New York: HarperCollins, 2001. This book is required reading for every businessperson. Chapter 3 about core values and chapter 11 about how to develop a vision are especially helpful for entrepreneurs.

Collins, Jim, and Jerry I. Porras, *Built to Last: Successful Habits of Visionary Companies.* New York: HarperCollins, 1997. This book provides much inspiration about the importance of culture and values in building successful businesses.

Conley, Chip. *Peak: How Great Companies Get Their Mojo from Maslow.* San Francisco: Jossey-Bass, 2007. This book provides an inspired approach to meeting the self-actualization needs of a company's stakeholders.

Dalai Lama. *Ethics for the New Millennium.* New York: Riverhead Books, 1999. This book sets forth an appeal for an approach to ethics based on universal rather than religious principles and provides a useful perspective for an entrepreneur who wishes to design a values-based culture.

Dooley, Deborah. *Journeying into Wholeness with Map and Skills.* Palo Alto, CA: Delphi Press, 2003. This book provides a coherent map of the development of human consciousness with five stages.

Freeman, R. Edward. *Strategic Management: A Stakeholder Approach.* Cambridge: Cambridge University Press, 2010. This book is credited with positing the stakeholder approach to thinking about corporations.

Gelb, Michael. *How to Think Like Leonardo da Vinci: Seven Steps to Genius Every Day.* New York: Dell, 2000. This delightful book expands the concept of whole-brain thinking by explaining the "Seven Da Vincian Principles" of *Curiosita, Dimonstratzione, Sensazione, Sfumato, Arte/Scienza, Corporalita,* and *Connessione.*

Goleman, Daniel. *Emotional Intelligence: Why It Can Matter More Than IQ,* rev ed. New York: Bantam Books, 2006. This classic work helps entrepreneurs understand and access their emotional intelligence.

Goleman, Daniel. *Working with Emotional Intelligence.* New York: Bantam Books, 1998. This book is helpful to those looking to stimulate their emotional skills.

Greene, Robert. *The 48 Laws of Power.* New York: Penguin Books, 1998. This book provides a working knowledge of the laws of power, which is an essential component of effective leadership.

Hall, Brian. *Values Shift: A Guide to Personal and Organizational Transformation.* Eugene: Wipf and Stock Publishers, 1994. This book presents a map of the stages of development of consciousness expressed though seven familiar leadership styles: authoritarian, paternalist, manager, facilitator, collaborator, servant and visionary.

Hamel, Gary. *The Future of Management.* Boston: Harvard Business School Press, 2007. This book raises many questions about the evolution of management.

Hawken, Paul. *The Ecology of Commerce: A Declaration of Sustainability.* New York: Harper Paperbacks, 1993, 2010. This book launched the dialogue on sustainable business practices.

Hawkins, David R. *Power vs. Force: The Hidden Determinants of Human Behavior.* Sedona, AZ: Veritas, 1995. This is the book for those who want to explore attractor patterns.

Jackson, Mick. *Temple Grandin.* Burbank, CA: HBO Films, 2010. This film profiles Temple Grandin, PhD, who is a genius in the field of animal intelligence. Grandin brilliantly applies her knowledge of how cattle's brains perceive their reality, to design humane stockyards and slaughterhouses that are optimized for the psychology of livestock. Grandin is my new hero. My hope for *Great from the Start* is to inspire humane businesses that are similarly optimized for human psychology.

Kawasaki, Guy. *The Art of the Start: The Time-Tested, Battle-Hardened Guide for Anyone Starting Anything.* New York: Penguin Group, 2004. This book is an excellent guide to building a successful startup company.

Klein, Jeff. *Working for Good: Making a Difference while Making a Living.* Boulder, CO: Sounds True, 2009. This book provides an entrepreneur with tools and techniques to develop a more conscious approach to work.

Livingston, Jessica, *Founders at Work: Stories of Startups' Early Days.* Berkeley, Apress, 2008. This book contains interviews with 32 founders of successful startup companies, which capture the alchemy of the entrepreneurial process and provide invaluable insights for any entrepreneur starting a company.

Mackey, John. *Passion and Purpose.* Boulder, CO: Sounds True, 2009. This pair of CDs provides an introduction to the principles of conscious capitalism and explores how businesses fueled by the entrepreneurial spirit can be forces for positive change.

Maslow, Abraham Harold. *Motivation and Personality,* 3rd edition. New York: HarperCollins, 1987. This is a classic work about motivation.

Maxwell, John. *The 21 Irrefutable Laws of Leadership: Follow Them and People Will Follow You,* rev ed. Nashville: Thomas Nelson, 2007. This book provides a useful set of principles to develop the skills of leadership.

McDonough, William, and Michael Braungart. *Cradle to Cradle: Remaking the Way We Make Things*. New York: North Point Press, 2002. This book provides a compelling alternative to the "cradle to grave" manufacturing model of the Industrial Age.

McGilchrist, Iain. *The Master and His Emissary: The Divided Brain and the Making of the Western World*. New Haven, CT: Yale University Press, 2009. This book analyzes the right and left hemispheres of the brain and explores the consequences of a world dominated by left-brain people. This extraordinary work establishes the urgent need for humanity to develop a whole-brain approach to organizing society and civilization.

Montgomery, John. *Introduction to Venture Capital Financing Agreements*. Westborough, MA: Cognistar, 2008. This three-hour video course explains the standard documents used in venture capital financing. Available at https://www.cognistar.com/MontHansen.

Montgomery, John. *Understanding the Venture Capital Term Sheet Process*. Westborough, MA: Cognistar, 2008. This hourlong video explains the term sheet process in venture capital financings. Available at https://www.cognistar.com/MontHansen.

Moore, Geoffrey A. *Crossing the Chasm*, rev ed. New York: Harper Paperbacks, 2002. This book suggests a unifying approach to marketing to help make a mainstream market emerge.

Mourkogiannis, Nikos. *Purpose: The Starting Point of Great Companies*. New York: St. Martin's Press, 2006. This book establishes that a meaningful purpose is essential to the success of any business.

Nesheim, John L. *High Tech Start Up: The Complete Handbook for Creating Successful New High Tech Companies*, rev ed. New York: Free Press, 2000. This book provides useful information about how to write a business plan.

Owen, James P. *Cowboy Ethics: What Wall Street Can Learn from the Code of the West*. Ketchum, ID: Stoecklein, 2005. The author, an investment banker, advocates that corporations adopt codes of ethics and govern their conduct accordingly.

Rao, Srikumar S. *Are You Ready to Succeed? Unconventional Strategies for Achieving Personal Mastery in Business and Life.* New York: Hyperion, 2006. This book inspires an entrepreneur to become aware of his life purpose and provides an introduction to the development of his consciousness.

Rath, Tom. *StrengthsFinder 2.0.* New York: Gallup Press, 2007. This useful book helps entrepreneurs identify and apply their aptitudes.

Riso, Don. *Personality Types: Using the Enneagram for Self-Discovery.* New York: Mariner Books, 1996. This book is an essential management tool to help a leader understand not only his own personality archetype but also those of his co-workers.

Robinson, Ken, and Lour Aronica. *The Element: How Finding Your Passion Changes Everything.* New York: Penguin, 2009. This inspiring book will help you identify your life's purpose.

Rock, David, *Your Brain at Work: Strategies for Overcoming Distraction, Regaining Focus, and Working Smarter All Day Long.* New York: HarperBusiness, 2009. This book provides an excellent introduction to the neuroscience of behavior.

Rosenberg, Marshall. *The Nonviolent Communication Training Course.* Boulder: SoundsTrue, 2006. 9 CDs and a succinct training manual provide an excellent introduction to nonviolent communication.

Rushkoff, Douglas. *Life Inc.: How the World Became a Corporation and How to Take It Back.* New York: Random House, 2009. This book provides an account of how corporations have become the dominant force of contemporary life.

Sanders, Tim. *Saving the World at Work: What Companies and Individuals Can Do to Go Beyond Making a Profit to Making a Difference.* New York: Crown Business, 2008. This inspiring book highlights our individual potential to make a difference.

Schachter-Shalomi, Zalman, and Ronald S. Miller. *From Age-ing to Sage-ing: A Profound New Vision of Growing Older.* New York: Grand Central, 1997. This book contains useful information about the power of mentoring.

Servan-Schreiber, David, *The Instinct to Heal: Curing Depression, Anxiety and Stress without Drugs and without Talk Therapy*. Emmaus, PA: Rodale, 2004. This book is a useful resource to help leaders manage fear and anxiety.

Sherwin, Elton B., Jr., *The Silicon Valley Way: Discover 45 Secrets for Successful Start-Ups*, rev ed. Palo Alto, CA: Energy House, 2010. This book contains valuable techniques used by successful entrepreneurs to develop their business plans.

Sisodia, Rajendra S., David B. Wolfe, and Jagdish N. Sheth. *Firms of Endearment: How World-Class Companies Profit from Passion and Purpose*. Upper Saddle River, PA: Wharton School, 2007. This book profiles companies that embody the principles of conscious capitalism; these "firms of endearment" beat the performance of the S&P 500 by a factor of 8 to 1 over a 10-year period.

Spence, Roy M., Jr. *It's Not What You Sell, It's What You Stand For: Why Every Extraordinary Company Is Driven by Purpose*. New York: Penguin, 2009. This inspiring book emphasizes the importance of a company's having a compelling purpose.

Strong, Michael, and John Mackey. *Be the Solution: How Entrepreneurs and Conscious Capitalists Can Solve All the World's Problems*. Hoboken, NJ: John Wiley & Sons, 2009. This book suggests how conscious entrepreneurs and capitalists can help solve big problems.

Thomson, David G. *Blueprint to a Billion: 7 Essentials to Achieve Exponential Growth*. Hoboken, NJ: John Wiley & Sons, 2005. This book is an excellent sequel to *Great from the Start* because it shows how great companies achieved exponential growth to $1 billion in revenue during the growth phase of their businesses.

Wilber, Ken. *The Integral Vision: A Very Short Introduction to the Revolutionary Integral Approach to Life, God, the Universe, and Everything*. Boston: Shambhala, 2007. This book provides an excellent, easy-to-read introduction to integral theory. In the context of integral theory, *Great from the Start* suggests how post-conventional entrepreneurs can design post-conventional companies. The legal architecture in chapter 20, for example, provides the structure of an integral corporate interior.

ACKNOWLEDGMENTS

In December 2007 I thought I had fully uncovered Gordon Campbell's blueprint. I decided to demonstrate it by launching a professional development program for entrepreneurs. I invited many of my friends from the venture capital ecosystem to present their wisdom to 40 startup companies. Geoffrey Moore encouraged me to proceed. Gordon Campbell, Roger Sanford, Nilofer Merchant, Vivek Mehra, Harry Max, Mike Edwards, Joe Watt, Ward Ashman and Ian Schmidt, Chris Melching, Bob Karr, Web Augustine, Dave Izuka, Jim McFadzean, Kathryn Gould, Chris Gill, Shrinath Acharya, Harry Quackenboss, Ram Jayam, Mark Orr, Steve Bengston, Saran Saund, Jim Hogan, Susan Russell, Dan O'Brien and Dick McIntosh, Ross Perich, Mark Zawacki, Bob Schoettle, Dan Sapp, Kathryn Coffey, Guy Kawasaki, Howard Hartenbaum, Tom Marchok, Tom Barsi, Ken Wilcox, Derek Blazensky, Ron Laurie, Leo Quilici, Brian Fitzgerald, and Dan Saccani—all volunteered to make presentations.

These experts presented to entrepreneurs in seven monthly sessions between January and July 2008. Dia North and her film crew—Shane King and Jason Wolos—captured the sessions on video. Saeed Amidi graciously hosted the program in the auditorium at his Plug and Play Tech Center in Sunnyvale, California. Susan Russell named the program Startworks.

The presentations were so inspired that it quickly became apparent that Startworks was not about educating the entrepreneurs but about capturing the career wisdom of the experts. Starting each session with a strong speaker inspired the other experts to rise to the same level of performance. After the program Cynthia Mitchell patiently transcribed more than 20 hours of videotapes.

The transcripts were so electric that I organized them into a book. Harry Max signed on as the developmental editor, Dan O'Brien became its graphic designer, and Janet Gift agreed to word-process the drafts, and Elizabeth von Radics became the copy editor.

I thought that writing a book would be easy. I was delusional, however, because the blueprint was entirely in my head and the book demanded that I distill it to writing. Happily, many people provided exactly the right advice or encouragement at the right time to inspire me to keep writing until I got it on paper so that others could logically follow it.

The good people of Languedoc, France, including Maurice de Coster, Gabrielle, Luc, Justine, Nick, Nancy, Christine, Richard, Gena, Tina, Philip, Noe, and Valentin, gave me their love and support to turn draft number five.

Many kind people read draft six and inspired me to start over. Bill Reichert showed me why it was too depressing to start a book describing corporate train wrecks. Kathryn Gould's recommendation to give the manuscript a "good editing" became my mantra. Jerry Scharf showed me what I was really trying to say. Jeevan Sivasubramaniam suggested how to better organize the ideas. Harry Max suggested better structure and pedagogy. Bruce La Fetra provided helpful guidance to improve the writing. Donna Carpenter showed me how to edit. Patrick Gaffney inspired me by sharing how he and Andrew Harvey had used a whole-brain approach to help Sogyal Rinpoche write *The Tibetan Book of Living and Dying*. My wife Linda saved the book by suggesting that I use an outline.

Many others provided invaluable feedback, including Geoffrey Little, Megan Caroll, Marsha Clark, Judy O'Brien, Judith Brown Meyers, Jeff Klein, Susan Hollingshead, Mark Richards, Jannie Wu, Andrew Kassoy, Patrick Hehir, Dan Appelman, Cousin Michael McCloud, Deborah Dooley, Dan Hansen, Jan Lewis, David Park, Tom Lane, Shirley Litsky, Zubin, Jack, Andrew, Laura, and my father, Parker Montgomery. Magatte Wade introduced me to Michael Strong, who invited me into the conscious capitalism movement. Dean Robert Klonoff and Professor Jennifer Johnson of Lewis & Clark Law School, Mark Finnern of the Future Salon, and Carl Nichols of the Haas School of Business at the University of California, Berkeley, allowed me to test the ideas in this book at their institutions.

The following presenters from the first C3 Summit—Catalyzing Conscious Capitalism—in November 2008, contributed quotes: Christiana Wyly, David Wolfe, John Mackey, Rajendra Sisodia, R. Edward Freeman, Chip Conley, Sir Ken Robinson, Srikumar Rao, Ron Pompei, Gerry McDonough, Robb Smith, Kip Tindell, Sally Jewel, Matt Goldman, Patricia Aburdene, Nikos Mourkogiannis, Gary Hamel, Jim Stengel, Tim Sanders, Terri Kelly, Roy Spence, Jeff Cherry, and Sunny Vanderbeck.

Phil Brittain kindly introduced me to David Hancock at Morgan James Publishing. David and his team, including Margo Toulouse, Rachel Lopez and Bonnie Bushman, turned the manuscript into a book. Elizabeth Parson prepared the index.

My partners and colleagues at Montgomery & Hansen made this book possible by indulging me leave from the billable hour and tolerating an iterative and extroverted creative process. Jon Noble and Dan Hansen helped produce the Startworks program. The entrepreneurs who attended Startworks provided the experts with an enthusiastic audience that inspired the extraordinary performances that became the basis of this book.

Writing a book, like building a company, is a team sport. I modeled the blueprint by surrounding myself with a superb team that patiently supported me while I found my voice. I thank them for making this book possible.

Special thanks go to Harry Max, who guided this book to the finish line, and to Janet Gift, who endured innumerable and illegible drafts with grace and good humor. *Great from the Start* would never have become a book without Harry and Janet.

Finally, I thank my wife, Linda, and my children, Spencer and Paige, whose love and support brought this book to life.

Appendix A

TRIMERGENCE'S THREE INTELLIGENCES SELF-ASSESSMENT TOOL

The Three Intelligences™ model is designed to build one's competency to activate, integrate, and apply our three primary intelligences: logic, emotion, and intuition. The principle of three intelligences "balance" assumes that most of us tend to use only one, or perhaps two, of our innate intelligences. Therefore we don't "run on all three cylinders." We can rapidly increase the quality of our relationship performance by maximizing these native capabilities. The three intelligences development process improves our ability to "speak the languages" of others, as each person has his own unique default intelligence aptitude. For example, having a default logic intelligence requires that you develop and use your emotion intelligence to fully connect with an emotion-oriented person. Trimergence's Three Intelligences Self-Assessment Tool provides rapid and practical feedback about one's three-intelligences balance by focusing on three areas:

- The balance and the activation of your three intelligences
- The levels of your three intelligences and implications of each intelligence on your life in general
- "Points to Consider" and a "To Do" list to develop each of your three intelligences

Reprinted with permission.

THREE INTELLIGENCES
SELF-ASSESSMENT TOOL

Directions

- This 30-item questionnaire is a subjective assessment specifically designed to activate and stimulate your self-observation.

- The assessment has a scale ranging from 1 (Never) to 2 (Rarely) to 3 (Sometimes) to 4 (Often) to 5 (Always).

- Read each statement carefully and circle the point on the scale that most closely fits how you relate to the statement.

1. I instinctively know what's best for me or for others; however, I may or may not follow these inner messages.

   1—Never   2—Rarely   3—Sometimes   4—Often   5—Always

2. One of my favorite pastimes is enjoying and appreciating many types of art.

   1—Never   2—Rarely   3—Sometimes   4—Often   5—Always

3. There are times when I "think out loud" with people. I have learned that others may not enjoy that I do this. They want me to get to the point.

   1—Never   2—Rarely   3—Sometimes   4—Often   5—Always

4. I reflect on how I feel emotionally when I am both alone and with others.

   1—Never   2—Rarely   3—Sometimes   4—Often   5—Always

5. When people talk to me about something I think is important and I don't fully understand, I can feel frustrated or anxious. At those times I may interrupt them.

    1—Never   2—Rarely   3—Sometimes   4—Often   5—Always

6. I can have a "gut sense" about life situations, but I may not be fully aware of the meaning of it at the time. Later I often find that my gut feeling was right.

    1—Never   2—Rarely   3—Sometimes   4—Often   5—Always

7. I sense I have an inner voice that I can trust. Sometimes this voice can be critical if I am unsure of myself. This can include judging that I have not done well enough.

    1—Never   2—Rarely   3—Sometimes   4—Often   5—Always

8. Sometimes I wonder why others seem unfeeling. At these times I can feel like an outsider or a foreigner with them.

    1—Never   2—Rarely   3—Sometimes   4—Often   5—Always

9. When I don't understand what people are talking about, I assume that they are not making sense. Then I judge them for not thinking clearly.

    1—Never   2—Rarely   3—Sometimes   4—Often   5—Always

10. I love it when I understand exactly how my life works with a type of elegant, internalized common sense.

    1—Never   2—Rarely   3—Sometimes   4—Often   5—Always

11. I can usually "read" people and intuitively determine whether to trust them.

    1—Never   2—Rarely   3—Sometimes   4—Often   5—Always

12. When I really connect with my message, I communicate it with passion. I almost don't have to think about what I am going to say. The words just flow.

    1—Never   2—Rarely   3—Sometimes   4—Often   5—Always

13. I can feel emotionally vulnerable if I let people know how I really feel about things.

    1—Never   2—Rarely   3—Sometimes   4—Often   5—Always

14. When people don't have clear, well-prepared thoughts, I can tune out. Then I start an internal multitasking thought process.

    1—Never   2—Rarely   3—Sometimes   4—Often   5—Always

15. I am very good at organizing my work, and I prefer not to have my workflow interrupted.

    1—Never   2—Rarely   3—Sometimes   4—Often   5—Always

16. I read people instinctively and usually sense what they need to feel more comfortable.

    1—Never   2—Rarely   3—Sometimes   4—Often   5—Always

17. I need the emotional "juice" of a relationship—the adventure of the emotional interaction. Without this I can lose interest in the relationship.

    1—Never   2—Rarely   3—Sometimes   4—Often   5—Always

18. I sense a connection with the larger "whole" of life, and I enjoy my relationship with nature.

    1—Never   2—Rarely   3—Sometimes   4—Often   5—Always

19. Sometimes people think that I want to control them. This can happen when I think they are not making sense. I will demonstrate that their logic is faulty in certain ways.

    1—Never   2—Rarely   3—Sometimes   4—Often   5—Always

20. I trust my response to situations, but at times I can overreact, losing my perspective. It can be hard for me to tell which way to respond when I react emotionally like this.

    1—Never   2—Rarely   3—Sometimes   4—Often   5—Always

21. If there is too much information to take in, I often need to withdraw. Then I take private time to make sense out of it all.

    1—Never   2—Rarely   3—Sometimes   4—Often   5—Always

22. I find that my emotions have information for me to learn from, but in the moment I am not always aware what those messages are.

    1—Never   2—Rarely   3—Sometimes   4—Often   5—Always

23. Sometimes people tell me that they think I am too "excitable."

    1—Never   2—Rarely   3—Sometimes   4—Often   5—Always

24. I trust myself and usually say what I think, even if I am concerned about others' reactions.

    1—Never   2—Rarely   3—Sometimes   4—Often   5—Always

25. If I told people everything that I sensed about either them or their situation, they might overreact. They may feel somewhat shocked by what I have to say.

    1—Never   2—Rarely   3—Sometimes   4—Often   5—Always

26. I prefer to use well-constructed and trusted models to make my decisions. I generally don't like to do things "by the seat of my pants."

    1—Never   2—Rarely   3—Sometimes   4—Often   5—Always

27. There are times that I just want to feel good and will do whatever it takes to maintain a positive emotional balance.

    1—Never   2—Rarely   3—Sometimes   4—Often   5—Always

28. If I hear a message that bothers me, I tend to tune it out. If I don't, I can feel sad or "down."

    1—Never   2—Rarely   3—Sometimes   4—Often   5—Always

29. When there is too much to think about, I can overanalyze or even become confused by too much information.

    1—Never   2—Rarely   3—Sometimes   4—Often   5—Always

30. I have hunches about things. At times I may tell others about them; at other times I won't.

    1—Never   2—Rarely   3—Sometimes   4—Often   5—Always

THREE INTELLIGENCES SCORE

On this page score your Three Intelligences Self-Assessment according to the legend. Find the number you circled for each question and write that number on the corresponding line below. Add the scores for each column and place that number on the Total line. On the next page, you will discover what your score means.

Logic		Emotion		Intuition	
Question #	Score	Question #	Score	Question #	Score
3		2		1	
5		4		6	
9		8		7	
10		13		11	
14		17		12	
15		20		16	
19		22		18	
21		23		24	
26		27		25	
29		28		30	
Total		Total		Total	

THE THREE INTELLIGENCES
SELF-ASSESSMENT FEEDBACK

The Three Intelligences Score Place your scores from the previous page in this table		
	Logic	Emotion	Intuition
Three Intelligences Score (Between 10-50 each)			
Three Intelligences Order (1,2,3)			
Three Intelligences Activation Activation Score Lower: 10-23 Middle: 24-37 Higher: 38-50			

Now put your Three Intelligences Score in the Three Intelligences circle and observe the balance and relative score of your three intelligences.

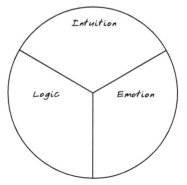

THREE INTELLIGENCES
INTERPRETATION SYSTEM

Introduction

The following paragraphs are designed to give you additional feedback about your scores on the Three Intelligences Self-Assessment Tool. These paragraphs correspond to your level of activation of these three intelligences. The paragraphs have two sections:

- A descriptive paragraph that defines how you may use that intelligence

- A "Five Points to Consider" paragraph designed to help you improve your use of that intelligence

Scoring System

Using the scoring table, you have already finalized your Three Intelligences scores as Lower, Middle, and Higher. The score legend is:

- Lower (10–23):
  You may have less of a tendency to utilize this intelligence.

- Middle (24–37):
  You appear to fit in the group of people who access and utilize this intelligence in a general manner.

- Higher (38–50):
  You use this intelligence quite often, which implies that this is your primary intelligence. Because you tend to use it so much, it may become a dominant intelligence, perhaps overshadowing the other two at times.

Finding Your Interpretive Paragraphs

Read through the following paragraphs and find the one in each of the three intelligences that coincides with your score. These three paragraphs are your feedback tools.

Interpretation Guidelines

1. Remember that this self-assessment tool is a subjective evaluation system. The Three Intelligences Self-Assessment is designed to stimulate your thinking and creativity. It is not as assessment of your personality.

2. Look for your overall score trend rather than pay too much attention to whether you are "higher" or "lower." As you review your scores, answer the following questions:

    a. What appears to be my dominant intelligence: logic, emotion, or intuition?

    b. What do I notice about the other two intelligences in relation to my dominant one? Are the levels close, or is there a significant variation? What do these variations mean?

3. These paragraphs are guidelines to stimulate you. They are not designed to be "right" or to "predict." Your ability to consider them and to use the information as a pathway to better understanding yourself within the Three Intelligences model is our key goal. In truth, no one knows you better than you know yourself! Your use of these paragraphs will facilitate the process of knowing yourself better.

4. "Higher, "middle," and "lower" do not imply that you do or do not have access to that intelligence. The scale is based on how much of that intelligence you identify with at this time. Thus your scores may fluctuate. In fact, it is not uncommon for people's scores to go up or down depending on when they complete the questionnaire.

5. Finally, the key goal is not necessarily to be at the "highest" level of each intelligence. Certainly, we want to improve our level of each intelligence, but overall balance in life is of key importance as well. Balancing our dominant intelligence with the other two is a pathway to obtaining greatest results. Therefore look at all of your scores to get an overall

picture of your three intelligences, then determine which intelligences you need to develop to attain three-intelligences balance.

Interpretive Paragraphs

Lower Logic (10–23)

"Making sense" of things doesn't appeal to you that much. You may tend to enjoy spending more time in the actual experience of what you do rather than analyzing it. This may cause others to question you, wondering if you are paying full attention to what they think is important. Deeper down, however, you may have a sense of what is going on that doesn't require you to rely so much on the logic of what is going on. In fact, you may actually think that being too logical at times can take away the fun or miss the point of what life is about. It's not that you don't want things to make sense as much as you just don't want to spend too much of your time analyzing and thinking.

Points to Consider

1. Observe your own thinking process. Notice your tendency to think in a linear, logical way. Notice if you find this skill difficult or easy.

2. Notice how much you read. Reading requires the use of logic because a book or an article has a beginning and end that requires logic to connect them together. If you don't read much, consider doing some easy reading as a way to stimulate your logic skill.

3. Observe others whom you find to be very logical. Notice the behaviors and skills that these people use.

4. Ask people you trust to give you feedback about your communication skills. Do you tend to stay "on track" in a logical manner, or do you move from topic to topic?

5. Determine if being more logical could help you in your job or personal life. If you made sense to others more quickly, would it enhance your success?

Middle Logic (24–37)

You probably like to do things in a way that is orderly and that everyone can understand. This sense of order is helpful because it reduces the possibility of miscommunication or misunderstanding of plans and directions. You might think that if only everyone would just think more clearly about what they are doing, we would all have an easier time of it. You enjoy analyzing and using your logical intelligence to follow work, reading projects, and even perhaps "whodunnit" types of TV shows or movies. After you are done figuring out your answer, however, you probably let your analytic mind relax and pay attention to other aspects of your life experience.

Points to Consider

1. Observe how you feel about having order in your life. Would you like more or less? Do you find that you can be too orderly and might sacrifice adventure for order?

2. Notice your reading habits. What do you tend to read? Is it easy reading, such as newspapers and magazines? Do you challenge your reading skills?

3. Watch your interactions with others. Do you become frustrated when others don't make sense? How do you communicate this to them, or do you tend to keep your frustration to yourself, perhaps in silent judgment?

4. Talk to those with whom you interact often and get their assessment of how you could improve your ability to think more clearly in a linear and logical manner.

Be more conscious of when you are underutilizing your thinking skills. Challenge yourself with more-difficult reading or movies that require more thought. Assess yourself to see if you are getting intellectually lazy and not pushing yourself to be mentally stimulated.

Higher Logic (38–50)

Elegant and precise logic is paramount to you. You probably feel quite exhilarated when things make sense, especially if you had predicted that they would or you solved a complicated puzzle or problem. This "analysis of the facts" is something that you not only enjoy but also find very stimulating and actually relaxing. You are able to take in a tremendous amount of information through your logical skills, and you love to have information flow in perfect order and be at your fingertips. When this doesn't happen, you can feel frustrated and possibly even judgmental toward those whom you feel are inhibiting making sense. These people may include those close to you or perhaps others over whom you have less control, such as politicians or other public figures who have a wide influence.

Points to Consider

1. Observe yourself and notice if you tend to rely on your thinking skill to the point where you may shut others out. As a result, you might be frustrated or impatient when others can't keep up with you.

2. Exercise your logical mind so that you focus not only on getting the most out of it but also on making the greatest contributions. Consider becoming part of groups that focus on major life issues, such as those found in university settings.

3. Make sure that your reading stimulates you to the point that you are fully challenged. You might find that you get tired from work and don't read enough. Remember that reading for you is like going to the gym: you may love it, but it still takes work to get fully buffed!

4. Make sure that you are connected with others from both the intuitive and the emotional levels. Our society stresses the value of logic, so you may find that you overuse that intelligence.

5. Ask others whom you trust about your balance of logic, emotion, and intuition. Make sure that you are not relying too much on your thinking skill to solve problems while missing key information in the other two intelligences. This is a common pattern for logic-oriented people, especially in intimate relationships.

Lower Emotion (10–23)

People may ask you how you feel, and you may not know how to answer. In fact, you might even begin your response by saying "I think." You may find it taxing to be around people who spend a lot of time talking about life challenges or who are focused on the more "touchy-feely" aspects of life. The theme of "talking about how one feels" in a relationship situation, or after a loss of some type, might leave you cold because you don't have a ready answer. It's not that you don't want to be aware of your emotional state; it is more that you may not know where to start. The emotional area may be somewhat of a mystery to you, and so you might tend to stay away from it because you don't have the language to describe it. This is not because you are "unemotional" as much as it is that you don't have easy access to this part of you.

Points to Consider

1. Remember that even though you may not "feel" your emotions, they are still there. Emotions can reside below the surface of our awareness. Therefore you *can* be in touch with them, but it might not be so easy at first. Talk to those who knew you as a child, such as a parent, about how you expressed your emotions in your early years.

2. Sometimes those who define themselves as "not emotional" are actually very close to their emotions, but they had to hide them from others because they felt too vulnerable. Ask yourself if you were more emotion oriented before and if there were situations that caused you to suppress your emotions.

3. Enjoying art is a great way to stimulate our emotions. A fascinating movie, a stimulating novel, or a great painting can evoke our emotions in many ways. Consider spending more time listening to music that you love as a way to bring your emotions to the surface.

4. Notice when you are around those whom you have defined as "emotional." You might feel uncomfortable around these people because you don't know how to respond to them. Observe and think about what you have learned at these times.

5. Consider your experiences in intimate relationships. Have you kept emotions at bay? If so, identify several ways that you could be more expressive to those you love. If you think your answer is "touchy-feely," that is probably a good sign!

Middle Emotion (24–37)

You can usually tell when you are angry or upset, and this is probably one of the key emotional messages that you understand about yourself. It might not be so easy, however, to perceive your more subtle emotions, such as sadness, joy, and those you experience in times of deeper intimacy with others. You might feel uncomfortable in these "emotional" situations, but at the same time want to better understand how you feel because you can see the value in connecting with that part of yourself. There may be times when others are in more-emotional states, such as sadness resulting from a loss, when you may not know how to support them, even though you want to. A deeper yearning to be in touch with your own emotions is something that you are conscious of and want to address.

Points to Consider

1. You may have found that you can access an appropriate emotional response in many life situations. Consider over the past year what you could have done even better to support others at the emotional level. You may find that you knew what to do at those times but felt inhibited to do so, such as giving a hug or kiss at the "perfect" time.

2. What are the main skills that you use to connect with others emotionally? List several skills that are common for you.

3. What feedback have you received from others when you have been in an emotional experience with them? What do they most appreciate about your approach? How can you do more of this?

4. Notice if you have any lingering self-judgment about being "too emotional." See if these judgments come from messages that others have passed on to you but which are not relevant to you now.

5. Consider stimulating your emotional skill by reading the works of others who have studied this area, such as *Working with Emotional Intelligence* by Daniel Goleman.

Higher Emotion (38–50)

You may at times feel a literal rush of emotions when you encounter certain experiences in life. Those that are more important, such as intimate relationships with family, children, or key colleagues, can evoke in you a powerful and sometimes overwhelming emotional response. On the one hand, you might find this difficult to manage because your own strong emotional response is hard to keep private within yourself. This may include outward expressions such as tears or even "jumping for joy" at times. The key difficulty you might experience is that others may judge or misunderstand you when you have these overt emotional responses. This is probably a main concern you have about being so close to your emotional state. You are happy to have this part of yourself accessible, although you might have concern that others don't know how to deal with this aspect of you.

Points to Consider

1. Notice if you rely too much on your emotional responses. Do you use them as a way to push others away or even to control them because they don't know how to respond to you?

2. When you are in touch with your deeper emotional messages, what do they say to you? What are you learning about yourself through this emotion connection?

3. What skills have you learned to use your emotions? Define these skills and learn to bring out those that are most constructive. How can you use your emotional skill without being *too* emotional?

4. Sometimes those who are highly oriented to emotion are focused on nurturing others because people always need love. You may find that you tend to love or nurture others excessively. What other ways can you support people?

5. Who are your key role models? What is it about these people that reflects the value of emotional skill? How have they used their ability to connect with others to everyone's advantage?

Lower Intuition (10–23)

There are times you may be quite surprised, or even blindsided, by situations that you did not predict. Perhaps in the past you received a message from another person that you never anticipated, such as a firing or the end of a relationship. Try as you might, you may attempt to figure out why these things happened to you, but you may not have a clear answer. Certainly, you have the desire to be more in tune with what is going on around you, but it may not come so easily. You also might enjoy your current approach to life, realizing that you don't have to be aware of so much and can just enjoy being yourself. You might think *If everyone had the freedom to just be himself and not bother each other, life would be so much easier.*

Points to Consider

1. Pay attention to others' body language and speech patterns. You can reduce the element of surprise by learning more from these cues.

2. Recognize that you have access to your intuition but may not know how to understand intuitive messages. Think back on times in your life when you had an "intuitive hit" and were right.

3. When watching a TV show or movie, experiment and see if you can predict what is going to happen next. Have fun following your hunch, and don't spend too much time trying to figure it out with logic.

4. Create a free day just for yourself without any plans at all. Get up in the morning and do whatever you want. At the end of the day, write down five things that you learned from having no plans.

5. Observe others whom you assess as being intuitive. Notice what they do and how they communicate. If you know them, ask them how they sense their intuitive messages. They may have developed skills or tools to be in touch with their intuition that they can pass on to you.

Middle Intuition (24–37)

You can fairly accurately sense others' intentions and are probably a good judge of character. You are not that often surprised by things that occur in your life, but sometimes you may read things wrong by not paying full attention to your "inner knowing." You might want to improve this ability to sense what is actually happening below the surface, but may not want to spend a lot of time on that endeavor because in general your approach works well enough for you. As a result, you may be periodically surprised when things don't turn out as you expected. You usually adjust to this, recognizing that life is ultimately a mystery. Sometimes others who seem to be able to read other people very accurately, with very little external information, can amaze you. This is something that you might want to do yourself, but you may not know exactly how.

Points to Consider

1. Remember times in your life that you had "been right" and followed your hunch. Think of how good this felt and how you might do this in your life right now.

2. Consider the times that you did not follow your intuitive hit and later assessed that you should have. What was your experience of that hit, and why did you not follow it?

3. When talking with someone you trust and are close to, notice what you sense as you interact with him. Begin to put these perceptions together, and ask him if you can disclose what you became aware of. *Note:* Make sure that what you say will not shock him!

4. When you wake up in the morning, write down several hunches for how the day will go. Before bed that night, read over what you wrote. Have fun noticing how your hunches predicted the day.

5. Learn from the masters! Find someone that is very intuitive, perhaps a parent or family member, and have him tell you what his experience is like. Pick a person who will share insights with you about what it is like to be intuitive.

Higher Intuition (38–50)

You may have an uncanny ability to just know what is going on and to predict what is going to happen next. This is not a magical skill so much as it is your ability to "tune in" to what is really happening below the surface. This may appear as a type of objectivity or even a clinical sense of precision. Your skill may even amaze others, since you can get so much from so little information. You may think this is all well and good, but you do not always follow your intuition in your own life. In fact, you may have found that you tend to overlook your natural intuitive messages to yourself in key life endeavors or challenges that you face. Thus a key goal to consider is how to use your intuitive abilities to help yourself more.

Points to Consider

1. Recognize that you may take your intuitive skill for granted, thinking that it is "just there." Remember that you can develop this skill even more by taking the risk to experiment. Talk to others of what you notice about them that is positive from your intuitive read. See if you are right. You will probably be pleasantly surprised!

2. Notice if you tend to rely too much on your intuition and don't include others in your thinking. You might assume that others know where you

are, but you later find out that they needed much more information, especially clear logic.

3. Build your intuitive capabilities by taking workshops or reading about how to improve your intuition. People of all backgrounds are recognizing the value of developing greater intuition, so there are more resources available.

4. Consider using meditation, prayer, or other internal exploration–oriented approaches to build your capacity to connect with your intuition.

5. Enjoy your gifts and use them wisely! Learn to trust yourself, not only in your relationships with others but with yourself! Think of those times when you did not follow your internal hunch in a relationship or business situation. Remember that you probably are correct when you follow your hunches!

THREE INTELLIGENCES SELF-ASSESSMENT FEEDBACK

Activation, Integration, Balance, and Application of the Three Intelligences

Trimergence
"I Am"

I exist, and do my best to understand myself and my life. This adventure challenges me and stimulates me to keep learning and growing.

Logic
"I Think"

I like to explore what makes sense and what doesn't. I enjoy using my analytic and logical skills as an adventure to understand how life works. When things don't make sense, I can become rattled and judge myself or others for not thinking clearly.

Personal Experience. When I make sense out of my life situations, I feel great! When people or situations don't make sense, however, I can feel frustrated and anxious at times. I become concerned that I may not have the right answer to make the correct decision. When this happens I can activate an analytic style that either helps me or creates more confusion like "analysis paralysis." At these times I may need to withdraw to make sense of things privately. Or I may assert to obtain the answers I need. Once I make sense of things, I respond with clarity and vision. I wish I could do this all the time!

Emotion
"I Feel"

I like to feel the emotional "ups" of life, but at other times I will feel the "downs." As a result, I will either throw myself into work or withdraw into my own emotional experience. Ultimately, I live for the "juice" of emotional contact with others.

Personal Experience.   I am at my best when I feel good about life and fully in touch with my positive emotions. When I can't get a handle on how I feel about things or am reacting emotionally, I can become frustrated and confused. Sometimes I want to hide my frustration from others because I find that they either don't understand me or may judge me for being too emotional. Then I either avoid my emotions through work or other activities, or I may take a dive into an uncomfortable "down" state.

Intuition
"I Sense"

I sense and trust a deep connection with myself and others. Sometimes I trust this deeper sense of "knowing," and at other times I don't. When I trust myself, I feel in touch with my deeper instincts and intuition.

Personal Experience.   I have a deep sense of inner knowing, which translates into a way of connecting with people and situations. As a result, I can experience a sense of inner control and well-being. Sometimes I don't trust my intuition and get off track. At these times I feel disconnected and derailed from my inner knowing. This can be frustrating and create an imbalance. Then I feel compelled to use emotion or logic to try to figure out what is going on.

Appendix B

STARTWORKS, INC.

CORPORATE GOVERNANCE COMMITTEE CHARTER

I.   MEMBERSHIP

The corporate governance committee of Startworks, Inc. (the "Company," and such committee, the "Committee") shall be comprised of at least two (2) members of the Board of Directors of the Company (the "Board") elected by the Board, which members shall include the Chairman and the CEO director, if any. The Committee shall continue in existence as provided in the Bylaws. The Committee is authorized and directed to engage such experts and advisers, including legal counsel, as the Committee shall deem necessary in the discharge of its responsibilities.

II.   QUORUM

A majority of the members of the Committee shall constitute a quorum.

III.   FREQUENCY

The Committee shall meet as required between the dates of regular Board meetings.

IV. FUNCTIONS

The Committee is the steward of the conscience and the collective intelligence of the Company. The Committee is empowered to work with the officers of the Company to (i) promulgate a set of corporate core values to be adopted by the Board of Directors and the Company as the core values by which the Company shall conduct and manage its business, (ii) integrate the core values into the Bylaws of the Company, (iii) periodically review the effectiveness of the Company's core values with its officers, and (iv) consider and propose, with the advice of the officers of the Company, any necessary revisions to the core values to be adopted by the Board and stockholders of the Company and incorporated into the Bylaws of the Company.

The Committee is empowered to work with the officers of the Company to use the three human intelligences—logic, emotion, and intuition intelligence— to create and maintain a whole-brain, creative, and collaborative culture.

The Committee members are the ombudsmen of the conscience and the collective intelligence of the Company on the Board and are encouraged to guide the Board to conduct its affairs in accordance with the Company's core values with its collective intelligence fully engaged.

VI. MINUTES

Minutes will be kept of each meeting of the Committee. Any action of the Committee shall be final, shall not be subject to review by the Board, and shall in all respects be binding on the Company.

ABOUT THE AUTHOR

John Montgomery is a corporate attorney and entrepreneur. He is the founder of Montgomery & Hansen, LLP, a Silicon Valley based corporate law firm, and founder of Startworks, a technology incubator serving the transition to a sustainable global economic system designed for humanity. He works primarily with high-potential entrepreneurial teams to help them translate their visions into successful companies.

In addition to being a frequent speaker on venture capital at such forums as the Future Salon, Haas School of Business, and NexGen, John leads continuing education programs about the process of raising venture capital. John is a co-chair of the legal working group behind Assembly Bill 361 recently signed by governor Brown, which establishes for-profit benefit corporations in California.

He is a student of non-dual philosophical systems, neuroscience, developmental maps of human consciousness, and organizational development. He recently co-founded Chrysallis, Inc., a human development company that aims to change the human development paradigm and support healthy, full productive lives for billions of people.

John holds a BA in studio art from Stanford University and a JD from Northwestern College of Law, Lewis & Clark College.

INDEX

BUY A SHARE OF THE FUTURE IN YOUR COMMUNITY

These certificates make great holiday, graduation and birthday gifts that can be personalized with the recipient's name. The cost of one S.H.A.R.E. or one square foot is $54.17. The personalized certificate is suitable for framing and will state the number of shares purchased and the amount of each share, as well as the recipient's name. The home that you participate in "building" will last for many years and will continue to grow in value.

Here is a sample SHARE certificate:

THIS CERTIFIES THAT

YOUR NAME HERE

HAS INVESTED IN A HOME FOR A DESERVING FAMILY

1985-2010
TWENTY-FIVE YEARS OF BUILDING FUTURES
IN OUR COMMUNITY ONE HOME AT A TIME

1200 SQUARE FOOT HOUSE @ $65,000 = $54.17 PER SQUARE FOOT
This certificate represents a tax deductible donation. It has no cash value.

YES, I WOULD LIKE TO HELP!

I support the work that Habitat for Humanity does and I want to be part of the excitement! As a donor, I will receive periodic updates on your construction activities but, more importantly, I know my gift will help a family in our community realize the dream of homeownership. I would like to SHARE in your efforts against substandard housing in my community! (Please print below)

PLEASE SEND ME _____ SHARES at $54.17 EACH = $ $_____

In Honor Of: _____

Occasion: (Circle One)   HOLIDAY   BIRTHDAY   ANNIVERSARY

       OTHER: _____

Address of Recipient: _____

Gift From: _____ *Donor Address:* _____

Donor Email: _____

I AM ENCLOSING A CHECK FOR $ $_____ PAYABLE TO HABITAT FOR HUMANITY <u>OR</u> PLEASE CHARGE MY VISA OR MASTERCARD *(CIRCLE ONE)*

Card Number _____ Expiration Date: _____

Name as it appears on Credit Card _____ Charge Amount $ _____

Signature _____

Billing Address _____

Telephone # Day _____ Eve _____

PLEASE NOTE: Your contribution is tax-deductible to the fullest extent allowed by law.
Habitat for Humanity • P.O. Box 1443 • Newport News, VA 23601 • 757-596-5553
www.HelpHabitatforHumanity.org